On Creating Competition and Strategic Restructuring

On Creating Competition and Strategic Restructuring

Regulatory Reform in Public Utilities

Edited by

Emiel F.M. Wubben

Associate Professor
Strategic Management and Business Administration
Wageningen University
The Netherlands

and

Willem Hulsink

Associate Professor
Entrepreneurship and Organisation Studies
Erasmus University Rotterdam
The Netherlands

BELGIAN-DUTCH ASSOCIATION FOR INSTITUTIONAL AND POLITICAL ECONOMY

Edward Elgar
Cheltenham, UK • Northampton, MA, USA

Published by
Edward Elgar Publishing Limited
Glensanda House
Montpellier Parade
Cheltenham
Glos GL50 1UA
UK

Edward Elgar Publishing, Inc.
136 West Street
Suite 202
Northampton
Massachusetts 01060
USA

A catalogue record for this book
is available from the British Library

ISBN 1 84376 371 0

Printed and bound in Great Britain by MPG Books Ltd, Bodmin, Cornwall

Contents

Figures

Tables

Contributors

Karel van Miert	Nyenrode University, The Netherlands
Johannes M. Bauer	Delft University, The Netherlands
David Parker	Aston Business School, Aston University, Birmingham; Competition Commission, Great Britain.
Volkert Schneider and Alexander Jäger	Universität Konstantz, Dept. of Politics and Management, Finland
Jens Arnbak Netherlands	OPTA, The Hague, Delft University, The
Tom Björkroth and Johan Willner	Åbo Akademi University, Turku, Finland
Willem Hulsink and Emiel F.M. Wubben	Erasmus University Rotterdam, The Netherlands Whulsink@fbk.eur.nl; Wageningen University and Researchcenter, The Netherlands Emiel.wubben@wur.nl
Leigh Hancher	Kennedy van der Laan, Amsterdam; Tilburg University, Tilburg, The Netherlands

Acknowledgements

The editors of this volume would like to thank the Association for Institutional and Political Economy (AIPE) for providing the editors the institutional setting to realize this volume in their series with Edward Elgar. We gratefully acknowledge the support of Versatel, E.ON Benelux, ERBS, the Strategy-department of the Erasmus University, ERIM and Grasp. Without their support this publication and the preceding conference, entitled 'Engineering Competition. On the interplay between supervising regulatory authorities, former monopolists and new entrants in liberalizing markets' would have been impossible to realize. Also many thanks go to the contributions to that conference by J. Pelkmans (EIPA, WWR), D. Parker (Aston Business School), J. Arnbak (OPTA), M. van der Heijden (Versatel), J. de Jong (NMa-Dte), C. Stoffaes (Electricité de France), J. Verwer (E.ON Benelux), and K. van Miert (Universiteit Nyenrode).

We are grateful to H. Schenk (University of Utrecht), J. Groenewegen (Erasmus University) and W. Naeije (former CEO ENECO-Energy) for their comments, suggestions and review of articles.

We would like to thank S. de Jong for getting this project started by organizing the conference for the editors. Finally, a special message of thanks goes to A. Sari for her time, patience and dedication in preparing a camera-ready copy of the original manuscript of this book.

Introduction

Willem Hulsink and Emiel F.M. Wubben

1 INTRODUCTION

This book is about the transformation of network industries or public utilities in Western Europe and the United States (US). A network industry provides a public or basic service by operating a large infrastructure system whose main characteristics are strongly increasing returns to scale, high levels of capital intensity, deployment of long-lasting industrial assets, and of vital importance to the economy. Examples are telecommunication, energy, transportation systems, water distribution, postal services, and broadcasting. Most of these network-based sectors were until recently a 'natural monopoly': economies of scale so large that competition is not viable. In the past public utilities were mainly organized through regulated franchisees and state enterprises. In return for such a privileged position (i.e. no or low levels of competition), those utilities were subjected to some form of direct or indirect government control: subject to economic regulation (e.g. prices/profit controls, entry and exit conditions) and social regulation (e.g. universal and continuous service provision), or more radical, integrated into the government administration.

From the 1980s of Ronald Reagan, Milton Friedman and Margaret Thatcher onwards, command and control governance became replaced by *laissez-faire*. For the government authorities in Europe and the regulators and regulatees in the US, the emphasis shifted from designing and running a monopoly to developing and making markets and to engineer and monitor competition. Alongside a former publicly-owned or regulated monopolist, entry and competition was now allowed (or even encouraged) in the domain of public utilities. While Europe saw a major shift from public to private ownership and the emergence of independent regulatory agencies over the last two decades, the US, with already a regulatory framework in place for more than 50 years, re-examined its practices, procedures and outcomes, and streamlined them through deregulation and new regulatory reform programs. Over the last two decades several national governments have embarked upon deregulating, liberalizing and privatizing their utility sectors (Derthick and

Quirk, 1985; Helm and Jenkinson, 1998; Parker, 1998). The key concept in this respect is *regulation.* There are different forms of regulation (Reagan 1987); from self-regulation through self-imposed codes of conduct for a specific industry or profession to externally imposed regulation whereby public organizations have legitimate coercive responsibilities in regulatory policy making. Two variations of externally imposed regulation may be discerned: public monopoly ownership and public regulation.

The first form works through direct public intervention whereby a state enterprise has the exclusive responsibility for the provision of particular services. Here the government controls the operational and strategic activities of the state enterprise, such as capital allocations, investment plans, pricing and personnel policy. Public ownership could also be conceived as a means of dealing with other market imperfections (national security, universal service provision, industrial innovation and adjustment, regional development etc.).

The second form works through administrative agencies that enjoy a considerable degree of independence from the industry and government in regulating a particular market. Public regulation refers to a package of legislative and administrative controls designed to structure and alter politically the operation of particular markets through an independent regulatory authority, while leaving private property intact. The role of such a regulator is restricted to that of referee in charge of general oversight and legal enforcement, reflecting a more judicial relationship between the state and the private sector.

Deregulation refers to an abolition or streamlining of government rules and legal provisions and hence, to an increasing reliance on market forces and self-regulation. In other words, it entails the process of reducing state control over an industry or activity so as to make it structurally more responsive to market forces (Baldwin and Cave, 1999). Freedom of action within a market can be greatly enhanced (e.g. with a loosening of profit and pricing caps), restrictions in a firm's freedom of entry into a particular market can be eliminated, and particular governmental objectives (e.g. securing minimum quality of service levels) are no longer realized by the government but through voluntary and joint activities by the sector.

The reasons for initiating deregulation programs can be found in complaints from industry experts about the administrative burden and intrusive red tape imposed by government, sunk costs and inefficiencies, and allegations of regulatory capture (the agencies are captured by those they are meant to regulate). For example, between 1938 and 1978, the Civil Aeronautics Board (CAB), granted with the exclusive regulatory authority over interstate air transportation, had never permitted another trunk airline to enter the market and had effectively prohibited price competition. After the 1978 Airlines Deregulation Act was passed, the previously sheltered American carriers were given almost complete freedom to set prices and easier access to new routes. Southwest Airlines and other new low-fare entrants furthermore contributed to the emergence of strong competition. The ultimate accomplishment in US airline deregulation was the abolition of the Civil Aeronautics Board (CAB) in 1984 and the transfer of its ongoing responsibilities for antitrust and international regulatory matters to the Department of Transportation.

Liberalization refers to the process of opening up state-controlled monopolies and transforming them into (more) open markets. Public services that were originally provided by a government entity or an exclusive franchisee are now contracted out to private firms (i.e. competition for the market). Access to previously sheltered markets is now partly or completely open for domestic and international private sector participation and facilities-based and/or service competition has emerged (i.e. competition on the market). For instance, the telecommunications markets in North America and Western Europe were gradually liberalized over a longer time span (5-15 years), generally starting with the market for terminal equipment, followed by value-added services and mobile telephony, and eventually completed by opening up voice telephony and public network provision to competition.

Privatization refers to the idea and practice of the transfer of productive assets from public ownership and control into private ownership through either public offering, management buy-out or traded sale (Veljanovski, 1989). In addition to the fiscal objective to use the receipts from the sale of public assets to reduce the government's debt, and the financial objective to open up the capital markets for companies, the decision to privatize has often been motivated by a desire to improve the management of public corporations by stimulating efficiency, innovation and customer responsiveness. It often implies a change in the legal form (from public to civil law), a replacement of senior management and a drastic corporate reorganization.

The utilities are transformed from departmental administrations to state-controlled or state-regulated corporations and granted access to capital markets and allowed to develop more flexible personnel policies. Especially in Western Europe, privatization is often carried out in two subsequent stages, namely corporatization and the sale of equity to the private sector. First of all, state-owned enterprises are re-organized according to private company law and incorporated outside their ministry. Although put at arm's length, the privatized company still has direct linkages with the government, that more often than not remains the key shareholder in the new situation.

This process of corporatization normally entails a restructuring of the company (e.g. better costing methods and cutting back on cross-subsidies, more transparent corporate governance structures, greater marketing effort) to prepare for competition and the next stage in the privatization process. In the second stage the assets of the company can be sold partially or fully to private investors or through the stock exchange. Eventually, some of the former publicly-owned monopolists have merged into an international and/or multi-utility holding company, as is the case with the European multi-utility giants Vivendi, RWE and Eon.

2 FROM MONOPOLIZATION TO DE-MONOPOLIZATION IN AMERICA'S UTILITIES

Paradoxically, most public utilities were pioneered by entrepreneurs and the services were provided by private companies (with the probable exception of Imperial Germany where the railway, postal and telecommunications systems were laid under state surveillance). After an early dominance of private enterprises in the first decades, governments responded by either regulating or nationalizing those essential services and facilities, as substitutes for competition (Brock, 1994; Noam, 1992; Hughes, 1988). As a consequence of poor service levels and serious underinvestment of the infrastructure and because of regional development and national security concerns, private enterprise and market forces were replaced.

European governments promoted public ownership (executed at the national or regional level, combining operational and regulatory tasks); the North-American governments advocated regulation as the best means to structure their public utility industries. In some sectors and countries, smaller private firms or community cooperatives, that complemented the dominant monopoly model by having technical and accounting agreements with the public or privately regulated network operator. Examples of such a *decentralized alternative* could be found in US and Scandinavian telecommunications: the small but numerous independent operators associated with the Bell system, and the quasi-hierarchical and hybrid telephone systems in Denmark and Finland (Davies, 1994).

While the European approach to organizing public utilities could be called interventionist and dirigiste, the American structure clearly reflected the tradition of economic or laissez-faire liberalism. Unimpeded by a guild, corporatist or absolutist legacy like most of the European countries, the US political economy was almost from the start committed to private rights and social individualism (entrepreneurial freedom and sanctity of contract), economic competition, and judicial review (e.g. resolving disputes through case-by-case adversarial litigation) (McCraw, 1981; 1984). The intra- and interstate railways were the first to see their sector regulated. When the abuse of economic power of the railroads and its frustrating impact on transportation efficiency was put on the agenda in the late 1860s, national and federal governments responded by establishing the first regulatory authorities, namely the Massachusetts Board of Railroad Commissioners (1869) and the Interstate Commerce Commission (1887). Further ingredients that shaped the US regulatory framework in the early 20th century were a strong hostility to a centralized government (hence the support for regulation of public services at the lower state-level) and the curse of big business, dealing with the structure and practices of large holding companies. While public ownership was dominant among the forms organizing and providing public services (e.g. water and electricity systems, airports) at state level, it was a non-issue at federal level. The US Postal Service is the exception to that rule.

For the regulation of public utility industries in the US, three practices stand out: anti-trust focus, the establishment of state-level public service commissions, followed by the creation of independent sector-specific regulatory agencies at federal and state level (McCraw, 1981). Following the first recognized, anti-competitive wave of mergers and acquisitions, the Sherman (antitrust) Act, originally passed in 1890, was offensively applied in 1911 in the break-up of the giant firms Standard Oil and American Tobacco.

Already in 1907, the states of New York and Wisconsin had set up public service commissions to regulate the activities of public utility holdings, soon to be quickly copied by all the other states. Until today, in addition to the federal agencies, national states, with their Public Service Commissions, play a key role in regulating utility services. For instance, the California Energy Commission was together with the Federal Energy Regulatory Commission (FERC) responsible for addressing and solving the power crisis of 2001. Although not entirely independent of the three constitutional branches (i.e. Congress, President, and the courts), the federal regulatory agencies and commissions were autonomous in terms of their budget from any of the ministries and independent of control by a single political party (Shapiro, 1997). Those bi-partisan and multi-headed administrative authorities were given considerable latitude in carrying out their mission.

In the genealogy of US regulation, three different phases can be distinguished, which spawned and shaped three different types of regulatory bodies (McCraw, 1981). The first wave of federal regulatory bodies emerged as a consequence of 'popular activism' and was initially designed to relieve the economic and social instability caused by the big trusts and the tremendous transformations of social and economic life at the end of the 19th century. The Interstate Commerce Commission (ICC), for example, was established in 1887 in part as a response to complaints from shippers about monopolistic pricing and route fixing by the big railroad companies. The second wave of regulation emerged in response to the anarchy of the market during the Depression in the 1930s and included the creation of industry-specific federal agencies with broad discretionary powers, such as strong price and entry controls in specific markets with the purpose of stabilizing the relationships among producers (e.g. finding a trade-off between reducing competition and achieving economies of scale by allowing monopolies and curbing them by constraining their profits). Furthermore, these regulatory agencies provided an administrative framework within which a large number of interest groups could bargain and settle disputes. For instance, the Federal Communications Commission (FCC), set up in 1934, was an independent agency responsible for regulating all interstate and foreign communication by means of radio, television, wire, cable or satellite. The FCC required common carriers to provide service upon request and at reasonable rates and to file tariff schedules for review and approval.

In the 1960s and 1970s, a third wave of liberal reform spawned social regulatory agencies, such as the Environmental Protection Agency (EPA) and the Occupational Safety and Health Administration (OSHA). They ought to deal with the social impact of business and not with their corporate and economic behavior *per se*. While economic regulation deals with small but important segments of the economy, social regulation regulates all industries. These 'social' agencies were largely oriented toward the values of consumers and other interests left out of producer-oriented representation (e.g. the promotion of safety for consumers, workers, and citizens).

With such an ever-extending regulatory machinery put in place, it was due to the economic crisis in the late 1970s and early 1980s that the Carter Administration, followed by the Reagan Administration, put into question the far-reaching influence of the state on the economy. Critics complained about a number of aspects associated with regulation: its enormous costs and ineffectiveness, unfair and unwieldy procedures, lack of legitimacy (unresponsiveness to democratic control), and the inherent unpredictability of the regulatory process and its final results (Breyer, 1982).

Weidenbaum (1979), for instance, warned against the encroachment of government power in the private sector, generating major inefficiencies throughout society and slowing down industrial innovation and development. He argued for strengthening the position of business through deregulation: cutting back rules and introducing cost-benefit analysis and budget review in government. The alternative of deregulation was successfully put on the political agenda by the economists, Stigler, Friedman and Coase, and the well-known industry experts Kahn and Bailey, who all saw deregulation as a way to cut back often unnecessary rules and hence to reduce social costs. Inspiration for their argument had been provided by Hayek (1944; 1945), who had conceptualized the economy as an ongoing process of discovery, competition, dynamic co-ordination and change.

Hayek's view on competition and dynamic was fully supported by the economist/regulator Kahn (1990, pp.353-354):

> The evolution of regulatory policy will never come to an end. The path it takes - and we should make every effort to see that it takes - however, is the path not of full circle or pendulum, which would take us back to where we started, but of a spiral, which has a direction. This is in a sense only an expression of a preference for seeking consistently to move in the direction of the first-best functioning of the market economy, rather than the second- or third-best world of centralized command and control.

The Chicago School economists Stigler, Friedman and Coase shared Hayek's belief in competitive capitalism as an engine of progress and thought about the detrimental effects of (too much) government intervention and public spending in the resource allocation processes throughout the economy. Friedman (1962) strongly promoted the organization of economic activity through private enterprise, operating in a free market, as both a device for achieving economic freedom and a necessary condition for political freedom. In the field of monetary policy, this would imply cutting taxes and government spending and controlling inflation by tightly constraining the growth of the money supply.

In a similar vein, Coase (1959), in his classic discussion of the rationale and procedures followed by the FCC in the allocation of the radio frequency spectrum, celebrated the virtues of private property and pricing. Given the fact that radio frequencies were at the time scarce resources, Coase suggested that it would be better if the use of the spectrum would be determined by the pricing system (instead of on the basis of 'first come first served') and would be awarded to the highest bidder. In that case, the property rights of any potential buyers could be determined by an auction and any transfer and recombination of them could be left to the market place. Like his Chicago colleagues, Stigler (1975) was mainly interested in the ways actual markets operate and how governments perform in regulating or undertaking economic activities. From his empirical studies on regulated industries he concluded that price and entry measures were primarily enacted and implemented in the interests of specialized producer groups. Stigler argued that regulation was ineffective in restraining monopoly power, as agencies were often captured by those industry groups they were supposed to supervise.

Kahn and Bailey, who together had been appointed at the CAB in the late 1970s, shared the Chicago School criticism of excessive government and cost-plus ways of thinking. Instead of suppressing the competition in aviation, any residual regulation should be made as consistent as possible with actual and potential rivalry and dynamics. A key device for Kahn in the deregulation of the airline industry was the marginal cost pricing philosophy: *I really don't know one plane from the other. To me they are all marginal costs with wings* (Kahn, in McCraw 1984: 224).

Another important concept in this respect was 'market contestability', without any mobility barriers (like sunk costs), as key requirements for introducing deregulation (Bailey and Baumol, 1984). Regulatory barriers that would impede (potential) competition ought to be identified and different ways had to be considered to reduce or eliminate them.

These claims for pro-competition policies were picked up and supported by leading politicians (from Republicans to Democrats), opportunity-seeking office-holders, and consumer activists, all responsive to concerns about high levels of inflation and taxation, government intervention, and inclined to free market ideologies. Although hindered by a relatively late and ineffective reaction from the affected industries to protect their vested interests and slow down far-reaching reform measures, entrepreneurial administrators, commissions and advisory working groups effectively advanced the ideas for deregulation and eventually implemented them (Derthick and Quirk, 1985). Evidently, aviation and telecommunications stood out in terms of carrying out radical institutional change, and improving productivity. In aviation, Kahn and Bailey not only stimulated new entry and competition, but also managed to dismantle 'their' CAB by 1984.

Another major accomplishment of deregulation in the US was the divestiture of AT&T in 1984, as the ultimate consequence of an antitrust suit instituted by the Justice Department. The quasi-vertically integrated AT&T/Bell system was separated into seven independent regional Bell operating companies providing local telephony, and the remainder of AT&T, including long-distance and international telephony, equipment manufacturing and R&D. Besides being forced to hive-off the regulated local telephony undertakings, the new-AT&T was now freed to take on indigenous competition from MCI and Sprint, enter the booming datacommunications market, and internationalize its operations. In the 1990s, deregulation turned into an administrative reform movement when the Clinton Administration with its 'Reinventing Government' program started to streamline regulatory and other administrative procedures even further, cutting red tape, and separating policy decisions from execution by divesting or introducing competition in service delivery (Osborne and Gaebler, 1993).

3 FROM MONOPOLIZATION TO DE-MONOPOLIZATION IN EUROPE'S UTILITIES

The collectivization of the provision of public utilities (e.g. telephony, mail, electricity, water and transport), that had started in most European countries at the end of the 19th century and lasted until the 1980s, had been institutionalized through statutory monopolies, authorized by central (or regional) governments and operated by state-owned administrations or municipalities. In Europe's mixed economies, the state has traditionally played a leading role in those key sectors of the national economy by acting as entrepreneur, direct supplier of services, lender of last resort and planner for the industry in question or the economy as a whole (Shonfield, 1965; Ambrosius, 1984; Jänicke, 1990). In those days, the European governments relied upon interventionist instruments, such as indicative planning, nationalizations and state monopolies, extensive public works and procurement programs, and demand creation/income redistribution policies. The increase of state intervention at the sector level was paralleled by the establishment of the welfare state at the macro-level.

In his *In Care of the State*, De Swaan (1988) has referred to the gradual rise of nation-wide, collective and compulsory arrangements, that structured the provision of both public services, social security and welfare systems. In the formation and implementation of these Keynesian macro-economic policies, the state apparatus was supported by the active participation of centralized labor and employers organizations, jointly combating inflation and unemployment, and securing substantial levels of economic growth (Shonfield, 1965). European governments and their recognized social partners had established tri-partite arrangements to settle wage/price levels, working conditions and labor market issues.

At the end of the 1970s, European public sectors were relatively large and characterized by an extensive bureaucracy, a substantial degree of public ownership, and ambitious redistribution and employment programs. Consequently, civil servants and their unions had substantial power: public sector employees had a strong legal and political position, based on the civil servant's statute, reasonable working conditions and extensive participation mechanisms. Political and administrative intervention by ministers, legislators, and civil servants in the day-to-day operations of the nationalized industries and interference with the pricing, personnel and investment decisions of public managers was frequent and all-pervasive.

What matters for state enterprise is political performance, in the words of a senior manager: *Running a nationalized company is like having a stockholder's meeting everyday* (Walters and Monsen, 1983, p.16). Nationalized industries and cross-industry state holdings (e.g. IRI Italy) proved to be failures: the capture of public managers by politicians and trade unions, a general over-manning of state monopolies, ambiguous and inconsistent corporate objectives and portfolio, poor coordination among the various public enterprises, and the absence of effective control over public enterprises by Parliament, the courts or the sponsoring minister (Majone, 1994a; 1994b). Especially in France, there was strong support for an active role of the sovereign state in national economy.

This has become known as the doctrine of *service public*: an activity which the sovereign state decides to conduct by itself, or at least, where its duty is to intervene strongly in order to correct deficiencies of private initiatives (e.g. defense, diplomacy, justice, social services and infrastructural public services) (Stoffaes, 1996).

From the late 1970s onwards, Europe's economies were hit hard by the economic recession and increasing competition from Japan and the Newly Industrializing Countries, resulting eventually in de-industrialization, long-term unemployment and cutbacks in public spending. European governments became concerned with how to adjust their stagnating economies to the new techno-economic and international conditions. With a relative decline in public investment and infrastructure spending in the 1980s, together with an increase of congestion in public infrastructures (e.g. communications and air transportation), European governments became painfully aware that the next round of investments had to be carried out by the private sector (OECD, 1993). The big challenge for national policy makers in the 1980s, became to prepare domestic firms, strategic sectors and the national economy as such for international competition, and to develop an appropriate mix of strategic responses (e.g. deregulation, privatization, innovation policy).

By the end of the 1970s, politicians, businessmen and intellectuals in Europe started to rediscover economic liberalism and, like their American counterparts, promoting supply side economics. Britain was clearly the first mover in this respect, not only in terms of preaching but also in practicing it. For instance, the economist Littlechild (1978) raised serious doubts about the large-scale and far-reaching state intervention in the national economy. He argued that private enterprise (laissez faire) and the smooth functioning of markets and competition would not only generate overall efficiency gains, but stimulate entrepreneurship and innovation. The *In care of the state* of a previous era was replaced by slogans in which an overambitious state was to be blamed for the economic crises and freeing market forces as the remedy for it: *Selling the state* (Veljanovki, 1987), *The retreat of the state* (Swann, 1988), and *The state under stress* (Foster and Plowden, 1996).

The UK governments showed great determination to replace state-controlled and monopolistic markets by a 'competitive order', where the dynamic play of market forces would be actively promoted. The belief was that regulation in this respect, imposed on just privatized and liberalized utilities, would only be temporary before workable competition would take hold. Initially supervisory powers would be delegated to newly created independent regulators, but ultimately, actual and potential competition would undermine monopolies and make regulation obsolete. One key policy innovation was introduced in that period, which was quickly and widely adopted in Britain and elsewhere, namely price-cap regulation: prices for a basket of services are set in advance for a longer period (3-5 years), allowing the firm to benefit from any cost savings made during that period.

The industry regulator faced the difficult role of promoting competition to cut back the monopoly on the one hand and constrain monopoly pricing on the other. Compared to the American system of rate of return or profit regulation, the economists Littlechild (1983) and Beesley (1992) argued that price-cap regulation was better in terms of efficiency and administrative convenience.

Despite the great efforts to privatize public utilities, to liberalize markets more or less radically (softly in telecoms and water, and drastically in railways and energy) and to formalize rules and regulation for those industries, the final outcome in the UK was *ordered competition*: a halfway house between government direction and a competitive order (Burton, 1997). Instead of dismantling artificial obstacles to entry and competition instantly, the British government gave clear priority to privatization and statutory regulation over liberalizing markets. At the actual time of privatization, basically no competition was allowed, yet even new market barriers had been erected by the various British governments (e.g. entry assistance, price-cap regulation, and duopolies).

On the European Continent, conservative and Christian Democratic parties followed the Anglo-Saxon path by giving priority to scaling back welfare provisions, contracting out public services and privatizing state-owned enterprises. In the late 1980s and early 1990s, the Social-Democratic parties were also converted to economic neo-liberalism and they too actively supported pro-market adjustment policies. In their responses to economic stagnation, European governments laid emphasis on curbing public expenditures, administrative reform and deregulation, decentralization of collective bargaining, and shifting resources from sunset to sunrise sectors.

Since the 1990s, all Western European governments are now in the process of gradually withdrawing from their active role in the provision of public services and are transferring assets from the public to the private sector. They have granted substantial managerial autonomy to former state enterprises and have separated operational activities from regulatory controls. The drastic policy changes implied a shift towards the (managed) liberalization of markets, the corporatization and privatization of the former monopolist, and institutional reform, in order to avoid the conflicting interests of the administration as market player and referee at the same time. The traditional state monopolies have often been replaced by a mixture of (more) market-oriented arrangements, such as new entry, the increase of competitive tendering and franchising, the introduction of yardstick competition and competition between different technological modes and capital market competition.

The traditional role of the state in Europe changed from being a producer of goods and services to that of a regulator whose main function is to ensure that economic actors play according to the agreed rules of the game. Originally, in the USA, and more recently in Europe, the supervision of utilities is the responsibility of independent single-industry agencies, dealing with the regulation of prices, enforcing licenses and ensuring quality of service, supported by transsectoral agencies to safeguard fair competition.

Compared with public ownership, characterized by active state intervention and political interference, the regulatory authority is not an acting party in the market, because private ownership is respected, and the execution of its administrative task is insulated from the potentially destabilizing effects of short-term party politics, electoral instabilities, and changes in government. In Western Europe there was until recently a reluctance to rely on those specialized, single-purpose administrative agencies; instead, important regulatory functions were assigned to the departments of the central government or to inter-ministerial committees (Majone, 1997a).

In this respect, Majone (1994a; 1994b) has typified the drastic institutional changes in Western Europe as a development from an interventionist state to a regulatory state. The interventionist model, based on an active and authoritarian role for the state in the national economy, has been replaced by a regulatory model, in which the state only stipulates the conduct of actors and the conditions under which the economic game is played.

Privatization and deregulation processes in Europe not only vary between Britain and Continental Europe, but they also differ between Western and post-communist economies, and among the countries within each group (Bös, 1993). This variety can be explained on the basis of differences in terms of ideology (radicalism/conservatism), scope and reach of public ownership (municipalities, regions, state), overall performance of the public sector, etc. For instance, the timing and degree of implementing structural reform in telecommunications showed a huge contrast between Britain, France and the Netherlands (Hulsink, 1999). The British 'first mover' strategy of carrying out privatization, liberalization and regulatory reform quickly and radically in the early 1980s, was followed by a more patient and cautious approach to transform the telecommunications market in France and in the Netherlands, stretching out to the mid-1980s.

In Western Europe, deregulation at the national level has often been followed by re-regulation at the EU-level. As a consequence, public utilities in Western Europe have lost their pre-existing statutory immunity from the Community's competition legislation and their business activities have become subject to the supranational anti-trust provisions of the European Union Treaty. The European Union's role in deregulating the domain of public utilities is mixed (Pelkmans, 2001). First of all, the European Union (EU) was (and still is) neutral with respect to property ownership; instead, all public and private entities are subject to the EU rules on competition. Secondly, in public utilities with no or limited cross-border trade, such as water and sewerage, there has been so far no major involvement of the EU in making those network markets competitive. Thirdly, the approach chosen by the EU was basically ad hoc and driven by the Competition Directorate of the Commission. It was only until the late 1980s, when the sketchy plans for liberalizing the European telecommunications and broadcasting had been drafted and Britain's radical privatization program was already implemented, that competition policy became gradually and actively applied in the EU (see chapter 2, this volume). In the 1990s and thereafter, most network-based markets in the EU have been liberalized or are in the process of being opened to competition with tightly-set deadlines.

The European Union's polity can be characterized by harmonization and decentralized administration and implementation. In these processes of approximating substantive rules in particular domains and transposing the relevant directives into national legislation, transnational networks of national regulators have been formed, with the European Commission acting as a co-ordinator. By exchanging information and sharing working standards amongst each other, they hope to achieve the necessary degree of uniformity in regulatory policy-making (Dehousse, 1997; Majone 1997b). Such a 'soft' regulatory system, based on information and persuasion, will not only make credible commitments possible, but also contribute to an effective enforcement of measures and objectives in their field. For instance, in the field of public utilities and anti-trust policy, the national regulatory authorities, together with the Commission, have raised their profile by coordinating their activities, pooling their experiences, and eventually embarking on a trajectory of mutual learning and benchmarking.

4 REGULATION AND CHARACTERISTICS OF NETWORK-BASED INDUSTRIES

Regulatory bodies have been created to ensure that these newly created competitive spaces function in a socially responsible way and that certain public interest requirements are met. They impose certain rules on the economic agents in the sector, concerning market entry/exit, conduct and/or corporate performance. So the overall structure of a particular market place (e.g. number of players and nature of competition), the provision and pricing of particular (set of) public services, and the input and output levels of the market players (e.g. profits, investments) are to be defined and upheld by regulation. The purpose of public regulation is to facilitate and to accomplish the realization of socio-economic goals like allocative efficiency and economic growth, price stability, and the provision of public goods by shaping the structural characteristics of an industry. The justification for administrative regulation has to do with market failures and market imperfections, that produce sub-optimal outcomes in terms of output and efficiency respectively (e.g. natural monopolies, externalities, excessive competition, and information asymmetry) and - to some extent - equity (e.g. universal service provision). One should distinguish between anti-trust, economic and social regulation. Anti-trust regulation aims at encouraging competition and curtailing the influence of monopolies, cartels and other restrictive business practices, that may disturb the proper functioning of markets. Economic regulation refers to the imposition of controls over prices, entry, exit, output, services rendered, markets served and profitability in particular industries. Social regulation deals with consumer protection, occupational health and safety, environmental protection (e.g. Wubben, 2000), etc.

Regulation has been defined by Selznick (1985, p.363) as '*a sustained and focused control exercised by a public agency over activities that are valued by a community'*. The element of 'sustained and focused control by a public agency' implies that regulation is more than merely passing a law; besides rule-making and rule-enforcement it also includes the responsibility of fact-finding in order to monitor these rules. Regulation on the one hand presupposes detailed and independent expertise of the industry to be audited and, on the other hand, an in-depth involvement in the regulated activity. The requirement of and the reliance on in-depth knowledge in carrying out this regulatory task, will sooner or later, result in the establishment of a specialized administrative agency, which is authorized for regulating a particular industry (Majone, 1994a; 1994b). These independent regulatory agencies, established by statute, operate on the basis of a legislative mandate in which their rule-making activities are stipulated, and use procedures that are fair, accessible and open ('due process'). Operating outside the line of hierarchical control or oversight by the central government, they are able to provide greater continuity and stability in policy making and implementation, than traditional government departments. The regulatory bodies, combining legislative and judicial powers that have traditionally been kept separate, differ from the central government and the courts by a collegial approach to decision making, an emphasis on professional expertise and political independence. The element of 'valued activities' in the definition indicates that the activities to be regulated are considered worthwhile in themselves: such as faith in private ownership and/or the promotion of competition. The regulatory approach aims at realizing a market's potential for furthering allocative efficiency, while at the same time correcting market imperfections through social and economic legislation to ensure objectives like fair competition, price control, consumer protection and universal service provision.

Regulation can be interpreted as a more or less formal system of rule-making, which operates though negotiation and bargaining between politicians, civil servants, industry, consumers and administrative bodies in the shadow of the law (Hancher and Moran, 1989; Veljanovski, 1991). Such a regulatory framework of organizations includes vertical relationships (e.g. goal setting, mandatory reporting, incentives and sanctions) and horizontal relationships (e.g. competition, cooperation, accommodation) (Baldwin and Cave, 1999). Public policy objectives, like universal service, price controls, innovation and fair competition are now sought after through different means, for instance through market coordination, administrative regulation and private law techniques. For instance, market coordination and regulation are now applied to improve efficiency, innovativeness, and quality of service and overall industrial performance. Bilateral contracts between the government and the franchisee and specific provisions in the articles of association are still used to prevent hostile take-overs or restrict foreign ownership (i.e. the so-called 'golden shares').

Many public utilities are network industries. Due to the capital-intensive character of infrastructural systems and their socio-political relevance for society, network-based industries have become 'administered' markets, where full competition is still constrained and market dynamics may not serve the public interest. There has to be a fit of the regulatory strategy to the particular characteristics of network industries: which of aspects in the overview of network-industry characteristics given below are relevant for the regulators framing their purpose(s) and selecting their method(s). For instance, in the process of opening a network-based industry to competition, the ownership of or control over so-called *essential facilities* (bottlenecks) by a monopolist, and especially abuse of these critical assets, can be detrimental. Since competitors are unable to provide these crucial facilities themselves or to develop a substitute, the regulator has to impose an obligation to give third party access and set fair interconnection requirements (Grieve and Levin, 1996). For instance, in the early days of European airline deregulation low-cost airlines Virgin and Easyjet had enormous difficulties getting decent landing slots at the London and Amsterdam airports: they faced strong opposition from the then tight coalition of the incumbent carriers (BA and KLM) and the national airport authorities (Heathrow, Gatwick, Schiphol).

In network-based markets effective competition is harder to establish than the proponents of deregulation suggest (Shepherd, 1998). The final outcome could even be another unacceptable situation of market dominance by a single firm or a tight oligopoly. Effective rivalry may be blocked because the (potential) impact of new entry is overestimated (often confined to shallow or niche entry) and the powers of the incumbent operators are seriously underestimated (e.g. past reputation, long-standing arrangements, extensive network facilities, superior knowledge, legal tactics, complex price discrimination, etc.). Major impediment to effective competition in a deregulating industry is still existing barriers to entry, complex dynamic pricing and mergers. Not only must barriers to entry and predatory pricing be identified after the competition gets started and addressed adequately, also anti-competitive mergers must be prevented. For example, the initial phase of airline deregulation in the US with free entry and competition was followed by a wave of mergers between the big carriers, and subsequently followed by systematic price discrimination, price raising, and a lack of free entry.

Public utilities have a number of characteristics, which set them apart from other industries. Trebing (1994) has stipulated the most important ones:

i networks require a heavy minimum threshold investment because of the need to interconnect with all customers in the service territory;
ii networks typically permit the development of multiple service at a lower cost than if each service were to pay its stand-alone cost because of joint product development;
iii there will be significant economies of scale from building capacity in advance of demand as long as that demand is properly forecasted;
iv adding a segment to a network typically increases traffic on all other segments of that network;
v networks provide inexpensive backup and increased reliability through routing alternatives, pooled reserves, and spreading outages;
vi the more comprehensive the network, the greater the potential for reducing the level of capacity to meet individual peaks;
vii advances in software and modernization improve network functionality and flexibility;
viii network size and new technology interact to permit new methods of packaging and transmitting service;
ix the incremental cost of adding a specific decreases as the size of the network increases;
x networks produce significant positive externalities (e.g. increase size of the market, and diminish the market power of an individual users).

5 CORPORATE STRATEGIES AND 'DAVID AND GOLIATH' COMPETITION

This collection of papers offers insights into the corporate strategies and stratagems in newly liberalized markets, the regulatory bargains struck between firms and public authorities, and the overall dynamics of markets and polities, and their ultimate outcomes. At first hand, the picture seems to be straightforward, the emergence of market entry and competition between new entrepreneurial firms and revitalized incumbent operators will eventually make government ownership obsolete and regulation – after an initial period of guiding the introduction of competition - redundant. Freed from a historic legacy and sunk assets, (prospective) entrants can choose whether or not to participate in a market which has been opened to competition and face one or more of the industry incumbent operators. Those incumbents may have a strong brand name, a dense and often nation-wide distribution systems and an installed customer base, but their infrastructure is often expensive, outdated (i.e. made up of legacy systems), and their service levels are poor and their set of products are limited. Although their entry opportunity involves high up-front investments with long pay-back periods and hence a strong need for continuous (re)financing, the new entrants stand a chance if they invest in improvements in operating efficiency, quality control, aggressive marketing, and spotting opportunities for price arbitrage. As some recent bankruptcies in the utilities industries illustrate (Enron, Worldcom, Railtrack, Sabena, Swissair), even aggressive established operators can simply stretch too far. Much to their surprise, regulators and governments have now realized corporate bankruptcies are part of the competitive process and that there is a big difference between the provision and the provider of public services.

The strategic choice between different governance modes of industry can be seen as a strategic game in which interests and values of the involved parties play a vital part and the political-economic organization of society is at stake. Regulated firms and industries, public agencies and other actors operate within the political and administrative process in exactly the same way they operate in the market (Owen and Braeutigam, 1978; Vietor, 1989; 1994). They seek to realize their corporate objectives by linking their strategic and operational behavior in the market place with their political strategies advocating their interests and influencing political decision making.

Or in other words, public or private companies that want to operate effectively in a regulatory environment must be active both in the market place and the political arena and complement their business activities with political action. The institutional environment, in which public service companies operate, entails both market and non-market (or political) components: they not only face competition and (may) rely on private agreements in exchanging resources, but they also have to represent themselves in the policy process where the rules of the regulatory game are defined and implemented (Emmons, 2000).

Firms that previously were hampered by government ownership and sheltered from competition, are now confronted with the impact of technological change, privatization and liberalization. As a consequence, former monopolists such as AT&T, British Airways, Belgacom, Schiphol Airport, Deutsche Bahn, and EDF have to come up with new strategies to organize and steer their business environment. Spurred by new external investors and shareholders, these state enterprises transform themselves into full service providers, driven by an entrepreneurial spirit, and facilitated by a decentralized structure and an international network of business partners. These operators face the two-fold task to realize the corporate goal of profit maximization and to comply with certain 'public interest' requirements (i.e. safeguarding the provision of key services). While modernizing the infrastructure and innovating the provision of regulated services, they diversify into new product and geographical markets (e.g. Internet access, waste collection, energy trading, facility management), and establish strategic linkages with foreign partners.

The sheer size and omnipotence of these hybrid companies, however, has caused concern about the lack of 'workable' competition' in newly liberalized markets. A characterization of *David and Goliath* competition seems to be more appropriate. New entrants, such as Mercury and Versatel (in telecommunications) and Virgin, Ryanair and Easyjet in aviation, have complained about the anti-competitive practices and the abuse of market dominance by the incumbent operators. Therefore, next to the market place, the political arena is the second environment in which regulated firms must compete by other means to advance their corporate interests. To be effective in the regulated environments, firms should adopt strategies, which secure a balance between improving market performance and obtaining institutional support from socio-political stakeholders.

Established operators could no longer rely upon their massive scale and scope of their assets and their historic strength, but they had to develop competitive capabilities in a more open market place (Kay, 2000). Incumbent operators are Janus-faced: they have to combine, both politically and strategically, the exploitation of staying a (de facto) monopolist in their home market and the exploration of becoming an aggressive competitor abroad or in new product/service markets. Besides by exogenous forces of emerging market competition and governments preparing for a corporate restructuring and an eventual privatization, the former monopolists will also be restructured by new shareholders and a stock market listing for the established companies, increasing visibility and accountability, and more commercial executives embarking upon a efficiency drive, (re)defining the core business, and pursuing risky differentiation and diversification strategies. As many incumbents have found out, entry in newly opened markets was more difficult than expected (often testing their managerial capabilities to the extreme and unexpectedly absorbing their scarce financial means).

A lot of the diversification strategies have ended in failure (dis-investments), or at best have generated mixed results (huge financial losses and bad publicity), having drawn management's attention away from core business operations. Also their internationalization strategies have often been a mixed blessing for them, manifested by huge investment and a high turnover in cross-border alliances and partnerships. Furthermore, those aggressive operators found out to their surprise that they were extremely vulnerable in their own backyard to unfavorable regulatory interventions and emerging competition eating away their historic competitive advantages.

Overall and in the long run, new entrants, however, will be at a distinct disadvantage. Such an industry with large networks relative to the size of a given market, considerable sunk investments, and high levels of concentration, will have substantial barriers to entry and contain a latitude to employ anti-competitive practices. New entrants may also be vulnerable to capacity shortfalls or bottlenecks associated with a sub-optimal infrastructure or caused by the dirty tricks of the incumbent operator and a regulator not yet in place or incompletely equipped.

Furthermore, the insurgents, already busy by achieving commercial viability and handicapped in accessing essential network facilities, face a profitable and diversified rival who may introduce complex pricing schemes (e.g. price discrimination, selective discounting and subtle risk/cost shifting). They are drawn into newly imposed price-cap and interconnection regimes, which are basically beneficial for the established network operators (allowing for tariff rebalancing, gradually scaling back cross-subsidies).

One of the many paradoxes in the domain of transforming the domain of public utilities is that the introduction of workable competition in those infrastructures needs to be designed and engineered. This process of engineering competition in the public utilities' domain is critical and complex, in a technical, economic, as well as political sense. Given the specific supply and demand characteristics of network-based industries, deciding upon the form, degree and pace of competition in the market place is no easy matter. The forces of the past and present may be hard to phase out: the sunk investments in and ongoing support for techno-administrative legacy systems, fierce political resistance against divestitures of businesses by managers, workers and trade unionists favoring gradual change, may hamper political decision making on implementing radical measures (Vietor, 1989; Emmons, 2000).

Furthermore, implementing those measures may be even more complicated (e.g. unbundling networks, services and even companies) and may demand highly advanced IT and control systems transfer pricing schemes (Sichel and Alexander, 1996). The results of deregulatory measures may even be counterproductive and the introduction of liberalization may lead towards new rules, often applied from adjacent areas (from sector to generic policies, i.e. antitrust policy) and higher discretionary levels (from national to supranational authorities: EU and World Trade Organization (WTO).

The impact of deregulation may even be counterproductive, such as pressing for greater competition but ending up in greater concentration and in setting up (or expanding the domain of existing) administrative agencies (Emmons, 2000). Besides constrained in their day-to-day operations, regulated firms are also hampered in their longer-term plans by governments and/or regulators setting limitations on their infrastructure and service investments and geographical expansion. The very complexity of regulation acts as a barrier to entry for new competitors but the same regulatory requirements also complicate product innovation and the use of distribution networks for the established operators. New entrants and incumbent network operators have to further their interests in both the market place and the political arena (Emmons, 2000). Executive boards of privatized firms actively seek to represent the demands of representing a new set of shareholders while facing and seeking to accommodate the restrictions and requirements regarding ownership of the past (e.g. universal service provision, golden shares directly or indirectly related to national security and sovereignty).

The new senior managers of the incumbent operators, most of them with private sector experience, now focus on defining the core business and adjusting the organization to improve efficiency and profitability, and expanding the scope of activities. They often adopt new organizational structures that permit more effective management of costs and more effective segmentation of customers: forms based on functional or geographic divisions are replaced by profit or cost centers organized around specific products and or customer segments.

As many new entrants and incumbent operators have experienced in the implementation of deregulation and privatization, the government and the larger political system continue to play a critical role in their performance. Despite corporatization and privatization, governments may still have substantial powers in the revitalized operator, such as holding a majority of shares in them (the French government in France Télécom), and minority shareholdings with golden shares which provide the governments with important decision making powers, such has the right to block mergers and acquisition and/or set prices for certain goods and services provided by the firm. Also the newly appointed regulatory authorities, which should overlook the initial stages during which competition will be created and then rule the industry and make the dedicated institution redundant, actively interfere in corporate decision making concerning the pricing, selection, availability and the quality of services. While lip service is paid to free markets and deregulation, the existing regulatory bodies are still persistent and proliferating.

6 STRUCTURE OF THE BOOK

The chapters by Karel van Miert and Johannes Bauer in Part one of this volume address the particularities of introducing deregulation and liberalization (or modifying regulation) in a utility world that is still characterized by partial competition and a persistent quasi-monopoly. Van Miert addresses the question of creating competition from the angles of the EU-context, the global trends, the reasons for liberalization, and the policy principles, over the past decade. The chapter depicts the process of de-monopolization as the result of ongoing strategic and tactical interactions among incumbent operators and insurgent market players, tough bargaining between those firms and supervisory regulators, and difficult negotiations between the national administrations and the EU Commission. In order to create some form of dynamic rivalry in those 'monopolistic' network-based industries, the emergence of new entry/exit and competition needs to be nourished and closely monitored and supervised: Van Miert suggests to use the concept of 'engineering competition' for this process. Bauer provides a critical analysis of the static premises upon which the tool-box oriented, pro-competitive stance is based. Whereas competition has an important role to play in infrastructure industries, its likely effects will be more heterogeneous and varied than anticipated in the past policy debates.

Part two discusses the results of a number of programs in which different 'public' infrastructures were privatized. David Parker looks at the various strategies pursued by the key players, the risks involved in the whole regulatory process, and their performance. Parker provides a lot of data trying to separate out the individual contributions of ownership change, competition, regulation and technological change in improving organizational performance. To make privatization a success, the role of the state becomes critically important especially when competition remains underdeveloped. Volker Schneider and Alexander Jäger argue that in analyzing the privatization of infrastructures the role of the state cannot be overlooked, and that an appropriate theory of the state in this area is barely needed.

Part three contains a number of country and sector case studies. These chapters seek to map out in detail how the interaction evolves over time between the supervisory bodies, the former monopolists and the new entrants in specific utilities markets. Jens Arnbak provides an overview of the policies for open network access in the field of European telecommunications where competition is finally taking root. Tom Björkroth and Johann Willner analyze the specific contributions of technical change and liberalization policies on the performance levels of the Finnish telecommunications industry. In their longitudinal case study on the restructuring of the Dutch water industry, Emiel Wubben and Willem Hulsink discuss the ambitious plans of the government to liberalize and privatize, ultimately followed by the painful conclusion of the whole exercise that the regional public water monopolies would be better left untouched.

The book concludes with a reflective note by Leigh Hancher, in which she tackles the ambiguous concept of 'engineering competition'. She suggests that we should be both aware of the shortcomings of designing and managing markets and the limitations on and problems with self-organization in regulation. In Hayek's terms, competition is in the domain of human action, while 'regulation' is a product of human design, and those two should not be mixed. Hence, as Hancher argues, 'engineering regulation', with a clear and intentional focus on devising an appropriate framework facilitating competition, is probably a better term.

REFERENCES

Ambrosius, G. (1984), *Der Staat als Unternehmer. Öffentliche Wirtschaft und Kapitalismus seit dem 19. Jahrhundert.* Göttingen: Van den hoeck and Ruprecht.

Bailey, E. and W.J. Baumol (1984), 'Deregulation and the theory of contestable markets', *Yale Journal on Regulation* 1: 111-137.

Baldwin, R. and M. Cave (1999), *Understanding regulation. Theory, strategy and practice.* Oxford: Oxford University Press.

Beesley, M.E. (1992), *Privatization, regulation and deregulation (2nd ed.).* London: Routledge.

Bös, D. (1993), 'Privatization in Europe: A comparison of approaches', *Oxford Review of Economic Policy* 9 (1): 95-111.

Breyer, S. (1982), *Regulation and its reform.* Cambridge MA: Harvard University Press.

Brock, G.W. (1994), *Telecommunication policy for the information age. From monopoly to competition.* Cambridge, MA: Harvard University Press.

Burton, J. (1997), 'The competitive order or ordered competition? The 'UK model' of utility regulation in theory and practice', *Public Administration* 75: 157-188.

Coase, R.H. (1959), 'The Federal Communications Commission', *Journal of Law and Economics* 2: 1-40.

Davies, A. (1994), *Telecommunications and politics. The decentralized alternative.* London: Pinter publishers.

Dehousse, R. (1997), 'Regulation by networks in the European Community: The role of European Agencies', *Journal of European Public Policy*, 4 (2): 246-261.

De Swaan, A. (1988), *In care of the state. Health care, education and welfare in Europe and the USA in the Modern Era.* New York: Oxford University Press.

Derthick, M. and P.J. Quirk (1985), *The politics of deregulation.* Washington DC: Brookings Institution.

Emmons, W. (2000), *The evolving bargain. Strategic implications of deregulation and privatization.* Boston, MA: Harvard Business School Press.

Foster, C.D. and F.J. Plowden (1996), *The state under stress: Can the hollow state be good government?* Philadelphia: Open University Press.

Friedman, M. (1962), *Capitalism and freedom.* Chicago: University of Chicago Press.

Grieve, W.A. and S.L. Levin (1996), 'Common carriers, public utilities and competition', *Industrial and Corporate Change* 5 (4): 993-1011.

Hancher, L. and Moran, M. (eds) (1989), *Capitalism, culture and economic regulation*. Oxford: Clarendon Press.

Hayek, F.A. von (1945), 'The use of knowledge in society', *American Economic Review* 35 (4): 519-30.

Hayek, F.A. von (1944), *The road to serfdom.* Chicago: University of Chicago Press.

Helm, D. and T. Jenkinson (eds) (1998), *Competition in regulated industries.* Oxford: Oxford University Press.

Hughes, T.P. (1988), *Networks of power. Electrification in Western society, 1880-1930.* Baltimore: Johns Hopkins University Press (1983).

Hulsink, W. (1999), *Privatization and liberalization in European telecommunications. Comparing Britain, the Netherlands and France.* London: Routledge.

Jänicke, M. (1990), *State failure. The impotence of politics in industrial society*. Cambridge: Polity.

Kahn, A.E. (1990), 'Deregulation: Looking backward and looking forward', *Yale Journal on Regulation* 7: 325-354.

Kay, J. (2000), 'Challenges of running a regulated business', In: *Mastering Strategy special of the Financial Times*, October 18,

Littlechild, S.C. (1978), *The fallacy of the mixed economy. Austrian critique of economic thinking and policy.* London: Institute of Economic Affairs.

Littlechild, S.C. (1983), *Regulation of British Telecommunications' profitability.* London: Department of Industry.

Majone, G. (1997a), 'From the positive to the regulatory state: Causes and consequences of changes in the mode of governance,' *Journal of Public Policy* 17: 139-167.

Majone, G. (1997b), 'The new European agencies: Regulation by information', *Journal of European Public Policy* 4 (2): 262-275.

Majone, G. (1994a), 'The rise of the regulatory state in Europe,' *West European Politics* 17(3): 77-101.

Majone, G. (1994b), 'Paradoxes of privatization and deregulation,' *Journal of European Public Policy* 1: 53-69.

McCraw, T. (1984), *Prophets of regulation: Charles Francis Adams, Louis D. Brandeis, James. L. Landis, Alfred E. Kahn.* Cambridge: Belknap Press.

McCraw, T.K. (ed) (1981), *Regulation in perspective. Historical essays.* Cambridge, MA: Harvard Business School.

Noam, E. (ed) (1992), *Telecommunications in Europe.* New York: Oxford University Press.

OECD (1993), *Infrastructure policies for the 1990s.* Paris: Organization for Economic Co-operation and Development.

Osborne, D. and T. Gaebler (1993) *Reinventing government. How the entrepreneurial spirit is transforming the public sector.* New York: Plume.

Owen, B.M. and Braeutigam, R. (1978), *The regulation game: Strategic use of the administrative process.* Cambridge MA: Ballinger.

Parker, D. (ed) (1998), *Privatization in the European Union. Theory and policy perspectives.* London: Routledge.

Pelkmans, J. (2001), 'Making EU network markets competitive', *Oxford Review of Economic Policy* 17 (3): 432-456.

Reagan, M.D. (1987), *Regulation. The politics of policy.* Boston: Little, Brown and Company.

Selznick, P. (1985), 'Focussing organisational research on regulation', In: R. Noll (ed.), *Regulatory policy and the social sciences*. Berkeley: University of California Press. pp.363-367.

Shapiro, M. (1997), 'The problems of independent agencies in the United States and the European Union,' *Journal of European Public Policy* 4 (2): 276-291.

Shepherd, W.G. (1998), 'Problems in creating effective competition', In: D. Gabel and D.F. Weiman (eds), *Opening networks to competition. The regulation and pricing of access.* Boston: Kluwer. pp.49-71

Shonfield, A. (1965), *Modern capitalism. The changing balance of public and private power*. London: Oxford University Press.

Sichel, W. and D.L. Alexander (1996), *Networks, infrastructure, and the new task for regulation.* Ann Arbor: University of Michigan Press.

Stigler, G.J. (1975), *Citizen and the state: Essays on regulation.* Chicago: University of Chicago Press.

Stoffaes, C. (1996), European Union deregulation and public utilities. *Key note address at the U.S.-Crest Franco-American dialogue meeting,* Washington, April 9, 1996.

Swann, D. (1988), *The Retreat of the State. Deregulation and Privatization in the UK and US.* New York: Harvester Wheatsheaf.

Trebing, H.M. (1994), 'The networks as infrastructure – The reestablishment of market power' *Journal of Economic Issues* XXVIII (2): 379-389.

Veljanovski, C. (ed.) (1991), *Regulators and the market. An assessment of the growth of regulation in the UK.* London: Institute of Economic Affairs.

Veljanovski, C. (ed.) (1989), *Privatization and competition. A market prospectus.* London: Institute of Economic Affairs.

Veljanovski, C.(1987), *Selling the state. Privatization in Britain.* London: Weidenfeld and Nicholson.

Vietor, R.H.K. (1994), *Contrived Competition. Regulation and Deregulation in America.* Cambridge MA: Belknap Press.

Vietor, R.H.K. (1989), *Strategic Management in the Regulatory Environment. Cases and Industry Notes*. Englewood Cliffs: Prentice Hall.

Walters, K.D. and R.J. Monsen (1983), 'Managing the nationalized company', *California Management Review* 25 (4): 16-26.

Weidenbaum, M.L. (1979), *The future of business regulation: Private action and public demand.* New York: Amacom.

Wubben, E.F.M. (ed.) (2000), *The Dynamics of the Eco-Efficient Economy: Environmental Regulation and Competitive Advantage.* Cheltenham: Edward Elgar.

PART ONE

Perspectives on Engineering Competition

1. Engineering Competition: The European Approach

Karel van Miert

I have been privileged enough to be in the European engine room during the nineties when engineering competition was an important policy issue. At the European level the topic became relevant for me from January 1989 onwards, when I became European Commissioner for transport under J. Delors. Until March 1999, with the fall of the European Commission headed by J. Santer. I was competition commissioner since January 1993. In this 11-year period I have been involved first in the liberalization of civil aviation, later in the telecom liberalization, and also in the energy field. We also tried moving the postal service sector, but this failed. The liberalization in all these industries was to a large extent a matter of applying competition policies in network industries. Today this is evident, but views were very different around 1990. What was the European situation then and what can we learn from European experience for the engineering of competition?

First, the general context. Of prime importance were the trends towards the market economy worldwide, the privatization process, the internal market policy, technological developments, globalization, rethinking the role of the state, and finally the trend of enhancing competitiveness for the sake of a dynamic European Economy and thus also full employment.

Let me specify the European context around 1989. We were moving in most European countries from a mixed economy towards a much more market driven economy. The wall between Eastern Europe and Western Europe fell triggering a gradual but unprecedented drive towards a market economy system. Such a trend obviously has a lot of consequences, both in terms of putting an end to monopoly situations and in terms of engineering competition in a given sector hitherto sheltered from competition. I believe it is a misunderstanding or a misgiving to think that this trend has ended, because the logic of the Economic and Monetary Union will have further effects in the coming years.

Parallel to this trend there was the privatization process, having also a very profound influence on economic structures. For example, Italy had to put an end to its old fashioned public holding system. The French, and even the Germans, had to review to some extent elements of their economic system including, amongst others, restructuring the banking sector. The relationship between public banks, enjoying a complete public guarantee and hence a higher rating, and the private banks is obviously a hot potato in Germany. But it is a real structuring issue.

Apart from these two powerful trends there was the political and economic goal to achieve the Internal Market. An internal European market and national monopolies are completely contradictory. Perhaps not everybody has seen this contradiction from the outset, but it became gradually crystal clear. So the internal market was an extremely strong engine propelling further liberalization and pushing towards an Economic and Monetary Union.

And obviously, next to the market trends and the privatization process, there is an enduring technological development. I recall arguing with the incumbent telecom operators. By 1993 when I became competition commissioner, most of the incumbents still vigorously opposed liberalization. Or they wanted to do it their own way, which was a euphemism for 'no liberalization'. We however substantiated that the technological development was already far ahead of their thinking. When it comes down to technological developments, an old fashion monopoly is completely out of step with radical innovations. I would also like to mention the changing role of the state. Instead of the old fashioned industrial policy, where the state pretended to run the economy, one way or another, gradually governments had to acknowledge that they couldn't do so, or at least no longer. So the role of the state changed drastically. But there shouldn't be a misunderstanding. The role of the public authorities remains crucial also in a more market driven economy. The more you liberalize, the more you need rules of the game and a strong authority to enforce the rules and assure fair competition. This is what I would call the 'Thatcher paradox'.

Regarding the question of competitiveness. When we started to think about the telecom sector, it appeared that we had a terrible handicap in Europe as compared, for instance, to the Americans. In telecom, as in other public sectors, not only where the tariffs much higher, but also the service was bad. Companies and individual users alike clearly lacked good quality service. When companies had to lease lines they paid in some instances 30 to 40 times, not percentages, more than competitors in the US. At that time we had a tremendous gap in terms of competitiveness. The following example was the situation in Belgium, but certainly not exclusively in Belgium. When I was nominated as a member of the Commission, I noted that when new colleagues came to Brussels and wanted to have a private telephone they were told they had to wait two, three, perhaps even more months. Could something be done about it? Yes, something could be done about it. If you had influence, political or trade union influence, and used it, then you got your telephone within 24 hours. But as an average citizen you had to wait. And if something went wrong you had to wait for days before it was repaired. Evidently, no one could pretend really that the monopolist was serving the public well. Maybe, one was pretending it was public service, but all to often it was the self-interest of a monopoly. Note that this was only twelve years ago, so movement was needed. And that's finally what happened.

But what where the policy principles behind that movement? From the very offset it was clear, certainly for the European Commission, that we needed to have a sector specific approach. The situation is structurally different sector by sector, for technological and for economic reasons. In the end you can't compare rail with civil aviation. Likewise for postal services or telecom services. The transfer of a solution from one sector to another doesn't necessarily work. Therefore we needed to engineer a very pragmatic approach; that is, a sector specific approach taking into account the characteristics of each sector of activities.

Furthermore, it was taken for granted that in order to make it a lasting success we should make it happen gradually. At least in the EU-constellation of that moment there was no support for a fix-it overnight approach. As a consequence, all these processes started with a so-called white book or whatever you call it, to discuss the matter with the utilities concerned, but also with the relevant stake holders, especially with consumers. Only after that round of consultations it was decided how to liberalize the particular industry. So that's the way it was being organized, and therefore it might have taken years. In the civil aviation sector we could bring it about within five years. But in the telecom sector it did take longer. It may be astonishing, but it is a fact of life.

One of the prime policy principles behind the Commission's liberalization policy of an industry was to guarantee the universal availability of services. The Commission never wanted to take chances with what we called universal service obligations. That means that the way you organize liberalization, the way you develop a policy in a given sector should always take into account the need that the entire population can be properly served. You must guarantee that the services are available to all. This principle would lead to the specific concept of universal service obligations. It brought me often into heated debates for instances in France, because universal service was highly criticized there. In France they stood by the term *service publique*. However, in some areas universal service means more than service publique. Some companies, like Gaz de France tended to take it easy with service publique.

In contrast universal service should be what it says, what it means. It functions as an obligation.

The need to integrate the European economies has also been a powerful element in the liberalization policies. By putting an end to country-by-country national monopoly situations and organizing competition amongst the remaining companies you integrate economies across the borders. It would also lead to enhancing the competitivity of the European economy. Ten years ago we had to acknowledge that we were in a rather bad shape and therefore having also a dramatically high unemployment level. So far for what the global setting is concerned.

Now, I would like to turn to the liberalization process as such. The first question was always can the market deliver the goods? Can it be done through the market mechanism or through the market functioning? Once we were convinced that that could be the case, the next question was to guarantee the provision of universal services, one way or another, either through competition or through specific requirements. For example, in the Telecom sector at least one operator should cover the whole of the territory. Once this guarantee could be provided, then the conclusion was crystal clear: we have to go for it.

Putting ideas on paper is one thing make them work is quite a different job. If I may rephrase the conditions presented in the paper by Mr. Arnbak. Assure access to essential facilities on fair conditions. Fight discrimination and abuse of dominance. Provide consumers with real choice, transparency of prices and fair conditions. Deploy truly universal service. And control mergers, acquisitions and leverage of dominance into downstream markets.

In this context the Commission has been issuing European directives and progress reports, for instance in the telecom sector. By using those instruments we regularly pushed the relevant national authorities to take their responsibility. And if they did not enforce the rules, if they did not make sure that it happened according to what has been agreed, we would say so publicly. And therefore, report after report, the Commission would make it plain that for instance in Belgium and Italy the government were lagging behind and denying the public and the economy the advantages of liberalization.

But why did liberalization happen in a given area and not in another? The explanation might boil down to economic relevance as well as public perception. In the telecom sector it was felt that we had an enormous competitive gap and widespread dissatisfaction of industrial and residential users. So we had a strong case against powerful incumbent monopolists and reluctant governments. It was much more difficult to get things across in the energy field, let alone the postal sector. And finally that is the way it evolved.

The need for sector specific regulation and sector and country specific regulators has also been fiercely debated. The way things evolved in Europe did lead to sector specific rules, for reasons which are not too difficult to explain. First of all the very pragmatic sector by sector approach. Second, the situation might be very different between member states, for example in the energy sector. And of course, thirdly, in order to get an agreement with the member states this sector and country specific regulation was something to be considered. For example, member states could only agree to a directive if enough room would be left for national regulation. Otherwise there wouldn't have been many agreements on the level of the council of ministers.

How do these national regulators function? As the process is on its way, evidently new problems occur, if only because some national regulators de facto do not have the real power to enforce European regulation. Or they take their time, e.g., for issuing licenses. This also introduces an element of unfair competition. It might even raise a new barrier to the single market. Furthermore, it might lead to the fact that in some areas national enforcement is working well, in others it remains a real problem. Finally, not everywhere is there full transparency. For instance, the question of cost accounting is still a troublesome one in some countries. As long as that has not been sorted out, you really run into trouble. The fact that the universal service funding schemes might be biased is another point leading to concerns in terms of fair competition. The national authorities are not necessarily functioning in line with each other. Now, this can be cured hopefully through a more in depth co-operation. It is already happening to some extent.

The question is do you need to keep this system indefinitely? Some argue that you can do away with sector specific regulations and regulators once the competitive environment has been finally established. Then it should be left to the competition authorities. This probably is too one-sided and too simple an answer. But on the other hand, when it comes to competition rules, it should not be left to sector specific authorities either. It makes a coherent competition policy almost impossible.

Take the energy market. For example, over the years many complaints have been voiced over EDF and often rightly so. Could one imagine that such competition issues would be left to national sector specific regulation? When EDF announced it wanted to buy London Electricity even the British started to complain, saying that EDF was still very much a French monopolist keeping the others out of the French market. One observes a similar situation in Germany and Italy since EDF got an important interest in ENWB in Baden-Wurtherberg and Montedison in Italy. There again the complaint is that EDF can't do in France what they can do in their country. There is indeed a real problem in terms of a level playing field, and in terms of reciprocity. Liberalization is a two-way street, not a one way street. This for the time being is not really occurring.

In this respect the role of the Commission consists of blocking mergers or acquisitions when they are creating or enhancing dominant positions in the relevant market. And that's exactly what was done. Very special attention must be paid to Mergers and Acquisitions by former monopolists, be it in the telecom, energy or postal service field.

The last topic I would like to go into is the relationship between competition policy, public investments in infrastructures and the environmental dimension. Competition policy is not just about free trade. This is a misunderstanding. It certainly was one of the biggest mistakes of Mrs. Thatcher. We were talking about a single market, which implies a lot of other things then free trade. Under Mrs. Thatcher it was given policy that the public hand should not invest in infrastructure and that it should be left to the private sector. Just observe the results now, including where it comes to railways. Liberalization is one thing, but global policy development is still a crucial task of public authorities. But even from the point of competition policy, eventually you have to accept state aid to favor some kinds of power generation for environmental reasons. And that's fair enough. Competition rules should accommodate for policy development. And this is certainly true when it comes to infrastructures. Obviously if the state has to back-off from being an entrepreneur the state has a very important role to play, as a regulator, an enforcer of the rules, as promoter of modern infrastructure and as guarantee of a free and socially balanced society. Therefore, the state should not be weakened but made more efficient, all for the sake of the good of the citizens.

REFERENCE

Miert, K. van (2000), (Mijn jaren in Europa) *My years in Europe*, Tielt, Belgium: Lannoo.

2. The Role of Regulation in an Era of Partial Competition

Johannes M. Bauer

1 INTRODUCTION

During the past two decades, telecommunications and energy policy was swept by a renewed belief in the superiority of competition as an economic organizing principle for these industries.[1] Legal and regulatory reforms of infrastructure industries have laid the groundwork for expanding the realms of competition. In the US Congress declared the Telecommunications Act of 1996 as a 'deregulatory, pro-competitive' piece of legislation and initiatives are pending to accelerate the liberalization of energy markets. Measures by the European Union and its member states have likewise expanded the realms of competition in infrastructure industries. There is a widespread consensus that regulation will have an important role to play during the transition period to more robust competition. However, many envision that regulation can be replaced by antitrust policy once infrastructure markets have developed fully competitive conditions.

This paper attempts to provide a critical analysis of the basic premises upon which this pro-competitive stance is based as well as key policy prescriptions derived from it. It will argue that, whereas competition has an important role to play in infrastructure industries, its likely effects will be more heterogeneous and varied than anticipated in the past policy debates. Recent observations, such as the glacial expansion of competition in local telecommunications markets or the recent wave of industry consolidation are compatible with this analysis. Competition is a process of rivalry among firms for something that not all can obtain simultaneously. Under certain conditions, but not always, competition among firms forces them to use resources efficiently (productive efficiency), produce the goods and services demanded by consumers (allocative efficiency), and innovate (dynamic efficiency). Economic research has worked out the conditions under which competition has such beneficial effects. One of the key insights of modern economics is that not all these goals of competition can be achieved simultaneously. Due to the unique economic features of networks industries competitive processes in energy and telecommunications are rather complex and multifaceted. Not all parts of these industries will support robust competition. Competitive and non-competitive market segments will thus continue to coexist.

In this new environment, the role and tasks of regulation change significantly. Rather than serving as a substitute for competition as was the classical view, appropriate regulation is now a complement or a precondition for competition to unfold. Paradoxically, whereas the notion of competition is embraced as a blueprint for an increasing number of practical policy decisions, there exist widely divergent views as to what constitutes 'competition' and how it impacts overall sector efficiency and stakeholders. Traditional economic theory and traditional regulation are strongly influenced by a static view of competition, in which most of the emphasis is placed on the outcome ('equilibrium') of the market process. Other models of competition emphasize the role of competition in fostering innovation and change or in coordinating activities in increasingly complex societies. Lastly, political theories of competition stress the role of competition in preventing the agglomeration of market power in the hands of a few players.

These differences do not just represent various stakeholder interests but are deeply rooted in alternative analytical models of the competitive process and its role in society. Not all of these models are equally appropriate to describe and forecast the events in deregulated infrastructure industries. Such differences would be largely irrelevant, if these different approaches all led to the same policy recommendations. Unfortunately, different analytical lenses result in different policy prescriptions. In the current policy debates an inappropriate notion of competition is often used in framing policy questions and answers, not only resulting in mistaken expectations but also in policies that are detrimental to the further evolution of competition. There is, therefore, an urgent need to better understand the forms and functions of competition in public utility industries.

This paper is an attempt to engage in such a broader debate. It intends to offer frameworks for the analysis and solution of problems rather than specific blueprints. While examples are largely drawn from the recent U.S. experience with regulatory reform the lessons are applicable to the European context as well. The next section of this paper briefly reviews concepts and functions of competition. It will become evident that competition is a more multi-faceted process than commonly perceived. The third section reviews the particular conditions of competition in network infrastructure industries. Section four discusses implications for practical regulatory policy if a more dynamic view of competition is adopted. The paper concludes with key lessons for regulators.

2 CONCEPTS AND FUNCTIONS OF COMPETITION[2]

Competition is essentially a 'rivalry between individuals (or groups or nations) and it arises whenever two or more parties strive for something that all cannot obtain' (Stigler, 1987). Firms compete in various forms such as market trading or auctions and with various instruments, including prices, costs, advertising, as well as research and development (R&D). The objects of competition can be profits, revenue growth, or survival in an industry. Competition often takes place between firms that are already established in a market ('actual competition') but it can also exist between incumbents and potential new entrants ('potential competition').

Competition as such is neither good nor bad but rather a means to achieve desirable ends. Under certain conditions competitive rivalry has beneficial implications for society at large. It forces firms to make efficient use of resources and produce the goods and services demanded by consumers. Over time, competition forces firms to introduce process and product innovations and thus increase the productivity of the industry. Competition facilitates efficient risk-taking by investors and reduces the accumulation of economic and political power in the hands of a few. Last but not least, decentralized decision-making in a competitive industry is often a more efficient way of coordinating complex transactions between multiple suppliers and consumers than more centralized control in a monopoly environment. However, competitive rivalry among firms does not always achieve these goals. Under certain conditions, notably the presence of a natural monopoly, significant economies of scale and scope, strong externalities, or public goods, market organization generally fails to achieve efficiency. If competition emerges among only a few firms, there may be a strong incentive for open or tacit collusion at the expense of efficiency. Moreover, unless effective counter measures are adopted, the highly capital-intensive network industries show an inherent tendency to consolidation and concentration with their detrimental competitive consequences.

2.1 Productive and Allocative Efficiency

Introductory chapters of economics textbooks and the trade press praise competition for its desirable effects on productive and allocative efficiency. Productive efficiency in an industry is reached if firms produce a given output with a least-cost combination of inputs (labor, capital, and materials). Allocative efficiency refers to the overall use of resources in an economy. It is achieved when all resources are dedicated to their most productive use and the bundle of goods and services produced best meets the preferences of consumers.[3] Adam Smith (1776) first pointed out the desirability of competition among many suppliers. Competition in decentralized markets, like an 'invisible hand,' aligns the narrow profit interests of suppliers with the interests of society at large. Merchants will only be able to increase their profits if they produce goods and services of value to society. Most importantly, decentralized markets coordinate decisions among many without the need for a centralized planning authority. In a decentralized economy the most important role of the government is to establish a legal and judicial system, in particular to assure property rights, and to facilitate the effective working of competition.[4]

The powerful metaphor of the invisible hand was later rephrased in more stringent mathematical terms by neoclassical economists, now the school with broad influence over regulatory and public policy-making. In the formalization, the process-orientation of early concepts of competition was eliminated and competition reformulated as the outcome of an atomistic market in equilibrium. In this situation, the market price is set at marginal costs and a level where average costs are minimized. The developments in the market dominate individual decision-making and all firms (and consumers) are price takers. Early economists were aware of the fact that this was a highly stylized limit case of real world markets and rather unlikely to occur in real world situations. Subsequent research focused on the properties of competitive equilibria and could prove powerful but highly abstract theorems. For example, welfare economics established that all competitive equilibria represent a Pareto optimal use of resources.[5] Likewise, every particular state can be reached as a competitive equilibrium by varying the initial endowment of actors. Thus, the notion of competitive equilibrium became equated with the outcome of a highly simplified complex system of markets. Despite the abstract nature of the theory, its conclusions regarding the desirability of competition became widely accepted and recently experienced a renaissance.

Early during the twentieth century major industries became heavily concentrated and the stylized nature of the competitive model was evident. Research began to focus on market structures with fewer suppliers and thus market power. In these market forms firms are not price takers any more but they can influence the market. Moreover, their actions become highly interdependent. The variety of possible outcomes resulted in a myriad of theoretical models. The development of game theory has greatly facilitated the study of such more concentrated markets. Regulatory theory has been greatly improved by these efforts and the development of information economics, which became the basis of the concept of incentive regulation (Laffont and Tirole, 1993). In their theory of contestable markets, Baumol, Panzar, and Willig (1982) have generalized the arguments derived under fully competitive conditions for market structures other than atomistic competition (see Shepherd 1984 for a critical analysis of the weaknesses of this approach). Despite these developments the emphasis remained on the outcome of a market interaction rather than the process of competition. Thus, an entire school of economic thought has essentially ignored the quintessence of competition: dynamic competitive rivalry.[6]

Another feature of the competitive model, developed fully by Kenneth Arrow (1951) in the two theorems of welfare economics, is generally under-emphasized. Competition is an optimization mechanism for reaching efficient outcomes. Its beneficial effect can materialize independent of the initial endowment of actors with resources. Thus, effective competition can achieve a Pareto optimum from any initial endowment of resources, be they distributed fairly evenly or unevenly among the participants in an economic system. In this sense, the outcome competition is fundamentally undetermined until the initial endowment with resources is specified. Economists often gloss over this issue by delegating distributional decisions to policy-makers. However, it is important to recognize that the initial conditions under which competition is introduced matter greatly. These include decision on a certain level of universal service obligations or rights of access to networks, services, and content. Contrary to the predominant view, which looks at non-price obligations as market distortions, these non-price decisions specify important preconditions for the competitive process and influence the overall evolution of the sector.

2.2 Competition as a Turbulent Process

The Harvard economist Joseph Schumpeter promoted the notion of competition as a turbulent process unfolding in time. From this perspective, the essence of competitive rivalry is that firms will attempt to strengthen their market position and to disadvantage competitors. Real world competition consists in tilting the playing field in one's own advantage. Strategies to that effect include achieving cost leadership, continuous innovation and the acquisition of patents and other exclusive rights, or pricing strategies that discourage competition. Firms may also mobilize political strategies to gain protection from potential competitors through regulation or legislation.

Schumpeter (1942) highlighted the importance of innovation for economic growth and prosperity with his colorful metaphor of capitalism as a process of 'creative destruction.' His perspective has not gained a strong foothold in mainstream economic research until recently. Schumpeter emphasized that the ideal of a competitive equilibrium in which the representative firm produces at least cost, prices equal marginal costs, and profits are at a normal level is only a desirable outcome in a stationary economy without technological change. It is not a meaningful yardstick in industries with significant technological potential, as innovation is spurred by the ability of firms to achieve temporary monopolistic profits, which are a premium for assuming the innovation risk. Schumpeter viewed a capitalist market economy as a process of 'creative destruction.' It is not price competition of the traditional sort that matters, he argued. Rather it is 'competition from the new commodity, the new technology, the new source of supply, the new type of organization (the largest-scale unit of control, for example) – competition which demands a decisive cost or quality advantage and which strikes not at the margins of the profits and the outputs of the existing firms but at their foundations and their very lives' (Schumpeter, 1942, p. 84).

In a dynamic perspective, temporary monopoly power and the concomitant supernormal profits are a precondition for innovative activities by firms. Deviations from the efficiency conditions of static equilibrium are not signs of inefficiency but prerequisites for the dynamic efficiency of the system. This perspective has radical implications for the optimal regulatory approach to network industries. Historically, regulation attempted to mimic the outcome of competitive market equilibrium. In contrast, Schumpeter argued that 'it is ... a mistake to base the theory of government regulation of industry on the principle that big business should be made to work as the respective industry would work in perfect competition' (Schumpeter, 1942, p. 106). The practical implications of this position will be explored more fully later in this paper. Suffice it to say that the main engine of competition is seen in deviations from the equilibrium position of markets. If one accepts that premise, policy-makers will have to distinguish between temporary market power, which accompanies competition in dynamic markets, and structural market power, which is a sign of a degenerated competitive process.

2.3 Competition as a Discovery and Coordination Process

Economists have highlighted several other features of competition as an economic organizing principle. The work of the Austrian School of economics, originating in the work of Carl Menger and Friedrich von Wieser focuses more on the informational aspects of economic processes. This approach stressed that economic agents do not know, as is assumed in the traditional competitive model, the totality of information relevant for their decisions, such as the true minimum cost of production, the potential for innovation, and so forth. The economic problem of society is a 'problem of the utilization of knowledge' and it is 'only through the process of competition that the facts will be discovered' (Hayek, 1945, p. 321; 1949, p. 96). Thus competition has its main role as a *discovery process* in which decentralized economic actors utilize their local information and create relevant information for other actors in the economy.

Kirzner (1992) has pointed out, market prices *communicate* information that has been discovered and thereby influence the direction of entrepreneurial energies. For instance, the fact that a firm can produce certain goods or services at a price below the current market price reveals information for all other producers and buyers about the possible costs of production. Likewise, an innovation reveals information about new processes or products. The advantage of a competitive organization of the economy, as opposed to a more controlled one, thus stems from its superior ability to process knowledge. Competition also works as a selection process by awarding larger market shares to more efficient firms and penalizing less efficient ones with shrinking market shares or even elimination from the market. Thus, from this informational perspective, a decentralized market organization of an industry may be desirable even under conditions that do not allow effective competition. Modern auction theory has provided a more formal backing for many of these arguments and supported the view of competition as a selection mechanism in markets with imperfect competition (Vickers, 1994).

3 COMPETITION IN NETWORK INDUSTRIES

Energy and telecommunications are network industries with economic characteristics that raise several unique issues. Technological change, such as distributed generation in electricity or the emergence of a data-centric network architecture in telecommunications, may lead to a radical reconfiguration of the network architecture of these industries. Competition in these industries will in part emerge from such new methods of providing substitute services. However, new service providers will have to succeed in competition with the incumbent service providers. Several aspects of the existing infrastructures affect the emerging patterns of competition. These features can bestow competitive advantages but also disadvantages on the incumbent service providers. There is a risk that in an attempt to mitigate these advantages or disadvantages, regulators will be tempted to micromanage the emerging competitive processes.

3.1 Forms of Competition in Network Industries

The vertical and horizontal integration of energy and telecommunications is to a large degree influenced by past regulatory decisions. The historical monopoly organization of the industry was premised on the existence of strong natural monopoly features and advantages of coordination between the different stages in the value chain. Recent policy experiments have demonstrated that the natural monopoly argument was overly broad and ill defined. However, the potential for competition varies greatly in the different segments of telecommunications and energy.

Moreover, even if the underlying market structure would allow competition it does not necessarily follow that sufficient market entry will occur to reach this structure. In order to enter a particular market segment, new competitors must face sufficient incentives to assume the risks associated with that segment. As will be discussed in more detail, the most important factors affecting market entry are the profit potential of a market segment and its growth potential. Actual market entry depends on the interaction of the cost and demand conditions of the specific market segment, the regulatory policies adopted towards that market segment and complementary market segments, as well as the corporate strategies of incumbents and new entrants.

Both energy and telecommunications can be envisioned as multi-tier industries. In telecommunications, a basic distinction is between network operation, services provision, and the supply of content. The network tier is best characterized as a network of networks, comprising local fixed networks, local wireless networks, long distance and international networks, satellites, cable television, as well as various data communications networks. Historically, these networks were engineered to provide a specific service such as voice, entertainment, or data. The digitization of information has broadened the capabilities of these formerly specialized networks and increasingly allows the transport of different kinds of information independently of the network platform. Broadband networks are the ultimate general service network infrastructure. In the electricity industry it makes sense to distinguish between generation, transmission, distribution, as well as ancillary services.

Competition can occur at different stages of the value chain. Most of the current discussion emphasizes competition for outputs such as voice telephone service or energy services to ultimate consumers. A detailed analysis of competitive processes in output markets needs to define various attributes, most importantly the nature of the output, the geographic location, and the time period during which it is provided. A competitive relation between outputs only exists if they are substitutes for each other. The degree of substitutability varies with the three attributes of outputs. Obviously, local phone service in location A is no substitute for a local phone call in location B. However, for a residential telephone user an evening call to a relative may be a close substitute for a call during peak afternoon hours. For a business user, on the other hand, peak and off-peak calls may not be substitutes at all. Likewise, in electricity the market for spot transactions is quite different from the market for long-term delivery contracts. Suppliers can thus compete for consumers by varying the term structure of their contracts. In fact, contract theory would suggest that the term structure of contract is influenced by the underlying technological relations (Helm and Jenkinson, 1997).

As these examples illustrate, competition at the output level can develop on one or more of the three attributes. Firms will use a variety of variables to compete against their rivals. Only in a structurally perfectly competitive market with its fully homogenous services, full market transparency, and ease of entry and exit will competition center on the price. In other market structures, the price of a good or services is only one – and often not the most important – dimension of competition. Firms will attempt to differentiate products and services along these three main dimensions by selecting particular locations, varying service quality, by offering different price packages, or by creating brand loyalty and other barriers against switching of suppliers. Many competitive strategies therefore reduce the substitutability between services and thus reduce the degree of competition between goods and services. The notion of effective competition intends to identify a degree of rivalry that is sufficient for the achievement of the benefits of rivalry among firms.

A basic distinction can be made between the provision of the physical network infrastructure and the services provided using this infrastructure. Market entry can be facilities-based or only limited to the services tier. For example, a new provider of long distance voice services can invest in own facilities, lease the needed capacity and other inputs from other facilities-based carriers and package it into a new service, or act as a pure reseller of existing services. New entrants also can pursue a mixed strategy of combining own facilities with leased capacity and pure resale. The network operations market and the services market differ significantly with respect to their investment needs and thus the risk of market entry. It is obvious that the regulatory framework of the industry influences the pattern of market entry. The Telecommunications Act of 1996, for instance, has created conditions that are rather conducive to service-based entry and perhaps discouraged the entry of facilities-based carriers. The specific mix between facilities and resale competition has strong repercussions on the longer-term evolution of competitive forces. Unfortunately, these inter-temporal links are not well understood yet.

In network industries, other forms of competition will evolve and can be utilized in restructuring strategies. Effective output competition will only emerge if the cost and demand conditions of the market allow a sufficient number of competitors to coexist. Where such effective competition in a market is not feasible due to natural monopoly conditions, competition *for* a market can serve as a substitute. Such methods have been used occasionally in network industries, for example, in forms of franchise bidding or more recently in spectrum auctions. As Williamson (1976) and others have pointed out, methods of franchise bidding and auctions have certain advantages but also disadvantages. Regardless, they can serve as useful tools to harness competitive forces in market segments that would otherwise not allow workable competition. Lastly, competitive forces can also be utilized at the level of inputs. The degree of vertical integration of network industries is not static and often competition for inputs can be introduced. Suffice it to say that in order for competition at the input level to work, the underlying market structure needs to support a sufficient number of firms.

3.3 Incentives to Enter a Market

Competition in a formerly monopolistic market can originate from three principal sources. First, firms operating in another geographic area but in the same industry may enter a market. Both domestic and international firms pursue such 'horizontal expansion' strategies. Thus the legal and regulatory framework governing entry into public utility markets by foreign firms will impact the evolution of competition. Second, new entry may come from firms with a presence in related or even unrelated markets. Examples of such 'product expansion' are the entry of energy companies into the provision of telecommunications services or the entry of long distance telephone service providers into cable television. Third, new entry may come from start-up companies. Each of these groups of potential competitors has unique advantages and disadvantages. Entrants with prior experience in energy and telecommunications may be able to build on their knowledge of the industry as well as potential economies of scale and scope between a potential new market and existing operations. At the same time they may be constrained by their existing management and operational routines that may have been shaped by the same regulatory environment than the incumbent's. As well, their existing capital base may have been developed during a regulated monopoly period. Firms that are new to a particular industry may be able to take advantage of new technologies and operating practices but may have to overcome significant initial learning costs before they can effectively compete.

The scale and form of market entry are influenced by the particular risk profile of a market, which in turn are dependent on its structural features. Empirical studies reveal that in a private capitalist environment the most important factors stimulating market entry are profit opportunities and market growth. On the other hand, market entry is negatively correlated to the absolute costs of capital required to reach the minimum efficient scale of operations (Siegfried and Evans, 1994). Entry may also be slowed or even blocked if the incumbent possesses effective deterrence strategies. Other things equal, the profitability of market entry, first, varies inversely with the efficiency of the incumbent. Somewhat paradoxically, effective regulation may contribute to a slower pace of market entry. Second, the profitability of market entry is influenced by the potential to introduce cost reducing innovations. One can thus expect that market entry is more vigorous in a technologically dynamic industry. Third, market entry may be induced if there is a potential to enhance revenues through strategies of price and service differentiation. Such approaches allow consumers to self-select an optimal plan, often enhancing welfare.

The traditional economic and management literature suggested that firms enter a market if the net present value (NPV) of an undertaking is positive. More recent analyses of the role and impact of uncertainty on investment decisions have cast some doubt on the validity of this simple criterion, except under very predictable market conditions. In the presence of uncertainty as to the future development of a market, firms will only pursue an investment project if its expected net present value is above a certain threshold (Dixit and Pindyck, 1994). The magnitude of this threshold depends on the specific type of uncertainty. Moreover, firms may structure an investment project in ways that reduce risk over time. A project may be postponed until more information is available. Alternatively, a market entry strategy with a lower risk profile, for example, resale as opposed to facilities based, may be followed.

Uncertainty may also work in the opposite direction and accelerate investment decisions if new entrants are in a race to establish the first presence in a market. Entrants who capture customers early on may be able to reap subsequent competitive advantages if consumers can be locked in through pricing and other strategies. The current investment strategies into broadband access facilities may fall into this category of a race for presence.

It is difficult to quantify the profitability threshold required to trigger actual market entry at the time of regulatory reform. However, it can be speculated that, other things equal, a certain threshold level is easier to reach in market segments with a high growth potential and/or with a high technological potential and innovation rate.

It is evident from this analysis that liberalization will most likely lead to uneven and selective market entry. New entrants will first target highly profitable and/or fast growing market segments and thus 'cherry-pick' the most lucrative subscribers. Regulators have long worried about selective market entry and its impacts on universal service obligations of the incumbent service provider. To avoid regulation-imposed financial impacts on the incumbent it is important that prices are subsidy free. It is further necessary that the incumbent firm have sufficient flexibility to react to market entry and that social obligations are funded in ways that do not systematically distort market entry decisions by placing the burden on the incumbent. Thin and slowly growing market segments will likely not see significant market entry. Even in areas that generally would allow competition, such as long distance telephone service, new entrants may gain market share only at a slow rate, say one to two percentage points per year.[7]

3.4 Market Entry Barriers

The incentive to enter a market is affected by the presence of exogenous and endogenous market entry barriers. Barriers to entry protect the position of the established firm to the detriment of consumers. Exogenous barriers to entry are embedded into the structure of a particular market whereas endogenous entry barriers are created by established firms to fend off competitors. Important exogenous entry barriers in network industries include the high capital requirements of network industries, economies of scale and scope, cost advantages enjoyed by the incumbent, or the exclusive control over strategic resources. Entry barriers can be both a cause and the effect of market power. Some of their effects can be mitigated by regulatory measures.

Major segments of the energy and telecommunications infrastructure are characterized by a high capital intensity. In particular, the local loop in telecommunications, or electricity generation, both potentially competitive market segments require high upfront capital expenditures. (Electricity transmission and distribution can be considered classical examples of natural monopolies.) Under certain conditions, the disadvantages of new entrants due to high upfront investment requirements can be mitigated through resale, unbundling and interconnection provisions. Such provisions allow new entrants to build facilities gradually without having to construct a full-scale network. However, this approach is more effective in telecommunications, where the costs of entering the services tier are often relatively low, than in electricity. In addition to capital requirements, network industries are characterized by economies of scale and scope that can only be captured by securing a large portion of the market. In telecommunications, larger firms also benefit from network externalities as customers generally realize higher benefits from subscribing to a larger network. Interconnection requirements in telecommunications have been motivated as an effective means to overcome these advantages of incumbency related to the scale of operations (Brock, 1996).

Incumbent firms have a broad menu of competitive strategies at their disposal to erect endogenous entry barriers and reduce the threat of market entry. Important measures include the setting of prices that discourage entry, investment into excess capacity to signal readiness to meet expanding demand, or strategies to increase the costs for consumers for switching to a new supplier. Whereas most of these measures are widely practiced legitimate business strategies, they may also be abused to distort competition. The unique economic features of network industries may, moreover, increase the freedom of the incumbent firm to utilize such approaches. In particular, the simultaneous presence of incumbent service providers in monopolistic and competitive markets and their ability to readily price discriminate between consumers with different price elasticities of demand raises concerns. Likewise, the control of incumbent service providers over bottleneck facilities that are complementary to services provided by competitors could be abused in an anti-competitive fashion.

If given the freedom to reduce prices, incumbent firms have a broad range of options to keep potential competitors at bay. Limit entry pricing refers to strategies in which the established firm sets prices at a level low enough to render entry by a new supplier unprofitable.[8] If entry is only a temporary threat, the incumbent firm may increase its prices again once the potential entrant has been fended off. Price differentiation can stimulate competition if it is practiced sporadically in a structurally competitive environment. However, in network industries, the established firms, often in command of a dominant market share, can readily price discriminate and thus maintain potentially anti-competitive strategies of price discrimination for extended time periods. Regulators therefore face the challenge to allow pro-competitive forms of price differentiation but prohibit strategies intended to quench competition.

Established firms have many other strategies in their arsenal potentially reducing the threat of new entry. In some cases the threat of retaliation alone may suffice to discourage entry. An incumbent may invest into excess capacity to signal a potential entrant that its output could be expanded quickly, depressing the market price and thus profit potential of entry. Firms can use advertising campaigns to increase consumer loyalty. They may be able to create switching costs for consumers by building their services around proprietary equipment standards. Market segmentation and packing of the product space with a variety of offerings may create additional difficulty for entry on a broad scale. Control over strategic resources, such as rights of way, patents, or proprietary technology may prevent new competition. Lastly, the established firm may have exclusive access to information that is critical for new entrants, for example, on customer load profiles or calling patterns. The ability of a new entrant to compete successfully may hinge on access to that kind of information.

Several options are available for regulators to prevent or at least mitigate the abuse of entry barriers. These include the structural separation of non-competitive and competitive market segments, the imposition of equal access obligations, or the establishment of non-discrimination requirements. As will be discussed in more detail below, in a competitive environment there needs to be strong evidence or at least a high likelihood of abuse to justify asymmetric treatment of service providers.

3.5 Assessing the Potential for Competition

From a regulatory point of view, a crucial question is whether a market segment has the potential to develop effective competition. This potential is lowest (highest) in those market segments where the minimum efficient size (MES) of a supplier compared to total market demand is high (low) (see table 2.1). In telecommunications the segment with the lowest potential for competition is the operation of local fixed networks. The main reasons are the existence of relatively high fixed costs of installing a local connection and economies of density. Costs of digging in ducts and cable are still the highest cost component of installing local connections. These costs are highest for fixed wire networks but do also exist for wireless local loop (WLL) technology and mobile communications networks. Economies of density emanate from the fact that the costs of installing local loops on a per capita basis is less if the population in a given geographic area is larger. Not only does this allow the construction of a local network with less cable it also allows the concentration of traffic into higher capacity facilities with lower costs per circuit or packet of information.

Current policy towards the local loop is predicated on the assumption that the availability of multiple technological platforms will allow effective competition even in the local loop. In the past, strong barriers to cross entry existed between potential providers of fixed local services, such as telephone, cable TV, and other utility companies. The elimination of these barriers in the Telecommunications Act of 1996 as well as the emergence of digital technology, which enhances the functionality of existing networks, may indeed lead to the co-existence of a sufficient number of providers of local access services. However, due to the existence of high installation costs, many users may ultimately be connected only to one fixed and, due to their mobility advantages, possibly one wireless network. As Armstrong (1997) has pointed out this implies that as long as one subscriber is connected to one specific fixed or mobile network (network 1), this network enjoys a monopoly over serving this customer. Users connected to another network (network 2) need access to the local loop of network 1 in order to communicate with users on that network. For this reason it can be expected that the local loop will continue to show certain natural monopoly characteristics. Thus, independently of the number of competitors in a location, some monopoly problems will persist. Appropriate policies for interconnection and open access are important to overcome these remaining pockets of monopoly power.

Table 2.1 Potential for competition in energy and telecommunications

	Potential for competition	
	Limited	**Medium-high**
Telecommunications	Local network operation	Service provision, interexchange, international network operation
Electricity	Transmission grid, distribution	Generation, energy services
Natural Gas	Pipeline transportation, distribution	Exploration, storage, energy services

In contrast to the local loop, there are probably no other areas in the telecommunications industry with strong natural monopoly characteristics. Whether these market segments will develop the features of effective competition depends on the salient cost and demand characteristics, regulatory policies, and corporate strategies adopted by incumbents and new entrants. The U.S. long distance market, for example, has long been characterized by a structure of tight oligopoly between AT&T, MCI/WorldCom and Sprint. A competitive fringe of more than 800 alternative service providers, most of them resellers has had only a limited impact on the pricing of services. Another example that is not a natural monopoly but plagued with forms of market power is the Internet backbone market, which is dominated by a few players. These market structures raise complicated issues but are perhaps better addressed by antitrust authorities than regulators.

Based on the current technology, the potential for competition in electricity markets is highest in generation markets. In contrast, the transmission grid and local distribution facilities will, for the foreseeable future, remain naturally monopolistic.[9] Competition in generation hinges on the regulatory regime implemented for the transmission grid and local distribution. Unlike in telecommunications, where a wave of technological change provides ample entry opportunities, the scope for competition in generation depends on the overall economic conditions in the energy markets. New gas fired generation technology is vulnerable to fluctuations in the price of natural gas. Moreover, in electricity market entry is often a function of embedded inefficiencies. Once these are eliminated, the market may start to reintegrate leaving the overall competitive outcome somewhat in doubt. A critical issue is the magnitude of coordination costs in a disintegrated electricity industry. The overall transaction costs are the outcome of two conflicting effects. Information technology allows more efficient coordination between the generation, transmission, and distribution stages and thus helps reduce coordination costs. On the other hand, the differentiation of the markets will increase coordination costs. Whether competition will have a positive net welfare impact will depend on the net effect of efficiency increases and transaction costs (Joskow, 1997).

4 REGULATION AND COMPETITION

Regulators face the difficult challenge of having to adopt policies facilitating market entry while prohibiting the abuse of market power by the incumbent. There is a danger that in an attempt to eliminate seemingly abusive conduct, regulators adopt policies that also suppress the emergence of competition. Motivated by a results-based rather than a procedural view of competition, public policy-makers may also strive to achieve certain outcomes through the micro-management of the competitive process. Legislatively mandated price reductions (e.g., electricity in California and Michigan) or market allocations (e.g., natural gas in Georgia) can seriously distort the working of market forces. In a partially competitive environment, regulatory decisions influence the further path of competition. For example, the permission of an incumbent provider of monopoly services to participate in competitive markets carries a higher risk of an abuse of market power (e.g., tacit forms of exclusion) than a clear separation of the two markets. From a public policy perspective it is thus important to recognize how the legal and regulatory regime of an industry influences the overall pattern of competition. This section discusses three key areas in which a more dynamic view of competition will lead to different prescriptions. They are the overall organization of the market, the treatment of bottleneck facilities at the wholesale level, and the design of regulatory policies for retail markets with continued market power.

4.1 Basic Principles

Competition is a dynamic process. Even where a market segment is structurally competitive, it will likely take some time before competition becomes a self-regulating process. The model of effective competition, outlined in this paper, provides criteria as to when regulatory oversight can be phased out. It provides less guidance for policy during a transition period to such a competitive structure. Nor does it provide conclusive advice as to how industries should be treated in which competitive and monopolistic market segments continue to coexist for extended time periods. Two approaches are widespread in dealing with the transition period to a more competitive environment. One approach is the maintenance of a traditional regulatory approach until competitive conditions have emerged. The criteria for determining when competition is sufficient are often vague and not applied in a consistent fashion (Bauer, 1999). The other approach is early deregulation in the belief that competition will eventually emerge. Neither approach is conceptually very sound in the light of the previous discussion.

In part, the difficulties of designing regimes for a transition to competition rest in the underpinnings of regulatory theory and practice in static economic theory. In part, they are associated with the incremental nature of the process of regulatory reform and the specific institutional framework in which it is embedded. The mandate of regulatory agencies is often defined as ensuring efficiency and fairness in energy and telecommunications. In a monopoly framework, regulators have the power to find a balance between these goals. In a partially competitive framework the reconciliation of these goals is more complicated. Competition leads to differentiation and creates winners and losers compared to the status quo ante, often appearing as a chaotic process. It is therefore helpful to review some basic principles that could guide regulatory policies in a more open market environment.

A key issue is whether the regulatory approach should treat all players in a symmetric fashion. Calls for asymmetric regulation originate from either the conviction that incumbent players would abuse their market power to expand their domination into competitive market segments or in the perceived need to help new entrants overcome some of their initial disadvantages ('infant industry' argument). Asymmetric regulation is widely practiced and often seen as a prerequisite to strengthen the forces of competition (Perucci and Cimatoribus, 1997). However, asymmetric regulation likely leads to a growing number of detailed regulatory interventions into the market, often with unknown net effects on competition and sector efficiency.

This risk has caused some authors to argue strongly in favor of symmetric regulation. Sidak and Spulber (1998), for example, propose three principles for the design of an overall regulatory framework, which would assure the evolution of fair and efficient competition. The *economic incentive* principle assures that no service provider is burdened with regulatory service obligations. The *equal opportunity* principle implies that incumbent players and new entrants should be allowed to pursue the same kinds of business strategies (e.g., price differentiation or diversification). Lastly, the *impartiality* principle requires that regulations are technologically and competitively neutral and apply to all market participants in the same way.

From the standpoint of competitive theory, a strong argument can be made in favor of symmetric regulation. An asymmetric framework may be justified if there is evidence that a more balanced approach would indeed thwart important public policy goals. A reliance on modern methods of regulation, such as global price caps, may facilitate a reconciliation of the seemingly contradictory goals of symmetric freedom to compete with the prevention of an abuse of market power. Katz (2000) has rightly emphasized that, as regulatory change causes administrative and transition costs, defining and implementing a symmetric regulatory regime only makes sense if these costs are outweighed by the associated benefits. Thus, under the unique economic conditions of network industries blanket calls for either a symmetric or asymmetric framework need to be replaced by more systematic analyses of the specific conditions of a market segment.

4.2 Overall Market Organization

As previous sections have illustrated, regulation cannot create an effectively competitive market; it can only create the conditions that allow competition to unfold. Whether the market will evolve into an effectively competitive market can often not be determined with a high degree of confidence at the outset. Thus, continued monitoring of the evolution of competition rather than blind faith is necessary. Public policy has most control over the legal framework of the industry. The design of market entry rules, of constraints on the organization and conduct of the major players, and of non-market obligations influences the unfolding of competitive processes. With regard to the overall market organization important regulatory variables are the degree of separation between potentially monopolistic and competitive market segments and the rules governing the participation of providers of monopolistic or oligopolistic services in competitive markets.

There are three basic options for approaching the overall industry organization, which differ with respect to the degree of separation they impose on the industry. First, monopolistic and competitive market segments can be structurally fully separated. In this approach providers of monopolistic services are not allowed to participate in the competitive markets. However, they may be part of a holding company with presence in both market segments or carry such operations out through a separate subsidiary. A case in point is Rochester Telephone, which was separated as a network company from the service provider Frontier Communications (now Qwest Communications). In this approach, one company can be present in both market segments, for example, through a fully owned subsidiary. Second, competitive and monopolistic operations may be performed by one company but treated separately for accounting purposes. Third, a firm may be free to participate in all market segments without any particular constraints.

Table 2.2 Optimal policies towards sector organization

	High potential of abuse of integration	**Low potential of abuse of integration**
Strong economies	Case-by-case analysis Best solution dependent on relative magnitude of effects	Freedom to participate in any organizational form best suited to exploit economies
Weak economies	Structural separation	Freedom to diversify in any organizational form

The key for making these decisions is in the assessment of a trade-off between the potential for abuse of a dominant market position and the potential efficiency losses due to synergies between the segmented parts of the industry. Incumbent firms may have a knowledge base and skills that would be lost if they were not allowed to participate in a competitive market segment. There may, further, be strong economies of scope embedded into the technology of the industry. In such cases the efficiency losses due to separation may be high. If a high potential for abuse exists, for example, because the regulator suffers from a serious information disadvantage, then a case-by-case assessment is necessary.

If, on the other hand, the risk of abuse of integrated operations is low, the established firms may be allowed to freely participate in competitive activities. This is the case if the regulator does not have a systematic information deficit and thus the conduct of the firm is easily observable or if regulatory incentives can be created that mitigate possible abuses. The optimal policy will depend on a detailed analysis of the costs and benefits of separation versus integration. If the efficiency gains from economies of scale and scope are low but the risk of an abuse of integration high, the default approach should be a structural separation. Firms can be free to pursue their activities in any organizational form if neither economic efficiency gains from integration are strong nor the risk of abuse is significant.

An asymmetric framework is therefore appropriate in the presence of strong economies of integration coupled with a high risk of an abuse of the dominant position. If there is not strong evidence in support of such a scenario, a symmetric framework seems to be the appropriate default solution. Regulators in different jurisdictions may interpret the structural conditions of the industry differently and also have varying degrees of risk aversion. Thus, their choices of best strategies may diverge. Nevertheless, the outlined framework would put many of the restructuring issues on a more solid ground and allow regulators to focus on the design of regulatory rules that mitigate potential abuses of market power.

In electricity, a high risk of abuse is likely given if a player has simultaneous control of generation as well as transmission and distribution facilities. The Federal Energy Regulatory Commission's (FERC) blueprint in Order 888/889 for only functional separation between competitive operations and the transmission system may therefore be inappropriate in the transition to a more open market environment. Likewise, a higher degree of structural separation between the network and services, especially in local telecommunications, would likely reduce conflicts between the incumbent firms and new entrants and allow a simplification of the regulatory framework. In all other cases it may be an efficient approach to establish a rebuttable presumption in favor of a symmetric framework. Stakeholders that are concerned about symmetry would have to come forward with supportive evidence. If such evidence cannot be produced periodic reviews of the experience with competition and antitrust measures can be used to cope with potential abuses of market power.

4.3 Interconnection, Unbundling and Openness

Due to the specific economic characteristics of network industries competition will not evolve evenly throughout the industry. As a result one or a few suppliers often control services that are complementary and necessary for the provision of competitive services. The existence of such essential facilities, such as the transmission and distribution networks in electricity, the distribution network in the natural gas industry, and the local loop in telecommunications, may raise complex regulatory issues. Moreover, even if competing network facilities exist, the layered nature of service provision raises complex issues with regard to standardization and openness. For example, wireless markets are generally considered effectively competitive and hence subject only to light-handed regulatory regimes. In Europe, the mandated adoption of the GSM standard by all carriers has stimulated competition between handset manufacturers, facilitated the deployment of services using wireless platforms, and reduced switching costs for subscribers. In contrast, U.S. policy was based on multiple standards and has resulted in significant switching costs, limited competition, and significant control of service providers over their customers' choice options with regard to terminal equipment and services. The problem was aggravated by the reliance on auctions, which increased the incentives of carriers to build 'walled garden' networks and likely reduced the welfare gains from mobile services. It has been suggested that more open access policies might help overcome this flaw (Noam, 2001).

A straightforward solution to the existence of bottleneck facilities is their provision by a structurally separated entity with an obligation to supply these essential services on a non-discriminatory basis. Complications arise if the entity supplying the essential facility also competes in the retail market requiring the input. Recent regulatory doctrine holds that such essential services should be priced at their forward-looking incremental costs. A recent example is the pricing of interconnection services in telecommunications. The Total Element Long Run Incremental Cost (TELRIC) method proposed by the FCC combines status quo and best practice assumptions. Whereas the existing location of wire centers is accepted, costs are based on the most efficient available technology (greenfield approach). The FCC's Order was stayed by the courts and later remanded to the agency by the U.S. Supreme Court for clarification. In the meantime, state Public Utility Commissions, following the mandate of the Telecommunications Act, set interconnection rates based on a range of forward-looking methodologies, including variations of TELRIC and Total Service Long Run Incremental Costs (TSLRIC). [10]

Brock (1996) and Katz (1996) discuss the economic rationales for the FCC's approach from a neoclassical perspective. In contrast to TSLRIC, TELRIC includes a portion of the common cost of the service provider and therefore addresses the problem of cost recovery.[11] As a forward-looking cost concept, it allows competitors to take advantage of existing economies of scale, scope and density. It also reduces the incumbent's advantage due to network externalities and reputation. From a static efficiency perspective this is a correct approach. The argument can even be interpreted in a dynamic fashion: new facilities-based market entry will only occur if the new service provider indeed has a more efficient technology, organization, or marketing available.[12]

However, for this argument to be correct, market entry would have to occur at the margin. Dynamic competitive analysis emphasizes that change in real-world markets does not occur at the margin but only if significant cost differences and thus profit opportunities exist. Therefore, the solutions adopted for interconnection pricing will likely deter facilities-based competition from new entrants. Kahn (1998) has pointed to this fact albeit without explicit reference to dynamic competitive models. He argues that interconnection prices and resale prices should be based on long run incremental costs (LRIC), based on the historical embedded costs of providing the service.[13]

Baumol and Gregory (1994) have promoted the Efficient Component Pricing Rule (ECPR) as a dynamically efficient approach to the pricing of essential facilities. Laffont and Tirole (2000) offer a more generalized treatment of optimal deviations from incremental costs in accordance with the cost and demand conditions of the incumbent and the new entrant. These proposals have several advantages, including the fact that they are compensatory and thus reduce the incentive of the incumbent firm to use exclusionary tactics other than the price to stall competition. However, they have also serious disadvantages. The ECPR is based on very strong and unrealistic theoretical assumptions. The generalized proposal by Laffont and Tirole requires detailed information that is often not available. A possible way out of this dilemma is the imposition of a broad price cap on the company providing the essential facilities. Such a global price cap would encompass wholesale and retail services and avoid some of the difficulties of earlier proposals. Unfortunately, global price caps do not prevent the incumbent firm from exerting a price squeeze and thus further monitoring is required.

Further applied research is necessary in the areas of access and interconnection pricing. However, a more dynamic competitive analysis illustrates that the currently widespread approach of pricing access at the level of the incremental costs of the most efficient available technology is likely to bias competition towards services-based market entry. Also it will likely trigger exclusionary actions from the incumbents, which will in turn increase the regulatory workload. This approach also raises the question of regulatory and deregulatory takings (Sidak and Spulber, 1998). Regulatory takings occur in a liberalized or a monopoly environment in which the regulator does not allow the firm to either charge its full long run incremental costs (LRIC) or to impute a reasonable markup over LRIC in the presence of a fixed cost. Deregulatory takings may occur if an incumbent firm has the mistaken expectations that its market will not be liberalized and thus applies a lower depreciation rate than would be calculated in the expectation of a liberalized market environment. The practical relevance of the deregulatory takings issue has been questioned (Trebing, 2000) but the larger issue of correct pricing of essential facilities in a dynamic setting remains relevant.

At a pragmatic level, therefore, a dynamic competitive perspective allows several conclusions with regard to the pricing of access. First, setting access prices at a level of fully embedded costs seems preferable to incremental cost pricing as it sends the correct signal to competitors considering facilities-based market entry. As was discussed earlier, in a dynamic context, competitors base their entry decisions among other things on the profitability of market entry. In a technologically dynamic environment, profitability, in turn, depends on the cost difference between the embedded technology and new technology. This decision is distorted if prices are set at the level of the most efficient technology and hence too little facilities-based investment will likely take place. The experience in local telecommunications markets largely confirms this conclusion. Another possible solution is to grant further pricing flexibility to the providers of essential facilities within the constraints of a global price cap. To mitigate the risk of a price squeeze, a maximum price level for a service could be pragmatically set at the level corresponding to the ECPR (Laffont and Tirole, 2000).

4.4 Regulation of Retail Markets

A third area in which a process-oriented perspective of competition would necessitate a different approach is the regulation of retail services. This is an area in which current regulatory practice comes closest to policies that are compatible with dynamic competition. It also illustrates some of the crucial choices faced by regulators. In an open market environment, prices are dynamic tools in the competitive process. They are utilized in addition to other competitive tools such as variations in the quality of service, the bundling of services, advertising, and customer support services. One would thus expect a greater differentiation in the qualities of service offered as well as in the prices charged for these services. As long as these developments are sufficiently transparent to consumers and their choice options are not restricted by unreasonable switching costs, market forces will support a welfare enhancing process of self-selection. For this reason, prices will not only be based on the costs of service but also reflect demand-side market conditions. Unlike in a regulated environment, neither the supplier nor the regulator will have to know the demand function in order to devise optimal prices. Rather, prices will gravitate towards market equilibrium in a process of trial and error.

The variation of prices in emerging competitive markets challenges traditional regulatory thinking, which often conceptualizes optimal prices as the static equilibrium price in a fully competitive market. Regulation needs to find a balance between permitting sufficient flexibility and avoiding abuse. In other words, regulation needs to be able to distinguish between temporary market power and structural market power. In the first case, an increase of a price above the costs of providing a service will lead to subsequent market entry (or at least a threat of market entry) followed by a downward price correction. In the second case, price increases are maintained over extended periods of time without any competitive response. In making this assessment, regulators need to look at the structural features of a market as well as the conduct and performance of the players in the market. Only lasting abuses of market power should result in a policy response.

The potential for abuse is related to the concentration of the market and to the effective competitive choices of consumers. Thus, where markets exhibit the conditions of effective competition, price regulation can properly be phased out. It may be necessary to establish provisions to improve market transparency and consumer protection. Where these conditions do not hold, some form of regulatory price control is required. Well-designed price cap plans do probably best meet the dual challenge of providing flexibility while protecting consumers against the systematic abuse of market power. In practice, this means that all services that are not provided under effectively competitive conditions should be integrated into regulatory supervision. Pricing flexibility under price caps should be more limited for services in which competition is limited. Thus, price caps should set a lid on the ability of suppliers to price discriminate against consumers without choice options.

(Flexibility can be allowed in situations in which a low price elasticity of demand is the result of high customer valuation and not the effect of a lack of competition.) For services in which no effective competition emerges, the overall level of prices under a price cap plan needs to be re-calibrated with cost information. This requires that the profitability of the firm operating under price caps needs to be reviewed as well. In addition, the structure of prices for non-competitive services needs to be periodically reviewed to avoid cross-subsidization between service classes or rate groups. Where operations under price cap plans increase the financial risk of a utility, this should be reflected in an increased return on equity around which the incentive plan is structured.

In the energy industries, transmission and distribution services are least likely to develop effectively competitive structures and thus will require continued use of cost data. In telecommunications, retail and wholesale access services may not justify the elimination of regulatory oversight in the near future. Unfortunately, many of the existing price cap plans fail to achieve the above stated objectives. Often, services that are not considered 'core' are excluded from price caps independently of the competitive structure of the market, allowing the exertion of market power in ancillary services, such as caller ID or call waiting. Second, the rules governing pricing flexibility are often unrelated to the underlying competitive structure of the market. Lastly, price cap plans are often introduced without appropriate provisions for their review. For example, utilities are shielded from a future scrutiny of their profitability or from a review of the subsidy-free nature of their prices.

4.5 Market Power and its Abuse

Market power is the ability of a firm to manipulate a market to its own advantage without triggering a competitive response. Market power can manifest itself in many forms besides an increase of the price above (marginal) costs. It can also be wielded through variations in the service quality, specific conditions placed into service contracts such as high surcharges for additional services, or through the bundling of services. In contrast to temporary market power, which is an intricate part of the competitive process, structural market power impairs the working of market forces. Obviously, structural market power will continue to affect electricity transmission and distribution as well as local markets in telecommunications. The empirical experience in network industries demonstrates that opening market entry does not eliminate market power even in structurally competitive segments. In part this is due to the fact that competition needs time to unfold. Markets may transit through extended periods of dominant firm structures and oligopoly before they reach an effectively competitive state (Shepherd, 1984).

An examination of the degree of market power needs to look at structural features of a market as well as the conduct of firms in these markets. A first step in assessing market power is the delineation of the relevant geographic and product market. Antitrust authorities determine the relevant geographic market typically by assuming a hypothetical 5% price increase in a specific location. All firms that can be expected to respond to such an increase are then considered part of the same geographic market. In terms of the product market, the relevant criterion is the degree of substitutability between products or services. In most cases, these definitions do not lead to sharp definitions of a market but rather clusters on a continuum of economic relations and it will require considerable skill and judgment to decide whether or not a particular activity ought to be included in the relevant market.

Economists have proposed several measures that facilitate the detection of structural market power. The most widely used are concentration measures. Concentration ratios (CR) measure the combined market share of a specified number of the largest firms.[14] This measure does not capture the size distribution of firms. The Herfindahl-Hirschman Index (HHI) avoids this problem by summing the squares of the market shares of the firms in a market. The index ranges from 0 for a fully competitive market to 10,000 for a monopoly. Currently, antitrust authorities use an HHI of 1,800 as a cutoff point above which a market becomes highly concentrated and needs close scrutiny. The HHI allows identification of markets with workably competitive structures (HHI<1,800). However, it cannot be concluded that a market is characterized by structural monopoly power if the index value is above 1,800. Only where a high HHI coincides with the existence of significant market entry barriers is this conclusion justified.

Economists have also developed several tests to assess whether an abuse of structural market power is taking place. Such an abuse can manifest itself either in prices that are significantly above costs or in prices that are below costs with the intention to drive competitors out of the market. Areeda and Turner (1975) have proposed to use pricing below marginal costs as an indication of such predatory behavior. Landes, Posner, and Lerner have developed an index that captured supply and demand-side conditions simultaneously. Like in the case of market structure measures, these indices are first warning signs but cannot replace a more detailed analysis of conduct in a market. Shepherd (1997) has proposed to consider as anti-competitive only selective actions by firms whose market share is significantly larger than their rivals' market share. With respect to pricing above costs, economic theory would suggest that market power be abused if prices are above stand-alone costs. In network industries with a high percentage of shared costs this test may lead to significant deviations of prices from incremental costs. From the perspective of dynamic competition the crucial question is whether or not pricing above incremental costs will lead to market responses. Structural market power thus only exists if no such response is triggered.

This should not belittle the fact that structural market power may be difficult to detect. Especially when services are sold and priced in different bundles, a supplier may have opportunities to disguise market power. Another possible difficulty arises from the fact that close coordination is needed between the different stages and layers of network industries. This is probably most evident in the electricity industry but it also applies to telecommunications, where interoperability often requires close cooperation between vendors. Long term contracts between suppliers at different stages of the value chain may partially jeopardize the competitive process and effectively constitute a tacit form of vertical integration. As is known from other industries, frequent contacts between players in an industry may result in tacit forms of collusion. As competitive processes unfold, it will be necessary to refine the tools of antitrust supervision in networks to recognize such forms of behavior.

Preventative measures play an important role in the transition to a more competitive framework. The growing wave of mergers, alliances, and joint ventures in energy and telecommunications raises concerns for the longer prospect of competition. Unfortunately, current merger review falls short of an effective test in this regard. Typically, a merger is assessed in its consequences for a particular geographic and product market. This test generally does not attempt to analyze the implications for competition in adjacent markets, which often is a key issue during the process of industry restructuring. For example, the mergers between the RBOCs are evaluated in their impacts on local telephone markets. As these markets, by their very nature, are spatially separated, mergers do not conflict with the standard concentration measures nor do they reduce existing competition (which is minimal to begin with). In contrast to the Department of Justice, which bases its review on the Horizontal Merger Guidelines, the Federal Communications Commission could use a broader public interest test. However, the FCC has not challenged any of the recent mergers presumably in the hope that they will intensify competition. The criteria used in this assessment are vague at best.[15] More thorough methods and systematic reviews, perhaps based on dynamic scenarios, are urgently needed.

Regulation and antitrust provide two sets of tools to control market power. However, there are several differences between the two. Whereas regulation generally consists in an ex ante review of proposed changes, antitrust review is typically invoked after an abuse of market power has occurred. At least in the past, regulation could be based on a substantial body of systematically reported data. In contrast, antitrust needs to produce evidence in a discovery process, which often fails to produce the data required to prove anti-competitive behavior. For that reason, the two policies must be considered as complementary rather than substitutes. Although there are also costs, there are potential advantages in having two sets of agencies involved in the review of competitive behavior. Regulation would predominantly be responsible for the non-competitive market segments and antitrust for the effectively competitive segments. In market segments with emerging competition regulation and antitrust will have to find forms of collaboration.

5 CONCLUSIONS

The new trust in competitive market organization requires a rethinking of some of the conceptual foundations of established regulatory doctrine. Explicitly or implicitly most of regulatory theory and practice is rooted in static economic models. Like these models, it emphasizes equilibrium outcomes of market processes, for example, when prices are set at average costs or forward looking incremental costs. In contrast to this approach, this paper emphasized a view of competition as a dynamic process. Competitive rivalry is essentially motivated by deviations from this equilibrium. Market entry opportunities are created by the inefficiency of an incumbent supplier or by new technologies that allow significant cost reductions or improvements in the quality of service.

However, competition does not occur at the margin but only if significant profit and/or growth opportunities exist. It is often a process of trial and error and may thus appear chaotic compared to the emphasis on reliability, non-discrimination, and universality of service that was typical for regulated monopoly. There is probably no 'best' regulatory approach and different models will, over time, show particular advantages and disadvantages. Differential regulatory regimes at the state and international level can help improve the limited knowledge on the interrelations between regulatory regimes and sector performance. It is safe to state that compared to the status quo ante, competition has potential benefits but also potential costs. Policy-makers are confronted with the difficult task of deciding whether the overall benefits of the competitive reorganization outweigh its costs and whether winners should compensate losers of the process.

Several lessons emerge from a more dynamic view of competition. First, regulation needs to replace its focus on market outcomes with a more dynamic perspective. While there are often no clear-cut 'correct' answers, the implications of certain regulatory rules on competitive processes need to be better understood. For example, it needs to be recognized that rules enforcing best practice incremental cost pricing on incumbent service providers will slow the emergence of facilities-based competition compared to embedded cost pricing. Second, regulation needs to permit corporate conduct that is typical for dynamic markets, such as forms of price differentiation, above normal profitability, or the bundling of services. Such generally legitimate conduct should only give raise to regulatory intervention if it is abused to thwart competition.

Third, where continued protection of the ratepayer is required due to a lack of effective competition, it should be achieved with price cap rather than other forms of regulatory oversight. Fourth, regulation needs to abstain from the temptation to micro-manage competition. Measures to allocate market share to new competitors or commitments by incumbents to enter certain markets will in the long run do more harm than good. Fifth, asymmetries in the regulatory treatment of incumbents and new competitors will need special justification. Sixth, in a more open market-based environment regulation and antitrust have complementary tasks. Last but not least, the expectation of broadly emerging competition will have to be replaced with a more realistic view of the roles and patterns of competition in network industries.

From such a perspective, it will become clear that in many segments of the industries the likelihood that effective competition will emerge is slim. Once it is accepted that competition leads to differentiation and not necessarily universal and affordable service will it be possible to adopt policies to cope with these potential disadvantages of competition.

NOTES

1. Several other factors are contributing to these changes in policy attitudes and approaches. Technological change, the saturation or near-saturation with basic utility services in many industrialized countries, the increasing diversity of services, and the global restructuring of business have rendered traditional monopoly arrangements unsustainable. The poor performance of publicly owned enterprises in the telecom sector, a perception of the failure of the public regulation of privately owned monopolies, and a generally more skeptical attitude towards the state, have put additional pressure on the traditional sector arrangements.

2. This section has greatly benefited from Vickers (1994).
3. For a more technical definition see Varian (1984).
4. Smith was well aware of the tendency of business people to conspire against the public whenever possible and saw an important role for public policy in its prevention.
5. A Pareto optimum is a state in which nobody can be made better off without making somebody else worse off.
6. It is indicative of this approach that one of the recent monographs on telecommunications competition, Laffont and Tirole (2000), continues to conceptualize competition as an equilibrium state and not a process of dynamic rivalry.
7. MCI entered the long distance market in 1969. Thirty years later, its market share was at around 25 percent.
8. In contrast, predatory pricing aims at eliminating an existing competitor by setting prices temporarily below costs. Losses during this period are then recovered through monopoly pricing once the competitor has left the market. The evidence in support of such strategies is rather inconclusive.
9. The evolution of distributed generation technologies may help overcome constraints imposed by the existing networks and allow a structurally competitive electricity market.
10. The database of the National Regulatory Research Institute contains key interconnection agreements from all states. Available at <http://www.nrri.ohio-state.edu>.
11. Many states that use TSLRIC in calculating the costs of interconnection allow the company a mark-up to cover common costs when prices are being set. See, for example, the practice of the Michigan Public Service Commission.
12. For arguments along this line see, for example, Beard, Kaserman and Mayo (1998).
13. An argument against the TELRIC approach could also be derived from the work on investment under uncertainty, for example, Dixit and Pindyck (1994).
14. Thus, the 4-firm concentration ratio (CR) measures the combined market share of the four largest firms, the 8-firm CR the combined market share of the eight largest firms.
15. In the case of the SBC-Ameritech merger, the FCC has imposed a list of conditions on the companies. Failure to meet certain targets could result in significant penalties. Such an approach of micro-managing competition is highly questionable.

REFERENCES

Areeda, P. and D.F. Turner (1975), 'Predatory pricing and related practices under Section 2 of the Sherman Act', *Harvard Law Review* 88, pp. 637.

Armstrong, M. (1997), 'Competition in telecommunications', *Oxford Review of Economic Policy* 13, pp. 64-82.

Arrow, K.J. (1951), *Social choice and individual values*, New York: John Wiley and Sons.

Bauer, J.M. (1999), 'Competition as a turbulent process', paper presented at the 27th Telecommunications Policy Research Conference, Alexandria, Virginia, September 25-27.

Baumol W.J., Panzar, J.D. and R.D. Willig (1982), *Contestability and the theory of industry structure*, New York: Harcourt Brace Jovanovich.

Baumol, W.J. and S.J. Gregory (1994), *Toward competition in local telephony,* Cambridge, Mass: MIT-Press.

Beard, T.R., Kaserman, D.L. and Mayo, J.W. (1998), 'The role of resale entry in promoting local exchange competition', *Telecommunications Policy* 22, pp. 315-322.

Brock, G.W. (1996), 'Local competition policy maneuvers', in: G.L. Rosston and D. Waterman (eds) *Interconnection and the Internet,* pp. 1-14, Mahwah, NJ: Lawrence Erlbaum.

Dixit, A.K. and Pindyck, R.S. (1994), *Investment under uncertainty,* Princeton, NJ: Princeton University Press.

Hayek, F.A. (1945), 'The use of knowledge in society', *American Economic Review* 35, pp. 519-530.

Hayek, F.A. (1949), 'The meaning of competition', in: *Individualism and economic order*, London: Routledge.

Helm, D. and Jenkinson, T. (1997), 'The assessment: introducing competition into regulated industries', *Oxford Review of Economic Policy* 13, pp. 1-14.

Joskow, P.L. (1997), 'Restructuring, competition and regulatory reform in the U.S. electricity sector', *Journal of Economic Perspectives* 11, pp. 119-138.

Kahn, A.E. (1998), *Letting go: deregulating the process of deregulation.* East Lansing, Mich.: Institute of Public Utilities.

Katz, M.L. (2000), 'Regulation: the next 1000 years', in: R.M. Entman (rapporteur), *Six degrees of competition: correlating regulation with the telecommunications marketplace.* A report of the Fourteenth Annual Aspen Institute Conference on Telecommunications Policy, pp. 29-53 (Washington, DC: The Aspen Institute).

Katz, M.L. (1996), 'Economic efficiency, public policy, and the pricing of network interconnection under the Telecommunications Act of 1996', in:

G.L. Rosston and D. Waterman (eds) *Interconnection and the Internet*, pp. 15-32, Mahwah, NJ: Lawrence Erlbaum.

Kirzner, I.M. (1992), *The meaning of market process*. London: Routledge.

Laffont, J. and Tirole, J. (1993), *A theory of incentives in procurement and regulation*. Cambridge, Mass: MIT-Press.

Laffont, J. and Tirole, J. (2000), *Competition in telecommunications* (Cambridge, Mass: MIT-Press).

Noam, E.M. (2001), 'Wireless: the next frontier of openness', paper presented at the 29th Telecommunications Policy Research Conference, Alexandria, Virginia, October 27-29.

Perucci, A. and Cimatoribus, M. (1997), 'Competition, convergence, and asymmetry in telecommunications regulation', *Telecommunications Policy* 21, pp. 493-512.

Schumpeter, J.A. (1942), *Capitalism, socialism, and democracy*. New York: Harper.

Schumpeter, J.A. (1954), *History of economic analysis*, edited by Elizabeth Boody Schumpeter, New York: Oxford University Press, 1954.

Shepherd, W.G. (1984), 'Contestability vs. competition', *American Economic Review* 74, pp. 572-587.

Shepherd, W.G. (1997), *The economics of industrial organization*. 4th ed. Upper Saddle River, New Jersey: Prentice Hall.

Siegfried, J.J. and Evans, L.B. (1994), 'Empirical studies of entry and exit: a survey of the evidence', *Review of Industrial Organization* 9, pp. 121-155.

Sidak, J.G. and Spulber, D.F. (1998), 'Deregulation and managed competition in network industries', *Yale Journal on Regulation* 15, pp. 117-147.

Smith, A. (1976) [1776], *An inquiry into the nature and the causes of the wealth of nations*. Oxford: Clarendon Press.

Stigler, G.J. (1987), 'Competition', in: J. Eatwell, M. Milgate, and P. Newman (eds) *The New Palgrave*. London: Macmillan.

Trebing, H.M. (2000) Review of J.G. Sidak and D.F. Spulber, 'Deregulatory takings and the regulatory contract', *Telecommunications Policy* 24, pp. 161-173.

Varian, H.R. (1984), *Microeconomic analysis*, 2nd edition, New York: Norton.

Vickers, J.S. (1994), *Concepts of competition*, Oxford: Clarendon Press.

Williamson, O.E. (1976) 'Franchise bidding for natural monopolies – in general and with respect to CATV', *The Bell Journal of Economics* 7, pp.73-104.

PART TWO

Empirical Overview Papers

3. The Dynamics of Regulation: Performance, Risk and Strategy in the Privatized, Regulated Industries

David Parker

1 INTRODUCTION

The public utilities[1], namely gas, electricity, water and sewerage, telecommunications and public transport developed mainly as a combination of private and municipal functions in the nineteenth century. The twentieth century, however, and particularly the years immediately after the Second World War saw large-scale nationalization. Therefore for most of the last fifty years in Europe state ownership has been the dominant mode of organizing and delivering utility services.

In the 1980s this began to change. This was because of growing discontent with the efficiency of service delivery in the public sector (Aharoni, 1986) and because technological change was creating opportunities for competition in supply where previously monopoly was expected to lead to the lowest costs of production. For example, combined cycle gas turbine generating sets significantly reduced the optimal scale in electricity generation enabling more firms to compete. In telecommunications new optical fibre and cellular technologies enhanced the scope for competition in that industry. All of this was occurring at a time when governments faced budgetary pressures and, more recently, limits on government borrowing laid down in the Maastricht Agreement, in the run up to the establishment of a common European currency. Governments have turned to restructuring and privatizing their utility industries so as to curtail state subsidies. European Commission Directives aimed at liberalizing markets, initially in telecommunications and electricity but now also in gas and railways, have added further impetus (for a more detailed discussion see Parker, 1998).

Within Europe the UK took the lead in utility privatization. The first major utility to be sold was British Telecom (BT), in 1984, a sell-off that attracted a surprising amount of City and public interest in the stock. This was followed by the privatization of British Gas in 1986, the water and sewerage industry in 1989, electricity in 1990/91, and the railways between 1995 and 1997. Coach and local bus transport in the UK was privatized during the 1980s. With the notable exception of the latter, which was structured as a competitive industry, privatization led to the establishment of dedicated regulatory offices to protect consumers from monopoly abuse until competition arrived. These regulatory offices are the Office of Telecommunications (OFTEL), the Office of Electricity and Gas Markets (OFGEM), the Office of Water Services (OFWAT) and the Office of Rail Regulation (ORR).[2]

The UK example has provided impetus for privatization in other parts of Europe. Privatization has grown in importance in the 1990s with large-scale programmes in Italy, Portugal, France and Spain in particular. Alongside privatization, new regulatory offices have been established, in part modelled on those in the UK and in the main part to some degree at arm's length from the government department that previously regulated the state-owned firms. This has been encouraged in the electricity and telecommunications sectors by European Commission market-liberalization directives. Transparent regulation of prices, including the terms on which new competitors can access the network of incumbent operators, is important if there is to be a 'level playing field' so that competition can develop.

This paper is concerned with performance, regulatory risk and strategy in regulated industries. First, the performance of the privatized utilities in the UK is considered in the light of claims about the benefits of privatization. Second, the discussion turns to the subject of regulatory risk, before looking at the implications of privatization, market liberalization and regulation for the strategies of utility enterprises. The paper concludes with a summary of the main points raised and that are relevant wherever utilities are privatized as regulated businesses. In summary the paper argues that it is difficult to separate out the individual contributions of ownership change, competition, regulation and technological change in improving organizational performance; that minimizing regulatory risk while achieving regulatory goals is complex; and that after privatization business success necessitates a fundamental review of strategy and operations.

2 PRIVATIZATION AND PERFORMANCE: EVIDENCE FROM THE UK

Table 3.1 provides a general schema setting out the case for privatization over state ownership. The schema is based on the usual arguments from economics that stress the superiority of private over public ownership in terms of capital and product market incentives (Vickers and Yarrow, 1988; Böss, 1991; Boycko, Shleifer and Vishny, 1996). So the argument goes, ownership is associated with 'low powered' incentives to be efficient because of the lack of capital market pressures on management to raise efficiency and because state-owned utilities tend to be monopolies or face highly regulated competition. In terms of the capital market, the state is considered to be a more benign supplier of capital for investment than private equity investors and loan creditors, who require an adequate return on their investments and loans. In terms of the product market, in private competitive markets inefficient suppliers fail, while in monopoly state sectors consumers cannot easily switch suppliers and enterprise losses can be financed from taxation.

Table 3.1 A schema for assessing regulatory and ownership structures

	State Owned Privatized &	**Regulated**	**Private Sector**
Market structure	Natural monopoly or competitive	Natural monopoly	Competitive
Capital market	State	Private	Private
Efficiency incentives	Low powered	Varies depending on nature of regulation	High powered
Form of state intervention	Micro-management	Macro-management	Well defined & protected private property rights
Regulatory risk	Usually high	Varies depending on nature of regulation	Low
Regulatory costs	Usually high	Varies depending on the nature of regulation	Low

The schema suggests that efficiency incentives will improve with privatization, leading to welfare gains. These gains will be in terms of allocative efficiency, as prices are more closely related to long-run marginal costs of supply, and technical efficiency, as costs of production are minimized. However, those advocating privatization often couch the discussion as a choice between monopoly state ownership and competitive private markets. In utility sectors the real choice, especially in the early years after privatization, is normally between state monopolies and private monopolies or at least firms that remain dominant in their markets for some time (e.g. after 15 years of privatization British Telecom still has around 76% of the overall market). In a monopoly environment the distribution of efficiency gains between economic rents to producers and lower prices and improved services to consumers ('consumer surplus') relies heavily on the effectiveness of the 'regulator'. Regulation becomes a form of proxy competition, with the regulator attempting to achieve allocative and technical efficiency in the industry in the absence of competition. Also, the form of the regulation can be crucial. For example, it can be shown that under cost of service regulation, where prices are adjusted based on allowed costs and an agreed profit, a publicly-owned utility, under pressure from government to minimize the burden on taxpayers, may pursue efficiency gains more vigorously than an equivalent private sector company. The private sector company passes cost increases on to consumers in the form of higher prices with no impact on its profits. This is consistent with de Fraja's (1993) suggestion that under certain regulatory conditions the public sector may be more efficient than privatized, regulated businesses. Much therefore turns on the interaction between the regulatory system and the structure of property rights for management incentives and disincentives.

Table 3.1 reminds us that state ownership is associated with day-to-day intervention by ministers and civil servants in the micro-management of enterprises, for example determining prices, investments and employment levels. Privatization with effective regulation is intended to alter the state's role to macro-management or establishing the regulatory framework or 'the rules of the game'. Management then manages their enterprises within the regulatory rules. This leads to a change in the operating environment for the management of the utilities. Previously they were accountable to government and subject to final decisions being made politically. Now privatized, the management are accountable to new stakeholders in the form of shareholders and private loan creditors (the capital market) and the new regulatory agencies. They may also face a more dynamic and hostile competitive market for their outputs. This can be expected to have a profound effect on management orientation, structures and processes, as discussed in more detail later under the heading of 'Strategy'.

An appraisal of the schema in Table 3.1 suggests, therefore, that privatization can be expected to lead to important efficiency gains but that the roles of competition and regulation may be crucial. In the UK a number of studies have been undertaken into the effects of privatization on performance, but it has proved problematic to separate out the effects of ownership, competition, regulation and technological change. Therefore it remains unclear how far privatization rather than other factors is responsible for the efficiency gains. According to some commentators (e.g. Millward and Parker, 1983; Kay and Thompson, 1986; Vickers and Yarrow, 1988) competition is likely to be more important than ownership, though arguably without privatization competition could not fully develop. Table 3.2 provides a summary of a number of the different UK studies. It is clear that many have found that privatization has not led to an obvious change in economic performance. In a number of cases performance improvements recorded continue a trend that pre-dates privatization. One explanation of the mixed results is as follows:

1. The greatest scope for efficiency gains occurs in the utility industries where previously monopoly suppliers existed. Where state industries operated in competitive markets there is less scope for management to make large efficiency gains after privatization. Presumably enterprises must have already been reasonably efficient to have survived in a competitive market, at least in the absence of continued state subsidies.
2. Competition and regulation are important in providing the necessary incentives for management to seek out efficiency gains following privatization. Therefore, until competition and regulation significantly impact efficiency gains may be limited.

These arguments are supported, for example, by the comprehensive study of UK privatization by Martin and Parker (1997). In this study, which revealed no consistent relationship between ownership and performance, a number of enterprises in competitive markets were included alongside two utilities, British Gas and BT.[3] Labour productivity growth in BT and British Gas fell after privatization, though it recovered sharply later. In both cases at first the regulatory pressures (including the price caps) provided generous scope to raise profits without major cost cutting. Also, competition did not begin to impact significantly until restrictions on market entry were gradually removed during the 1990s. In the face of tightening regulation and more competition, however, productivity responded. The average annual rise in labour productivity was around 15% in BT and 6% in British Gas in the early to the mid-1990s. Since then the continued growth of competition has spurred further productivity gains. Waddams Price and Weyman-Jones (1996) have also found evidence of higher productivity growth in British Gas since privatization.

This trend emphasizing the roles of competition and regulation is also born out by the record of the UK electricity industry.[4] Here competition was introduced at privatization and was quickly extended. Burns and Weyman-Jones (1994) in an early study concluded that the 12 regional electricity distribution companies had become more efficient after privatization but this was a continuation of a longer-term trend. A more recent review of the industry as a whole has concluded that 'productivity in the industry has almost doubled since privatization' (Electricity Association, 1998, p.55). Another into electricity generation found that substantial cost reductions had occurred (Newbery and Pollitt, 1997). In electricity like the other utility industries the efficiency increases are a reflection of the sharp reductions in employment achieved. Employment in the industry fell from 127,300 at privatization to around 66,000 by 1996/97. Over the same period transmission operating costs have fallen by nearly 40% (*Financial Times*, 18 October 1999). In BT employment declined from around 238,000 at privatization to 124,700 by 1999, and in British Gas from about 92,000 at privatization to 70,000 by 1994.

Turning to the water industry where there is still very little competition, Shaoul (1997) concluded that significant efficiency gains, meaning lower costs relative to output, occurred before privatization. Initially after privatization employment in the industry rose. In 1990/91 the average number of employees in the water supply and sewerage companies was 45,863. By 1993/94 this had grown to 58,270. More recently numbers have fallen and the water regulator's latest price proposals imply that the water companies will need to achieve operating efficiency gains of almost 16% over the next five years (*Financial Times*, 12 October 1999, p.6). What appears to have happened in this industry is lax regulation at the outset plus a lack of competition combined to keep efficiency incentives relatively weak in the early years.

In the case of all of the privatizations, results may well have been affected by technical change. This is particularly so in telecommunications and electricity generation where there have been some notable technological improvements, as noted earlier. One way forward is to compare the performance of the UK utilities with those overseas and able to capitalize equally on the new technologies. In this respect O'Mahony's (1998) work on comparative productivity levels in the electricity, gas and water sectors in the US, France, Germany and Japan compared with the UK is of interest. Table 3.3 reproduces some of the results. It is evident that the labour and total factor productivity gap between the UK and the other countries has narrowed, but that in most cases this narrowing dates back to the late 1970s or before. That is to say, the catching up in productivity pre-dates privatization, a result

Table 3.2 UK privatization: a summary of efficiency studies

Author(s)	Industry(s)	Main Performance Measures Used	Findings
Hutchinson (1991)	17 UK firms in several industrial groupings	Labour productivity, profitability and technology mix	Privately-owned firms outperformed comparable state-owned firms in the 1970s and 1980s in terms of profitability only. Less certain whether privatization had improved performance.
Bishop and Thompson (1992)	9 privatized enterprises across a range of UK industries. Includes BT, British Gas and electricity supply	Labour productivity and TFP, 1970/80 compared with 1980/90	There was higher growth in labour productivity in BT but the growth in TFP fell in the 1980s. In British Gas labour productivity grew at the same rate in the 1970s as the 1980s, while the growth of TFP declined. Electricity supply saw a fall in both labour productivity and TFP growth.

Table 3.2 continued

Haskel and Szymanski (1993)	12 privatized firms between 1972 and 1988, including BT, British gas, electricity supply and water	Estimates of productivity growth (output per employee)	In the main productivity has grown faster in the 1980s. Competition is a significant causal factor.
Burns and Weyman-Jones (1994)	Electricity distribution	Multiple input, multiple output model of before and after privatization using mathematical programming techniques	The 12 electricity distribution companies have been more efficient since privatization, but this continues a long-term historical trend. There is also a greater diversity of performance amongst the 12 since privatisation.
Parker (1994)	British Telecom (BT) 1979/80 to 1993/94	Productivity and employment costs in total costs	Labour productivity grown faster since privatization, but the record for TFP is much less impressive. Employment costs have declined as a percentage of all costs, continuing a trend that dates back to before privatization.

Bishop and Green (1995)	6 privatized enterprises including British Gas and BT	TFP and financial data 1989/94	Competition rather than ownership is important. Growth in TFP in BT was in part due to technical change.
Waddams Price and Weyman-Jones (1996)	Gas industry, 1977/78 to 1991	Malmquist indices of productivity growth	Post-privatization productivity growth was around 5/6% per annum compared with 3% a year before privatization in 1986. Differences remain in technical efficiency amongst British Gas's regions.
Newbery and Pollitt (1997)	Electricity generation	Various	Labour productivity has more than doubled since 1990, mainly due to shedding labour. Real unit costs have declined.
Shaoul (1997)	Water industry	Cost and output data	Greater efficiency gains, meaning lower costs relative to output, occurred prior to privatization.

Table 3.2 continued

Martin and Parker (1997)	11 privatized organizations studied including BGas and BT. Years before and after privatization included.	Labour productivity, TFP, various financial ratios and data envelopment analysis (DEA)	Mixed results with labour productivity growth evident but TFP growth lagging behind.
O'Mahony (1998)	Sectors of UK economy including electricity, gas and water	Labour productivity and TFP in the UK relative to US, France, Germany and Japan	Productivity gap declined in 1995 compared to 1989; but evidence of a closing gap from the 1970s except relative to France.
Parker and Wu (1998)	UK steel industry compared to steel producers in 6 other countries.	DEA analysis of relative input- output efficiency and productivity figures.	A large improvement in relative performance occurred in the British steel industry before the privatization. This was followed by a decline.
Parker (1999c)	British Airports Authority – largest airport operator in the UK privatized in July 1987	DEA analysis of the relative performance of BAA pre and post-privatization and the relative performance of its individual airports compared with other airports in the UK.	No evidence that privatization had a significant effect on performance. Performance improvements were a continuation of a longer-term trend.

consistent with the findings of a number of the studies in Table 3.2. For example, Parker and Wu (1998) found that comparing the British steel industry with a number of other steel industries around the world, the relative performance of British Steel declined after privatization. British Steel had improved its performance in the last few years of state ownership.

Table 3.3 Comparative productivity results: electricity, gas and water sectors, 1979/95

	UK=100					
	Labour Productivity (output per hour)			**TFP**		
	1979	**1989**	**1995**	**1979**	**1989**	**1995**
US	474	345	245	247	190	176
France	238	255	173	101	110	99
Germany	202	156	103	149	116	97
Japan	180	155	107	117	88	73

Source: O'Mahony, 1998.

O'Mahony's study covers both labour and total factor productivity (TFP). A full analysis of production efficiency would ideally include estimates of changes in TFP. Labour productivity gains may result from substitution of capital for labour. Calculating TFP is complex, however, requiring accurate data on capital and other inputs with TFP representing the residual output not explained by the additional inputs. Where TFP measurement has been attempted in privatization studies, the results generally suggest that the efficiency gains have been smaller than for labour productivity (e.g. Martin and Parker, 1997). This could well reflect the greater ease with which labour inputs are adjusted after privatization compared with reconfiguring capital stock; previous over-manning under state ownership; and the tendency for City investors to want to see quick and visible evidence of cost cutting (Cox, Harris and Parker, 1999). It could also simply reflect the difficulty in calculating TFP and resulting inaccuracies in the statistical results.

Productivity and cost studies are concerned with measuring changes in production efficiency. One further set of benefits from privatization and competition should be greater allocative efficiency. Allocative efficiency is the extent to which prices reflect marginal costs of supply. This efficiency is notoriously difficult to measure directly requiring considerable data on market demand and cost functions. But it can be assessed in terms of how far since privatization prices have been aligned with costs. Across the UK regulated industries both regulation and competition have encouraged the companies to remove cross-subsidies and end price discrimination. Therefore in the former monopoly markets prices have become more closely aligned with supply costs suggesting higher allocative efficiency. It is also the case that consumers have benefited from efficiency gains through lower prices.

In most of the UK regulated industries prices have fallen since privatization reflecting the gains in production efficiency already mentioned. The following examples are selected to reflect the general nature of the price changes since privatization (a more detailed account can be found in Parker, 1999a, p.127). Taking telecommunications first; since privatization average charges have fallen by around 40%; though this change certainly results from technology and competition in addition to ownership change and regulation. Turning to the gas sector, the next to be privatized after telecommunications, between 1986 and 1997 domestic gas bills fell by an average of 2.6% a year, again in real terms. More recently the gradual introduction on a regional basis of competition in domestic gas supplies, from 1996, has led to further cuts of up to 20%.[5] Real industrial and commercial gas prices have fallen over the same period by about 5% a year.

In the electricity market the decline in charges for domestic consumers in England and Wales has been around 26% in real terms for domestic consumers; while the reduction for industrial and commercial consumers has been even larger, totalling between 25% and 34% (*Financial Times*, 18 October 1999).[6] The main exception to this impressive track record on charging is in the water and sewerage industry. Here domestic charges have risen sharply since privatization, by over 40% in real terms for average unmeasured water and sewerage bills (less for measured or metered services). This has been in no small part due to the need to fund investments to modernize the system after years of under investment in the state sector and to meet the requirements of the EU water quality directives. But it is also likely to reflect the lack of competition in water. The water regulator has now indicated that he expects to see a future reduction in prices to consumers and the government is currently exploring ways to introduce more competition into the industry. The ability of the water industry to raise charges in the past may well have blunted management's incentive to pursue cost cutting in this industry to the same extent as found in telecommunications, gas and electricity.

Service quality improvements are particularly difficult to summarise because service quality is multi-dimensional. Nevertheless, there is no evidence that lower manning and price reductions have been at the expense of service quality even though this is always a potential danger under a price cap system of regulation where management is incentivised to cut costs. Indeed, there is evidence of an improved quality of service since privatization across the utility sectors with the possible exception of the railways, where service failures still occur on too regular a basis (for a review see Parker, 1998). Space precludes a detailed analysis of service measures here; but suffice to say that in all of the regulated industries, including the railways, the regulators have negotiated service performance standards with the companies and penalties and compensation payments to consumers for service failures. Over the years the regulators have set more exacting service standards that have delivered service improvements.

In summary and notwithstanding some of the findings summarized in Table 3.2, the UK's experience does suggest that for those industries previously populated by monopoly state enterprises privatization has been associated with efficiency gains. This in turn has led to benefits to consumers in terms of lower prices, except in water, and improved services, except perhaps so far on the railways. More problematic is to know to what extent such improvements *result* from privatization, from regulation and competition, or from other factors notably technological change and changes in input prices (e.g. fuel costs). A number of the studies in Table 3.2 were unable to reject the null hypothesis that ownership has no effect on performance, though this may simply reflect the difficulty of separating out ownership from other causes. One recent study has suggested that price reductions in electricity would have been even larger had the industry remained a state monopoly (Branston, 1999). This study, however, is acutely sensitive to assumptions made about the performance of the enterprises had they remained in the state sector, which is ultimately an unknown. Less difficult to interpret are studies that show a disparity in the distribution of the welfare gains between different consumer groups (e.g. Hancock and Waddams Price, 1995; Waddams Price and Hancock, 1998). The above price figures are averages masking variations in the price changes between different consumers. State ownership is associated with cross-subsidies and 'no undue discrimination' clauses that lead to uniform pricing. Privatization, especially when coupled with competition, can be expected to lead to prices more closely related to the marginal costs of supplying particular users. This outcome has also been promoted by the regulators in the UK. As a result, users with lower marginal costs, usually larger users, have tended to receive bigger reductions in charges than smaller, often poorer consumers that are more costly to serve. In this sense it has not proved possible for regulators neatly to separate the pursuit of economic efficiency from the social consequences of their decisions (Baldwin and Cave, 1999, pp.80-81).

A full analysis of the welfare gains from privatization needs also to address the distribution of the economic benefits between consumers and investors. Profitability was buoyant in the privatized utilities especially in the early years after privatization. For example, the rate of return on capital employed in the water industry rose from an average of 9.8% at privatization in 1989 to 11.1% by 1996/97; in electricity the increase was larger, with average returns rising from around 4% in generation and 6.5% in distribution and supply to around 11% and 8.8% respectively, between 1990/91 and 1995/96. As a result, and because the shares were floated at attractive prices, investors benefited from large, sometimes spectacular rises in share values. Recent calculation (Parker, 1997) suggests that while there has been a variance in returns over the years and across the regulated industries, in general individual investors who bought shares in the privatized utilities at flotation obtained returns on their investment up to the end of April 1997 exceeding 10% *per annum* in real terms[7] The average return in the water sector was 24% and in the electricity distribution and supply sector 38% a year. The latter figure was buoyed up by take-over bids in the mid-1990s for distribution and supply companies in England and Wales.[8] Table 3.4 summarises the findings from the study, showing the returns obtained by investors if the shares were sold at the end of the first day of trading, after 1 year, 5 years and if the shares were still held on 30 April 1997.

Returns to investors in the UK following privatization were high and it seems higher than government anticipated at the time of the sell-offs (otherwise presumably the government would have held out for a higher price for the shares at the time of their sale). The high profits and shareholder returns can be attributed to the companies exploiting their market power in the face of lax regulation or to government under-estimating the scope for cost savings following privatization (e.g. Boardman and Laurin, 1998; Dnes, et.al., 1998). Opinion seems to be divided on which of these explanations is the more important; probably both apply. What is clear is that the regulators have been able to respond fully only when the price caps have come up for reconsideration, at so-called ‘periodic reviews’ (though some regulators, notably the water regulator, intervened earlier and in the other industries companies were successfully cajoled from time to time not to increase their prices by the maximum permitted under the price cap). The periodic review timetable involves price reviews normally every five years. This has meant a time lag of up to five years from the time extra efficiency savings were made (savings above those factored into the price cap) to the time these savings could be properly reflected in lower consumer prices. In the meantime, shareholders gained.

Table 3.4 Summary of the returns to investors (internal rate of return)

	% Returns to investors selling after:						
	1 day	**1 year**		**5 years**		**Still held at 30/4/97**	
BT (1)	35	84	(+69)	20	(+6)	14	(+3)
BT (2)	5	22	(+5)	10	(-3)	12	(-2)
BT(3)	5	5	(-4)	-	-	8	(-5)
British Gas	10	24	(+20)	15	(+9)	11	(+2)
Water and Sewerage (average)	20	39	(+45)	23	(+18)	24	(+16)
RECs Average	23	41	(+29)	40	(+27)	38	(+25)
Powergen (1)	22	29	(+26)	30	(+19)	29	(+18)
Powergen (2)	3	9	(-14)	-	-	16	(-3)
National Power (1)	22	22	(+19)	28	(+17)	30	(+19)
National Power (2)	4	6	(-17)	-	-	23	(+4)

Notes:

1. Figures in parentheses show gains relative to movement of the FT- All Share Index over the same period. Returns are to individuals investing. Due to special incentive schemes the return to institutional investors is slightly lower.
2. All returns are real returns deflated using the RPI.
3. 1-day return is an absolute IRR (not annualized). It shows the gain from first day's trading on the selling price (the shares were invariably sold at a discount to encourage the spread of share ownership). All other periods reflect annualized returns.

Source: Parker, 1997.

The lag in adjusting prices under the UK price cap regime is the reason that returns to investors in many of the utility stocks have been lower in more recent times. The price caps have been tightened in telecommunications and gas on a number of occasions since the 1980s (in telecoms in 1989, 1991, 1993 and 1997, and in gas in 1992, 1994 and 1997).[9] In 1995 the X factors were tightened in both the electricity and water sectors and the price caps are subject to renewal again in April 2000. The current plans of the electricity and water regulators will mean sharp price reductions to consumers from 2000 and hence lower profits to the companies. For example, the water regulator has called for domestic water bills to fall by 13.7% from April 2000 with the bill expected to be 15% lower in real terms by 2005. This follows ten years since privatization in which water charges have risen. This suggests a future shift in the distribution of the efficiency gains from shareholders to consumers in this industry. More generally, across the regulated industries regulatory tightening is leading to profitability reducing towards a normal level or equivalence to the cost of capital.

3 REGULATORY RISK

The above performance results are a reflection of changes occurring in the privatized, regulated industries in the UK. Overall the results suggest that while the separate contributions of privatization, competition, regulation and technology remain unclear, in telecommunications, gas and electricity in particular there have been some large efficiency improvements, especially since regulatory and competitive pressures intensified in the 1990s. Initially investors benefited from high returns on their investments in the privatized utilities, but over time the balance of the distribution of the efficiency gains has been moving in favour of consumers, though with some consumer groups benefiting more than others. At the same time, however, the performance studies in Table 3.2 confirm that efficiency gains following privatization are by no means guaranteed. Performance may be disappointing where competition and regulation do not change following privatization in such a way as to stimulate management to improve the operation of their business.

The following discussion looks at the changes in the operating environment faced by the privatized, regulated industries and in particular the nature of regulatory risk. An appreciation of this environment is necessary for an understanding of the context in which management strategies are formulated and implemented in regulated sectors, as discussed later. Regulation involves a complex balancing act between advancing the interests of consumers, the interests of investors in the incumbent utility, and the needs of potential competitors. This involves inevitable tensions. Under a well-functioning regulatory structure, whatever its precise form, there should be scope for regulators to use their judgement and there should be scope for 'discovery' and 'learning' as the markets change and adapt (Burton, 1997). But at the same time a well-functioning regulatory structure avoids high levels of regulatory uncertainty or *regulatory risk*. All privatized companies face normal *commercial risk* to do with producing and investing in the private sector, but regulated enterprises face an additional risk that relates to the threat from regulatory intervention. The objective of regulation should be to protect the consumer, while providing an environment where the industry can invest with a high degree of confidence that profits legitimately made are not eroded by vexatious regulation. Otherwise, regulation will seriously distort management strategies.

Regulatory risk arises from the nature of the regulatory rules and practices. Rules establish the degree of inherent risk by determining the extent to which regulatory interventions are discretionary. The more rule based the regulation, the less the scope for regulatory discretion. Practice enters into regulatory risk through the interpretation the regulator and others (notably government) place on the rules. Related to practice are the *information asymmetries* inherent in regulation. The companies can be expected to have superior information about their costs of production, future investment plans and price elasticities; while the function of the regulator is to encourage companies to supply this information so that proper regulatory decisions can be made on prices, profits and the quality of service. For example, only when the regulator has a good idea about the price elasticities of the companies' outputs, their cost functions and investment plans can prices be set so as to achieve a normal rate of return on capital. At the same time, the regulated companies must enter into investment programmes often involving appreciable sunk costs. Once having invested, the regulated companies can suffer from 'hold up' (Hart and Moore, 1986). In the absence of contrary rules the regulator could drive down prices towards the short-run marginal costs of production leading to financial losses.

Wherever there are sunk costs, as inevitably there are in network industries involving large, dedicated investments in pipes, transmission lines, water treatment plants and so on, the regulated companies are at risk. This regulatory risk arises from uncertainty about the future actions of the regulator at the time of the investment. Comparing two regulatory regimes, everything else being equal, that which has the lower regulatory risk will have the lower cost of capital. The degree of correlation between returns on a company's shares and returns in the stock market as a whole is estimated using a coefficient called Beta. The basic premise is that investors require a higher expected return on any investment (a 'risk premium') in order to compensate them for the higher risk to returns on that investment, as measured by the variability of those returns. A comparison of beta values for electricity and water utilities in the USA and UK shows that the US utilities are judged by investors to have a lower risk (Grout, 1997). Whereas UK utilities tend to have beta values of around 0.6 upwards, US utilities tend to have values significantly lower than this. For example, one study found that the beta value for the gas sector was 0.84 in the UK but 0.2 in the US. The comparable figures for the water industry were 0.67 and 0.29 and for telecommunications 0.87 and 0.52 (OXERA, 1996).

A number of factors determine beta values. But the lower regulatory risk implied by the beta values for regulated utilities in US financial markets is, in part, a product of rate of return regulation compared with price cap regulation (Alexander and Irwin, 1996). Rate of return regulation establishes a target rate of return. While not exactly guaranteeing a given profit, this method of regulation is intended to be more certain in terms of the profit outcome than is the case in a price cap regime. Another reason for the lower beta values in the US relates to the maturity of the regulatory system. As a regulatory system ages the more learning or knowledge about the way it operates and its consequences results. Such knowledge reduces investor risk. The US has a mature regulatory system, whereas those in Europe are relatively new and untested.

In the UK at privatization the goal was to design a regulatory system that would, over time, minimize regulatory risk while maximizing efficiency incentives. This has not proved easy to achieve. Where regulation is new there is a need to establish a regulatory system that permits flexibility to accommodate learning about regulation, even at the cost of some regulatory unpredictability. But changes in the regulatory rules and practices lead to clashes with the regulated companies. For example, in 1999 the water and sewerage companies argued publicly with their regulator (OFWAT) over cost of capital calculations and future investment needs during negotiations over revised price caps. More generally, the following have been particular areas of disagreement:

1. The rights of regulators to obtain information which they consider they need to regulate effectively – this reflects the information asymmetry in regulated markets;
2. The proper valuation of capital stock, asset values and the setting of appropriate rates of return, which enter into the setting of the price cap (this has been complicated in the UK by the discrepancy between the market valuation of the company at privatization and its net book value, known as the 'discount' at privatization);[10]
3. The extent to which the regulator should be allowed to alter 'the rules of the game', particularly in the UK through a change in the company's

operating licence or through a change in interpretation, for instance over what is the level of depreciation charge that should be permitted to enter into a company's cost structure when setting prices;

4. The extent to which regulators should favour new operators over the incumbent firm so as to promote competition. The regulator may need to tilt 'the playing field' to encourage new entrants in the face of market dominance by the incumbent operator. In the UK the telecommunications regulator protected the second network provider, Mercury Communications, from competition from other new market entrants until 1991 to allow it to become established. The regulators have also intervened to ensure that new entrants can access the incumbent's network at a reasonable charge by regulating network access charges. Regulators will have to regulate and police market entry where the incumbent firm retains ownership of an essential asset, notably the network (Armstrong, Doyle and Vickers, 1996).

Above all it is important to recognize that regulation influences the nature of the markets that evolve. Instead of resources being attracted to areas of greatest need, with potentially the highest welfare gains, they may be attracted to areas where access is permitted or short-term profit is highest given the regulatory constraints. This means that regulated industries operate in a different external environment to other privatized firms. Managers in privatized, regulated companies must manage their businesses in the face of commercial pressures and regulatory interventions. The impact of regulation on strategy in privatized industries is now discussed.

4 STRATEGY

Privatization, competition and regulation force management to reconsider how best to manage their businesses. In effect, managers need to reconceptualize the basis on which they do business and develop strategies accordingly. In the face of information asymmetries and regulatory risk, management involves the normal analysing, planning and reaction to market signals, as well as an on-going interaction with the regulatory office. In this section of the paper the discussion turns to the inter-relationship between competition, regulation and organizational performance from the perspective of strategy formulation and implementation in privatized companies.

Regulation can be viewed as a game played out over time between the regulator and the regulated company. This is likely to be played with particular ferocity during the early years of privatization, with regulator and regulated posturing and re-positioning in the light of events. Following privatization the dynamics of regulation involve both the regulator and management learning about regulation and the optimal strategies to adopt. The regulatory offices will need to appoint staff who will take time to learn about the markets they are regulating and how the dominant companies behave. The companies will need to learn how best to manage within the new regulatory system and this may require the recruitment of new management with regulatory expertise.

The regulated companies face market structures that are distorted by decades of state ownership and by regulatory constraints relating to the development of competition, including network access codes and pricing and profit limits. The complexity of regulation can act as a barrier to entry especially where regulation costs fall more heavily on small companies than the large, dominant incumbent. The complexity is reflected in the direct costs of the regulatory office, which may, as in the UK, be met from operating licence fees levied on the turnover of the companies, and compliance costs in terms of the costs born directly by companies in servicing the regulatory system. The latter are often unquantified (there are no publicly available figures for the UK) but are likely to be appreciable. Compliance costs arise in terms of the direct costs of administering the regulation (providing returns to the regulator, replying to the regulator's questions, etc.) and indirectly in terms of distortions to the enterprise's corporate strategies including pricing, outputs and investment.

The privatized company will need to learn how to operate now that it is no longer directly accountable to a government department (or part of a government department). This requires new networks of relationships to be developed: 'The institutional change brought about by privatization has the effect of reshaping sectoral networks and constructing fresh relationships between established actors' (Dudley, 1999, p.53). This involves formulating new frames of reference involving new resource dependencies and a 'reframing' of strategic orientation and priorities. This can extend to an attempt to change the 'culture' within the organization away from public sector ways of operating, involving a complete review of management needs, operational goals, organizational structure, nature and location of the business, reporting and internal communication, and human resource management policies (Parker, 1995a & 1995b). There may be a need for new leadership alongside new methods of remunerating staff (more performance related), financial restructuring and new financial systems (Andrews and Dowling, 1998). But in particular, the regulated companies will need to reorientate to meeting the needs of different stakeholders, including consumers who may now have a choice of suppliers and the regulators, who can seriously impact on the development of the business.

The regulated company will need to develop internal systems and structures that support change, such as a new emphasis on marketing as markets are opened up to competition, while retaining the confidence of the regulator so as to avoid unpredicted and damaging regulatory interventions. At the same time, because the regulated company will hold information necessary for effective regulation, notably market and cost data, it is in the interests of the regulated office to cultivate an atmosphere of co-operation with the company. In this environment cheating is most obviously an optimal strategy where it is a one-shot game with no on-going relationship. In practice, regulation is normally an on-going or 'non-finite repeat game', where it is to be expected that 'cheating' will be penalised by the other party through future non-co-operation or 'tit-for'tat' reaction. Regulation involves a tension between the desire of the company to benefit its investors and the desire of the regulator to benefit consumers. But co-operation is optimal provided both parties see this as having a higher continuing pay-off than conflict. This does not rule out occasional argument between the regulated and the regulator, but this is unlikely to amount to a complete breaking-off of relations because the regulator needs the company to co-operate in providing information; while the company needs to head-off damaging regulatory interventions. While there have been disagreements between the regulators and their industries in the UK, sometimes heated, relations have never been allowed to deteriorate to the point where dialogue completely breaks down.

In the face of asset specificity it might be expected that the regulator would act opportunistically. As noted already, companies with high sunk costs may be subject to 'hold up'. Hence regulatory rules, such as legislation in the UK that requires that the regulator must ensure that the companies are able to finance their services, are there to reassure investors that the regulator will not be allowed to act opportunistically and undermine the enterprise's long-run existence (though he may allow competition to do this in time). Without such assurance investors could refuse to invest (e.g. fail to buy the privatization shares) or require a hefty risk premium leading to a higher cost of capital in the industry (or a much lower share price at privatization). Similarly, in the face of information asymmetries the regulated company could act opportunistically and withhold or distort information that the regulator needs to regulate efficiently. Some reluctance to provide information that could be damaging to the company, for example leading to a tighter price cap, is to be expected; but within the regulatory game such strategy is bounded by the net advantages of maintaining the co-operation of the regulator. As a consequence, opportunistic behaviour or 'self-seeking with guile' (Williamson, 1985) is unlikely to be the optimal strategy for companies to follow or to follow for long. As Lapsley and Kilpatrick (1997, p.4) comment:

> At the heart of the effective regulation of utilities sits the question of trust: the extent to which consumers, employees and the government can trust the individuals selected to act as regulators. In particular, the extent to which they can be trusted to discharge their discretionary powers effectively and the extent to which the regulator can trust the regulatee to act in a manner which may not exploit any advantage, e.g. informational, actual or perceived, which it has over the regulator.

Therefore maintaining a degree of trust as the basis for co-operation with the regulator is a constraint on management strategies in regulated environments. Strategies need to be formulated with cognisance of the rules of the regulatory regime and with a view as to whether they are likely to provoke the regulator to intervene. The UK experience suggests, for example, that aggressive competition against new entrants is likely to produce a regulatory response. Regulated companies do not have the same freedom to determine prices, outputs and capital programmes that exist for other private-sector enterprises. At the same time, regulated companies will be able to capitalize on their growing knowledge of how to manage in a regulated environment and seek competitive advantage by exploiting this expertise. For instance, UK water and electricity companies have extended their businesses overseas as part of a 'globalization'strategy, carrying over their knowledge of UK regulation into other regulated environments. An alternative strategy that may be pursued, possibly simultaneously, is to diversify into non-regulated but related activities; for example water companies in England and Wales have bought into waste management. In essence, what is happening is companies are developing a core competence in managing regulated businesses worldwide and using what they believe to be their core competence in managing assets to expand outside the scope of regulation. In both cases, however, there can be no guarantee of success. The water companies have lost large amounts through unwise diversification.

Dominant state-owned utilities gained their dominance not through competitive advantages in the market place but through legislative fiat. They may have few if any true competitive advantages when faced by a commercial environment. For this reason, if they are to survive, privatized utilities need to adapt quickly to the new agenda. Management need to identify the value drivers in their business in the new operating environment and develop resources or capabilities accordingly (Hosein, 1999). This is consistent with a 'resource-based' view of the firm that sees competitive advantage lying not simply in terms of competitive positioning in the market place, but in terms of internal capabilities or competencies. Resource-based theory suggests that firms must continually enhance their resources and capabilities to take advantage of changing market conditions (Mahoney and Pandian, 1992; Eriksen and Mikkelsen, 1996; ed. Foss, 1997). This places the emphasis on privatized firms requiring new competencies including asset and human resource management capabilities. In terms of competitive positioning, organizations may attempt to capitalize on their head-start in the market and build upon brand recognition, to differentiate their offer from that of the new, competing companies. Branding enables firms to adopt a differentiation strategy with premium prices for premium brands. Where this is not possible, and it may not be for a number of the products produced by utility firms (how do you brand telephone calls, tap water, gas therms or electricity kilowatts?), firms tend to be driven towards a lowest-cost supplier strategy for survival (Porter, 1980). In the UK, water, electricity and gas suppliers have tried to develop brand recognition, but with the exception of the incumbent supplier in a region who may retain some customer loyalty, branding has been of limited success. In telecommunications BT has arguably been more successful in its branding strategy, though even here many customers have been inclined to switch to cheaper providers. In an increasingly competitive environment it is little wonder that the privatized utilities have been driven into major cost-cutting programmes. A lowest cost strategy means a desperate 'downsizing' to enable a supplier to price more cheaply than its competitors.

In the UK some privatized firms have embarked on rapid and ruthless cost cutting and restructuring, including hiving-off parts of their business. Others have adopted a more incremental approach with only gradual changes in structure. Some have anticipated change, while others have delayed their response. Research into change management in the water industry in England and Wales has shown that discontinuous or punctuated change programmes can be equally as effective (or ineffective) as more continuous change methods (Dean, Carlisle and Baden-Fuller, 1999). This confirms that there is no one formula for successful change management in regulated markets, anymore than there is in a competitive one; though it can be expected that the pressures on management to implement change will increase as regulation and competition intensify. This is evidenced by the experiences of BT, which went through numerous reorganizations in the 1980s and 1990s, and British Gas, where at privatization its management naively believed that the company's market dominance was safe. After 1992 the company had to restructure extensively in the face of competition and regulatory pressures.

Other research (Harris, Parker and Cox, 1998; Cox, Harris and Parker, 1999) has detailed how companies react in different ways and at different times to the new commercial pressures by realigning and reassessing their supply-chain management. Some of the results from this research, which involved 28 privatized firms including British Gas, seven water companies and 10 electricity utilities, are given in Tables 3.5 and 3.6.

Table 3.5 Timing of the changes in the structure of procurement

Timing of Change	No. of Companies	%
More than 3 years before privatization	2	7
0-3 years before privatization	5	18
During year of privatization	3	11
0-3 years after privatization	9	32
More than 3 years after privatization	7	25
No change	2	7
Total	28	100

Source: Cox, Harris and Parker, 1999, Table 4.2, p.51.

Table 3.6 Procurement tools and techniques most commonly used before and after privatization

Purchasing Tools & Techniques	Before	After
Writing tender specifications	13	12
Organizing Bids	19	18
Negotiating	17	24
Awarding contracts	23	23
Expediting	17	13
Inspection of goods on arrival	10	10
Vendor Accreditation	11	20
Formal Vendor Selection Mechanisms	9	23
Benchmarking/'Best Practice'	3	22
Purchasing Portfolio Analysis	3	22
Strategic Source Planning	3	21
Purchase Price Cost Analysis	7	19

Strategic Supplier Alliances	3	17
Partnership Sourcing	2	20
Network Sourcing	1	11
Relational Competence Analysis	1	10

Source: Cox, Harris and Parker, 1999, Table 4.18, p.67.

In the study only two out of the 28 privatized firms reported no significant change in the methods used to procure inputs. Where changes occurred most had been undertaken within the three years before or after privatization (Table 3.5). This indicates a search for new methods of procurement in the face of the new competitive and regulatory pressures introduced by privatization. The research found that initially the chief driver of change was cost reduction especially through reducing employment. Often only later was procurement policy reconsidered in terms of a strategic appraisal of how value could be best added to the business by managing the supply chain more effectively. This sometimes meant employing new heads of procurement from outside the organization to introduce new ways of working. In time this led to more strategic methods of procurement, including benchmarking best practice, strategic supplier alliances and network sourcing. Prior to privatization these methods were used by very few of the firms studied.

Most of the purchasing techniques were traditional and concerned with order contracting, processing, expediting and inspecting (the top seven items in Table 3.6). In summary, the study found evidence that procurement practices which sufficed under public ownership, where costs and speed to market were less important, proved inadequate when the companies had to survive in more competitive markets and in the face of tightening regulation. Another study (Parker, 1995a & 1995b) has detailed the wider internal changes in management and organizational structures that occurred in a number of privatized companies in the UK as they attempted to come to terms with operating in the private sector .

Finally, when markets are opened up to competition after a history of restricted entry, in the early stages of market liberalization industries tend to become fragmented with lots of new players. Over time, however, the marginal players are forced out and the industry re-consolidates (e.g. US airlines). This is proving true of the UK telecoms, gas and electricity markets and is likely to be true of many of the newly liberalized markets in Continental Europe. Looking specifically at the incumbent companies, they may be expected during the reorienting of their businesses to seek out possible economies of scale and scope and higher levels of dynamic efficiency (in terms of innovations in products and processes) through acquisitions and alliances. On the one hand, the motivation may be entrepreneurial in terms of expanding the business and taking maximum advantage of the new open environment to increase shareholder value. On the other hand, restructuring may simply be defensively motivated with a view to protecting markets from competition. Acquisitions and alliances may eliminate possible competitors and produce formidable barriers to entry in the form of size and market coverage. Certainly telecommunications has seen an explosion of alliances over the last ten years of which Concert (BT, AT&T and others) and Global One (France Telecom, Deutsche Telecom and Sprint of the US) are but two examples. More recently there has been increased activity in the form of mergers and takeovers. The aborted bid by Deutsche Telecom for Telecom Italia, that was eventually sold to Olivetti, is a portent of what is likely to evolve in terms of consolidation in the telecommunications sector in Europe over the next few years. In the UK both the water and energy industries have been affected by numerous takeovers since privatization.

5 CONCLUSIONS

For much of the twentieth century state-owned utilities have been favoured over privately owned suppliers. In the last fifteen years the pendulum has swung the other way favouring privatization and state regulatory structures for monopoly activities. This study has been concerned with the issues of post-privatization performance, regulatory risk, and strategies for survival in a regulated environment. The main conclusions are:

- Privatization is associated with performance improvements, especially in terms of increased labour productivity. This is reflected in healthy returns to investors and in time lower prices to consumers. It is difficult, however, to separate out the individual contributions of ownership change, competition, regulation and technological change to this performance improvement. What can be said is that where privatization is not accompanied by more competition, or regulation that produces similar pressures on management to raise efficiency and benefit consumers, the incentives for management to pursue efficiency gains are greatly diminished.

- Regulatory risk should be minimized while achieving the regulatory goals so as to encourage investment. At the same time, it is to be expected that regulatory 'discovery' or 'learning' will occur in regulated markets, especially in the early years, leading to changes and adaptations. There is a balance to be achieved between regulatory risk and the need for regulation to evolve so as to better protect consumers and maximize efficiency incentives. On the basis of the evidence from the UK there is an inevitable tension between the regulated and regulator, leading to occasional disputes over appropriate practices. In privatized, regulated markets it is to be expected that there will be a conflict between management's wish to pursue shareholder value and the regulator's concern to protect consumers from monopoly abuse.

- Regulation is a non-finite repeat game in which it is to be expected that it will usually be in the interests of both the regulator and regulated parties to maintain co-operation, though this does not rule out disagreements from time to time. In this environment the management of privatized companies need to learn how best to manage within the regulatory rules so as to achieve shareholder value. Success no longer depends upon favours from the state but upon operating successfully in regulated and increasingly competitive markets. Management will therefore need to assess (a) what are the value drivers in the new business environment, (b) how best to align structures and processes, including supply chains, to maximize value, (c) how best to anticipate competition and regulatory interventions that may impact on value, and (d) the scope for acquisitions, mergers and alliances for both defensive and offensive purposes in the market place.

Above all, management need to recognize that the current market dominance of their firm probably owes very little to competitive success and much more to the legal privileges that are now being removed. Once markets are liberalized the incumbent former monopolies are extremely vulnerable unless they can identify and develop the competencies necessary to thrive in regulated and increasingly competitive markets. They have an advantage. Their existing size and market penetration provides time to undertake the strategic reappraisal and to experiment with strategies. The incumbent should benefit from economies of scale and scope, learning curve advantages, control of strategic assets and customer switching costs. But in the longer-term such advantages are unlikely to provide a sufficient protection against the effects of competition and regulatory pressures. The histories of BT, British Gas and the electricity companies in the UK since privatization are already educational in this respect.

NOTES

1. Alternatively referred to as the 'network industries'. The term public utilities is preferred because many industries have networks, such as banking and retailing.
2. Until very recently gas and electricity had their own dedicated regulatory offices, the Office of Gas Supply (OFGAS) and the Office of the Electricity Regulator (OFFER). To reflect changes in the industries that led to the establishment of companies supplying both gas and electricity, these two offices were merged to form OFGEM early in 1999. Other industries notably pharmaceuticals and financial and professional services have their own regulatory systems which are excluded from this study.
3. The airports operator BAA was also included but is not discussed here.
4. This discussion excludes the railways because these were privatized only recently and it is too soon to pass judgement. Coach and bus transport is excluded because the industry is competitive and deregulated.
5. Since the domestic market was liberalised one in four domestic consumers has switched from the former monopoly supplier, British Gas, to a new supplier.
6. The electricity industries in Scotland and Northern Ireland are separately structured and competition has been less intense. In Scotland the reduction in domestic charges up to 1997 was about 7% and in Northern Ireland a miserly 0.4%.
7. The end of April 1997 was chosen because May saw the election of a Labour Government. This government imposed a £5.2bn. 'windfall profits' tax on the utilities, including the main airport operator BAA, in an attempt to recoup some of the large profits made.
8. The figures quoted are internal rates of return based on capital gains, dividends and amounts invested; for the method of calculation see Parker, 1997.
9. Price reviews have occurred more frequently than every five years because of changes in the competitive environment faced by BT and British Gas.
10. This has been a particular problem in the case of British Gas, where the market to asset value ratio (MAR) at privatization was 60%, and the water and sewerage sector, where it was 10%. The regulatory book value (RBV) determines allowed depreciation charges and returns to investors and depends upon which capital valuation is used. Where acquisition costs are used windfalls to shareholders are removed but as the assets at privatization are eventually replaced prices must rise, reflecting (higher) replacement costs (Newbery, 1997; Vass, 1997,

1999). The result is an inter-generational redistribution of income in favour of current consumers who do not pay the true long-run marginal costs of their supply. The implications of a change in valuation can be very significant. When the assets of the gas transmission operator, Transco, were adjusted to allow for the discount at privatization, following a Monopolies and Mergers Commission inquiry (MMC, 1997), the result was a write-off to reserves of £4.9 bn..

REFERENCES

Aharoni, Y. (1986), *The Evolution and Management of State Owned Enterprises*, Cambridge MA: Ballinger.

Alexander, I. and T. Irwin (1996), 'Price Caps, Rate-of-Return Regulation and the Cost of Capital', *Private Sector*, September, 25-28.

Andrews, W.A. and M.J. Dowling (1998), 'Explaining Performance Changes in Newly Privatized Firms', *Journal of Management Studies*, (35) 5, 601-617.

Armstrong, M., C. Doyle and J. Vickers (1996), 'The Access Pricing Problem: a Synthesis', *Journal of Industrial Economics*, 44.

Baldwin, R. and M. Cave (1999), *Understanding Regulation: Theory, Strategy and Practice*, Oxford: Oxford UP.

Bishop, M. and M. Green (1995), *Privatization and Recession – the Miracle Tested*, Centre for the Study of Regulated Industries, London.

Bishop, M. and D. Thompson (1992), 'Regulatory Reform and Productivity Growth in the UK's Public Utilities', *Applied Economics*, 24, 1181-90.

Boardman, A.E. and C. Laurin (1998), 'The Performance of Privatized British Public Utilities and the Windfall Profits Tax', mimeo, Faculty of Commerce, University of British Columbia.

Böss, D. (1991), *Privatization: A Theoretical Treatment*, Oxford: Clarendon Press.

Boycko, M., A. Shleifer and R.W. Vishny (1996), 'A Theory of Privatization', *Economic Journal,* 106, March, 309-19.

Bradbury, R. and D.R. Ross (1991), *Regulation and Deregulation in Industrial Countries: Some Lessons for LDCs*, Washington D.C.: World Bank.

Branston, R. (1999), 'A counterfactual price analysis of electricity privatization in England and Wales', paper presented at the European Association for Research in Industrial Economics Conference, Turin, 4-7 September.

Burns, P. and T. Weyman-Jones (1994), 'Regulatory Incentives, Privatization and Productivity Growth in UK Electricity Distribution', *CRI Technical Paper 1*, London: Centre for the Study of Regulated Industries.

Burton, J. (1997), 'The Competitive Order or Ordered Competition?: The 'UK model' of utility regulation in theory and practice', *Public Administration*, 75 (2), 157-88.

Cox, A., L. Harris and D. Parker (1999), *Privatization and Supply Chain Management: On the effective alignment of purchasing and supply after privatization*, London: Routledge.

De Fraja, G. (1993), 'Productive efficiency in public and private firms', *Journal of Public Economics*, 30, 15-30.

Dean, A., Y. Carlisle and C. Baden-Fuller (1999), 'Punctuated and Continuous Change: the UK Water Industry', *British Journal of Management*, 10, special issue, S3-S18.

Dnes, A.W., D.G. Kodwani, J.S. Seaton and D. Wood (1998), 'The Regulation of the United Kingdom Electricity Industry: an Event Study of Price-Capping Measures' *Journal of Regulatory Economics*, 13, 207-25.

Dudley, G. (1999), 'British Steel and Government since Privatization: Policy 'Framing' and the Transformation of Policy Networks', *Public Administration*, 77 (1), 51-71.

Electricity Association (1998), *Electricity Industry Review*, London: HMSO.

Eriksen, B. and J. Mikkelsen (1996), 'Competitive Advantage and the Concept of Core Competence', in N.J. Foss and C. Knudsen (eds), *Towards a Competence Theory of the Firm*, London: Routledge.

Financial Times, 12 October 1999, 'Planned water price cuts threaten 9,000 jobs', p.6.

Financial Times, 18 October 1999, 'Competition remains the top priority', p.23.

Foss, N.J. (ed.) (1997), *Resources, Firms and Strategies: A Reader in the Resource Based Perspective*, Oxford: Oxford UP.

Grout, P. (1997), 'The Foundations of Regulatory Methodology: the cost of capital and asset values', paper presented at the CRI Conference, *The Financial Methodology of 'Incentive' Regulation - Reconciling Accounting and Economics*, London, 5 November.

Hancock, C. and C. Waddams Price (1995), 'Competition in the British Domestic Gas Market: Efficiency and Equity', *Fiscal Studies*, 16 (3), 81-105.

Harris, L., D. Parker and C. Cox (1998), 'UK Privatization: its impact on procurement', *British Journal of Management*, 9, special issue, S13-S26.

Hart, O. and J. Moore, (1988), 'Incomplete Contracts and Renegotiation', *Econometrica*, 56, 755-85.

Haskel, J. and S. Szymanski (1993), 'The Effects of Privatization, Restructuring and Competition on Productivity Growth in UK Public Corporations', Department of Economics Working Paper no.286, London: Queen Mary and Westfield College.

Hosein, D. (1999), 'Where are the Utilities Going Next?', *Business Strategy Review,* 10 (2), 37-42.

Hutchinson, G. (1991), 'Efficiency Gains through Privatization of UK Industries', in K. Hartley and A.F. Ott (eds), *Privatization and Economic Efficiency: a Comparative Analysis of Developed and Developing Countries*, Aldershot: Edward Elgar.

Kay, J. and D.J. Thompson (1986), 'Privatization: a Policy in Search of a Rationale', *Economic Journal*, 96, 18-32.

Lapsley, I. and K. Kilpatrick (1997), *A Question of Trust: Regulators and the regulatory regime for privatized utilities*, Edinburgh, Institute of Chartered Accountants of Scotland.

Mahoney, J. and J. Pandian (1992), 'The resource based view within the conversation of strategic management', *Strategic Management Journal*, 13, 363-80.

Martin, S. and D. Parker (1997), *The Impact of Privatization: ownership and corporate performance in the UK*, London: Routledge.

Millward, R. and D. Parker (1983), 'Public and Private Enterprise: Comparative Behaviour and Relative Efficiency', in R. Millward, D. Parker, L. Rosenthal, M.T. Sumner and N. Topham (eds), *Public Sector Economics*, Longman: London.

MMC (1997), *BG plc*, London: Monopolies and Mergers Commission/HMSO.

Newbery, D. (1997), 'Determining the Regulatory Asset Base for Utility Price Regulation', *Utilities Policy*, 6 (1), 1-8.

Newbery, D. and M.G. Pollitt (1997), 'The restructuring and privatization of the CEGB – was it worth it?', *Journal of Industrial Economics*, XLV (3), 269-304.

O'Mahony, M. (1998), 'Britain's competitive performance: an analysis of productivity by sector, 1950-1995', London: NIESR.

OXERA (1996), *Regulation, Structure and Risk: an International Comparison*, OXERA: Oxford.

Parker, D. (1994), 'A Decade of Privatization: the Effect of Ownership Change and Competition on British Telecom', *British Review of Economic Issues*, 16 (40), 87-113.

Parker, D. (1995a), 'Privatization and Agency Status: Identifying the Critical Factors for Performance Improvement', *British Journal of Management*, 6 (1), 29-43.

Parker, D. (1995b), 'Privatization and the Internal Environment: Developing our Knowledge of the Adjustment Process', *International Journal of Public Sector Management*, 8 (2), 44-62.

Parker, D. (1997), 'Price cap regulation, profitability and returns to investors in the UK regulated industries, *Utilities Policy*, 6 (4), 303-15.

Parker, D. (1998), 'Privatization in the European Union: an overview', in D. Parker (ed.), *Privatization in the European Union: Theory and Policy Perspectives*, London: Routledge.

Parker, D. (1999a), 'Regulating Public Utilities: Lessons from the UK', *International Review of Administrative Sciences*, 65, 117-31.

Parker, D. (1999b), 'Regulating Public Utilities: What other countries can learn from the UK experience', *Public Management,* 1 (1), 93-120.

Parker, D. (1999c), 'The Performance of BAA Before and After Privatization', *Journal of Transport Economics and Policy*, 33, part 2, 133-46.

Parker, D. and H.S. Wu (1998), 'Privatization and Performance: A Study of the British Steel Industry under Public and Private Ownership', *Economic Issues*, 3, part 2, 31-50.

Porter, M.E. (1980), *Competitive Strategy: Techniques for Analyzing Industries and Competitors*, New York: Free Press.

Shaoul, J. (1997), 'A critical financial analysis of the performance of privatized utilities: the case of the water industry in England and Wales', *Critical Perspectives on Accounting*, 8, 479-505.

Vass, P. (1997), 'The Methodology for Resetting X', in P. Vass (ed.), *Regulatory Review 1997*, London: Centre for the Study of Regulated Industries

Vass, P. (1999), 'Accounting for Regulation', in P. Vass (ed.), *Regulatory Review1998/99,* London: Centre for the Study of Regulated Industries.

Vickers, J. and G. Yarrow (1988), *Privatization: an Economic Analysis*, Cambridge MA: MIT Press.

Waddams Price, C. and R. Hancock (1998), 'Distributional Effects of Liberalizing UK Residential Utility Markets', *Fiscal Studies*, 19 (3), 295-319.

Waddams Price, C. and T. Weyman-Jones (1996), 'Malmquist indices of productivity change in the UK gas industry before and after privatization', *Applied Economics*, 28 (1), 29-39.

Williamson, O.E. (1985), *The Economic Institutions of Capitalism: Firms, Markets and Relational Contracting*, New York: Free Press.

4. The Privatization of Infrastructures in the Theory of the State: an Empirical Overview and a Discussion of Competing Theoretical Explanations

Volkert Schneider and Alexander Jäger[1]

1 INTRODUCTION

During the last three decades, infrastructural sectors of advanced industrial societies have changed in an unprecedented way. Not only becoming larger and larger in scale, their interdependence and the dependence of economies and societies on the various large technical support systems have increased significantly. In less than one generation, the information revolution and the introduction of computer technology into virtually all segments of modern society have changed how economies function, how governments provide internal and external security, and how everyday life is organized. Whether we are simply turning on the lights at home, boarding a train or plane, or making a phone call, we all rely on nested infrastructural systems providing energy and computing power. As shown in California in 2001, without electricity no information and communications system will function. Without computers and telecommunications networks most business activities will stop.

The change in the institutional organization of many infrastructures that has occurred over the last two decades is closely related to the increasing importance of infrastructures to modern societies. Up until the last quarter of the past century, most of them were governed by monopolistic structures tightly controlled by the state. In the meantime, in an increasing number of countries many areas of infrastructures have opened for market competition, and some of them have been finally privatized. These changes, starting during the late 1970s, came about in several waves and became stronger and stronger during the last decade. Most dramatic were changes in telecommunications. Initially restricted mainly to the most advanced industrial countries, the shock wave of these transformations are now reaching the developing world. Recent data from the ITU shows that in the last two decades the traditional telecommunications provider has in more than 80 countries been – at least partially – privatized. In most of the countries markets have been opened, competition has been introduced, and new independent regulatory agencies have been created.

In order to understand the significance of this institutional transformation we have to bear in mind that in almost all countries the control over communications infrastructures had been an exclusive prerogative of the state. These arrangements had lasted for centuries. Since the rise of the modern nation state in 16th century continental Europe, the state had played a key role in the provision of communication infrastructures and the control of communication contents. During these ages postal and telecommunications systems had been highly relevant for military purposes as well as for internal security. The provision of long-distance communication facilities was considered to be a major component in the 'logistics of power' of the state (Mann, 1984). Especially in geopolitical contexts such as those found in continental Europe, where the system of nation states originally was based on the military control of increasingly large territories, communications was a key aspect of growing state power. In almost all countries the provision and operation of communications systems became legally protected state monopolies, and the respective administrations and public enterprises had been important components of the public sector.

However, this institutional division of labor between state and society, which had been immutable for centuries, began to change radically within only two decades. Many observers in the social and political sciences understand this 'retreat of the state' (Strange, 1996) as a manifestation of the process of globalization and its negative effects on the erosion of state sovereignty. The general argument in this discourse is rather simple: Competitive pressures are pushing nation states to compete, with industrial, infrastructural and tax policies used to attract investment by multinational companies. The power of nation states to set autonomous political goals and priorities is increasingly being limited. While the political left is dramatizing this decline in autonomy and is suddenly discovering the nation state, 'the coldest of all monsters' (Nietzsche), as the last fortress against the terrorizing world market, neo-liberal economists welcome this development, because it promises to lead to more economic freedom. Some neo-liberals even see revolutionary aspects in this development. They expect that system competition could reverse the hypertrophy of the public sector in advanced industrialized countries, thus break up the 'tyranny of the status quo' (Friedman, 1982).

Indeed, a number of developments seem to point in this direction. The public sector saw a dramatic expansion up until the 1980s, although this trend has been reversed during the last decade.

Current worldwide initiatives to re-dimensionalize the public sector, to 'reinvent government' and to privatize former public services are thus largely seen as necessary adaptations to cope with global pressures. In the meantime, most of the industrialized countries, as well as an increasing number of the developing nations, have launched some kind of reform programs to restructure their public sectors, with core initiatives in most cases are targeting infrastructures.

In this chapter we will deal with the theoretical question, of why the state is retreating from one of its key functions in modern society, i.e. provision and control of infrastructures. To give an impression of the size and magnitude of the problem, we start with an empirical map of liberalization and privatization processes in some infrastructural areas (telecommunication, air transport, posts and electricity) within OECD countries – except the eastern countries. Much of the overview is based on the regulatory reform data collection of the OECD. In the second part we raise the question of why these restructuring processes take place and why they vary among the different countries. We will enter into this debate by first investigating the relationship between state and network bound infrastructures in general. In the subsequent section different reasons for the state's responsibility in infrastructures will be sorted out. In addition, we also will deal with the question of co-evolution of the state and infrastructures and the evaluation of state's changing role in this area. In the final part we discuss different explanatory approaches for the re-dimensionalization of the states role in the infrastructure sectors that we have observed in section 2.3.

2 FROM PUBLIC TO PRIVATE CONTROL OF INFRASTRUCTURES

Before entering the description of the different changes in the provision and management of infrastructures and the related repositioning of the state, we will first clarify some important notions we use in this paper. The first is the concept of infrastructures, the second is the notion of privatization and its different meanings and forms.

2.1 The Concept of Infrastructure

The term infrastructure has its origins in the military and describes the totality of those buildings, installations and communication networks necessary for supplies, especially in regard to the sending of goods and messages. The term is borrowed from the Romance Languages, where it refers to the immovable parts of the transportation system, such as the substructure of railways (track) and the network of air routes (airports) (Jochimsen, 1966, p.100). Infrastructure as 'sub- or basis structure' refers to support structures and basic resources. Infrastructures form necessary preconditions for private investment and consumption, and are hence conceived as an important locational factor.

The broad definition of the term infrastructure distinguishes material and immaterial infrastructures. The latter can be further divided into personal (skills and human capital) and institutional (legal norms and traditions) infrastructures. A more limited notion of infrastructure focuses on material infrastructures, like buildings, installations, equipment and setting-up especially for transportation, communication and energy supply. Network bound infrastructures such as energy, transportation and telecommunications are regarded as infrastructure sectors in the classical sense (Wille, 1993, p.17).

Lately the term 'complex technical systems in the infrastructure sector' has appeared more often in the social sciences with respect to extensive techno-structures like transportation-, communications- and energy supply systems etc. (Mayntz/Schneider, 1995, pp.73ff.; cf. Mayntz, 1988; Mayntz/Hughes, 1988). This term refers to large and complex systems, in which multiple actors and artefacts, that are often geographically spread, are acting in combination in a structured and a highly complex manner. It should also be pointed out that these systems are increasingly computerized and coupled with technology (Schneider, 2001, pp.31-34).

2.2 Meanings and Forms of Privatization

Until the 1980s, most infrastructures in most of the countries of the developed world had been controlled by the state. In Europe and former European colonies this generally happened by either integrating the provision and operational functions into state bureaucracy itself (i.e. as part of public administration) or in the form of public enterprises. In the United States, on the other hand, a specific model of public control had been developed in the beginning of the 20th century. This combined the acceptance of private property with some form of political control. In terms of regulation, this model contained independent regulatory agencies where controlled firms became constrained in investment and pricing behavior. Thus in the United States providers and operators of infrastructural systems always kept their private status and regulation did not replace economics by politico-administrative decision-making. Regulation has only had the effect of placing external behavioral restrictions on private business management. Regulatory reform in the United States therefore means something quite different then privatization in Europe.

Under such a perspective, privatization has to be understood on the one hand as a transformation of property rights regimes, and on the other hand also as a reduction of public control. In the study of economics, property rights are conceived as an enforceable authority to undertake particular actions in a specific domain (Commons 1968, Coleman 1990). Property rights define possible actions that individuals can take in relation to other individuals regarding some 'thing' or 'good'. A given property regime is therefore a specific combination or 'bundle of rights' to act with regard to a given object (Coleman, 1990, pp. 45-64; Ostrom & Schlager 1996; Ostrom, 2000). With respect to these different rights Coleman (1990, pp.45-64) distinguishes between the right of use, right of consumption, and right of disposal. Ostrom (2000) includes rights of access, rights of withdrawal, management rights, rights of exclusion, and rights of alienation.

Specific ownership regimes depend on the specific *combination* of these different rights and the *allocation* of these rights among actors. Rights may be concentrated or distributed on social actors. If the same single actor holds all different rights to a given good, we have a complete private property regime. If all are distributed on all actors, we have a public or common property. In complex regimes, such as in the American case of regulation by independent agencies, most of the rights that are associated with private property may be concentrated on private actors, but some rights – e.g. to set prices for services – are distributed on political actors in a public decision-making structure.

Ownership also can be expressed in more abstract terms as the right to control the outcomes of events that are connected to or embodied in a given good. Ownership implies a given structure of rights of control (Coleman, 1990). From such a perspective public property is a structure of 'rights of control' in which control is distributed among public decision-makers representing the people as the ultimate sovereign. Outcomes in infrastructures governed by public property systems are thus determined by public decision-making systems (as complex systems of decisions rules; cf. Scharpf, 1997).

Privatization from this perspective then, is a transformation of the property regime in the sense that rights of control are reallocated. Rights of control, which more or less have been dispersed in a public decision-making structure, now become concentrated on a single private person, private organization or a collectivities of share holders partially controlling such a private organization.

Such a transformation can be achieved by explicit and implicit privatization. Explicit privatization means that the structure of property rights of the whole infrastructural system will be transformed towards private control. This can be done in different degrees and levels of effectiveness. By mere *formal legal privatization*, by which, for instance, a public administration or state enterprise gets a private law status, public control would not necessarily be abolished or significantly reduced. Control could just be exerted in a different form. However, if rights of control are re-allocated in the sense that public control would actually be substituted by control through private actors, this transformation would be called *material privatization.* There are further arrangements besides this in which the whole complex of infrastructure provision and operation is divided among several actors and sequences in an infrastructure's value chain (e.g. *franchising* and *contracting out*).

2.3 Patterns of Change in Three Infrastructural Sectors

In the following section we will describe in more detail the development towards implicit and explicit privatization and the enhancement of private control in the major infrastructure sectors in 26 OECD countries. We have already claimed in the introduction, that this process of 're-dimensionalizing' the role of the state in infrastructures started during the late 1970s and has developed and spread through several waves. The first wave of liberalization and deregulation had been triggered by the deregulation movement in the US, which first affected the telecommunication and the aviation sectors in particular. The most significant changes in these areas occurred during the 1980s and 1990s. A second wave of liberalization and privatization had now started in the mid 1990s, now affecting the railway, postal, and electricity sectors. In the following section we will give an overview on these transformations.

2.3.1 Telecommunications

Telecommunications was the first sector in which the provision and operation of infrastructural systems had been privatized. Telecommunications is also the sector in which this restructuring process has been most radical, and where the broadest social and economic implications of this process can be observed. This is perhaps the reason why it is up to now the best-researched sector, containing the most complete data for our analytical purposes.

The transformation in telecommunications started in the form of implicit privatization through liberalization by the removal of regulatory constraints and burdens (deregulation) in the USA. Most of the key decisions during the 1970s leading to such market openings had been made by either the American Federal Communications Commission or by various Courts, challenging existing entry barriers and other regulatory constraints in the telecommunications domain. In the early 1980s this process culminated in the well-known divestiture of the former private monopolist AT&T. In the following years Britain and Japan followed the American example. Since the late 1980s and the early 1990s most of the other countries in our data set liberalized their telecommunications domains, with many of them also formally and materially privatizing their incumbent operator organizations. As shown in Figure 1, the privatization process showed the pattern of typical bandwagon diffusion process in which an increasing number of countries choose to follow this strategy.

Figure 4.1 The diffusion of privatization in telecommunications

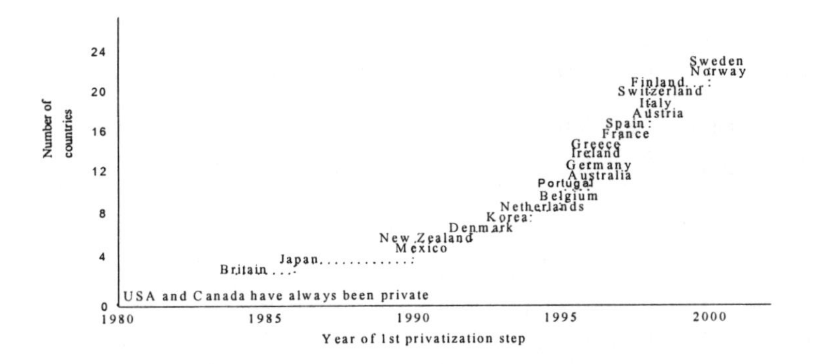

The current situation with respect to the control structure in telecommunications is shown in Table 4.1, where the most relevant information on the current shape of the sector is put together. The different data show the degree of explicit and implicit privatization: how far the incumbent infrastructure provider and operator is privatized (formally, materially); how strongly a privatized firm still is controlled by the state and how large the market share of the incumbent organization of the most important markets in this sector is.

Table 4.1 Privatization and competition in telecommunications

Country	Equity (in %) of incumbent PTO owned by public authorities			Year of privatization[1]	Share of the incumbent PTO: Basic voice 1998[1]			
	2000[2]	1998[1]	1992[1]		Local	Trunk	International	Digital mobile
Australia	50.1[3]	66.6	100	1996/97	99.4	82.13	62.8	47.8
Austria	75 – 1 share	100	100	1998	100	100	100	.
Belgium	50 + 1 share	51	100	1995	100	100	100	.
Canada	0	0	0	Always private	100	.	.	0
Denmark	0	0	89	1992	100	95	75	.
Finland	54.2	77.8[4]	100	1998	28	40	66	69
France	61[5]	62	100	1997	100	100	.	53
Germany	58[6]	61	100	1996	98	.	.	43
Greece	51	65	100	1996[7]	100	100	100	0
Iceland	100	100	100	No privatization	100	100	100	100
Ireland	0[8]	50.1[8]	100	1996/97	100	100	100	35
Italy	3.46	5	>50	1998	100	100	100	.
Japan	0	65	>66	1986	97	64	64	51
Korea	58.9	71.2	>71	1993[9]	100	90.6	68.2	0
Luxembourg	100	100	100	No privatization	100	100	100	100
Mexico	0	0	0	1990	100	81.2	.	.
Netherlands	43.25	43.8	100	1994	99.7	80	80	60
New Zealand	0	0	0	1990	99	77	72	.
Norway	79 (2001)[10]	100	100	2000[10]	100	100	95	.
Portugal	10	25	100	1995	100	100	100	.
Spain	0	0	35 (1991)	1997[11]	100	97	97	.
Sweden	70	100	100	2000[12]	93	83	68	80
Switzerland	65.5	100	100	1998	100	100	100	100
Turkey	100[13]	100	100	No privatization[14]	100	100	100	.
U.K.	0	0	22	1984	89	76.2	49	.
U.S.	0	0	0	Always private				

Table 4.1 (continued)

Sources/Notes:
[1]OECD International Regulation Database;
[2]http://webnet1.oecd.org/pdf/M00005000/M00005368.pdf; ...370.pdf; ...371.pdf; ...372.pdf; ...374.pdf; ...375.pdf; ...382.pdf; ...383.pdf; ...384.pdf; ...385.pdf; ...390.pdf; ...391.pdf; ...393.pdf; ...394.pdf; ...395.pdf; ...397.pdf; ...398.pdf; ...400.pdf; ...401.pdf; ...402.pdf; ...403.pdf; ...405.pdf; ...407.pdf; http://www.oecd.org/daf/corporate-affairs/privatization/trends/1999.pdf;
[3]http://www.theaustralian.news.com.au/common/story_page/0,5744,2390019%255E7583,00.html;
[4] http://www.feem.it/web/activ/wp/abs01/26-01.pdf, http://webnet1.oecd.org/pdf/M00005000/M00005375.pdf;
[5] Germany 2001: 43% (http://www.german-way.com/german/privat.html);
[6] France 2001: 56% (http://www.german-way.com/german/privat.html);
[7] http://www.feem.it/web/activ/wp/abs01/26-01.pdf, http://www7.itu.int/treg/profiles2/cntryprfiles/Build_EU_Guide.asp, http://www.invgr.com/ote/advertisment.htm;
[8] http://www.idg.net/idgns/1999/06/14/IrelandToSellEntireStakeIn.shtml;
[9] http://www.feem.it/web/activ/wp/abs01/26-01.pdf, http://www.afajof.org/Pdf/meeting/2001/d'sousa_megginson_nash_paper.pdf;
[10]http://biz.yahoo.com/ifc/no/news/121100-1.html;
[11]First tranche privatized in 1924;
[12]http://www.helios-tech.co.uk/papers/3G%20review%20-%20Pt4%20Network%20Operator%20Information.pdf;
[13]http://www.oecd.org/dsti/sti/it/cm/act/tel-reg/etel-tur.pdf;
[14]planned (http://news.bbc.co.uk/hi/english/world/europe/newsid_1327000/1327828.stm).

Figure 4.1 and the data in Table 4.1 point towards interesting developments. On the one hand it is shown, that there is a clear trend and convergence towards a privatized and liberalized structure (measured by government ownership in the incumbent or largest operator and by measures of market concentration).

On the other hand, one can see that there is still significant variation between the different countries in the way in which liberalization has really materialized. An immediate expression of this variation is given by Figure 4.2, where the ownership patterns of the operator(s) are depicted. Here the picture is mixed: in about a half of the countries, the operators are completely or almost completely (Portugal, Italy) privatized, in the other half of the countries they are partially (mostly about a quarter to 50%) privatized. Only in the two very small countries Iceland and Luxembourg and in Turkey (plans for privatization!) the respective companies are still under full governmental control.

Figure 4.2 Governmental ownership of largest operator (PTOs), 2000 (%)

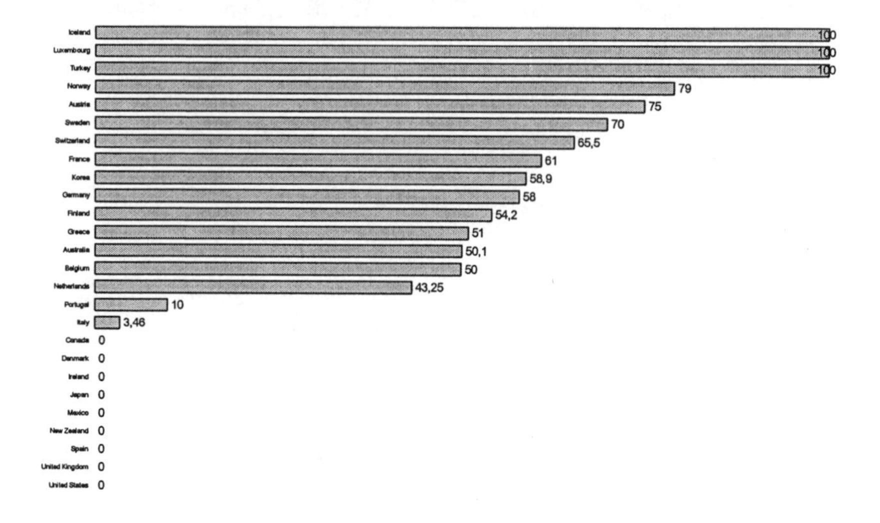

2.3.2 Airlines

The privatization in the airline industry is an example of institutional changes in the area of transport infrastructures. Although the degree of private control in this sector in 1998 was currently greater than in telecommunications, the transformation was less radical here because most of the incumbent operator organizations had already had a private legal shape, or at least the structure of a relatively independent public corporation. In telecommunications, on the other hand, most of the operator organizations were public administrations.

The transformations in aviation have also been triggered by policy changes in the United States at the end of the seventies. At that time the industry resembled a public utility, organized either as a regulated industry or as a state company. A turning point was the American Airline Deregulation Act of October 1978, which first lead to wide-ranging deregulation during the Ronald Reagan presidency.

During the 1980s, almost all airline companies formally privatized their organizational structures. In the following years the majority of our 25 countries also sold significant shares of capital in the stock market (column 1 in Table 4.2). By the year 1998, only the less developed EU member states,

Greece, Ireland, and Portugal, still had full governmental control of their airline sectors.

Table 4.2 Private and public control in the airline industry

Country	Government ownership in largest airline firm (%) 1998	Domestic deregulation 1998	Concentration of airline industry (Herfindahl Index) 1997		Open Sky agreements 2000
			Domestic	International	
	1	*2*	*3*	*4*	*5*
Australia	0	●	0.50 (1995)	0.88 (1995)	-
Austria	52	●	0.97	0.50	1995
Belgium	34	●	1.00	1.00	1995
Canada	0	O	0.52	0.52	-
Denmark	50	●	1.00	1.00	1995
Finland	60	●	0.60 (1995)	1.00 (1995)	1995
France	95	●	0.55	0.92	-
Germany	0	●	0.70	0.96	1996
Greece	100	O	1.00	1.00	-
Iceland	0	●	1.00	1.00	1995
Ireland	100	●	0.44	0.97	-
Italy	86	●	0.35 (1995)	0.59 (1995)	1999
Japan	0	O	0.59	0.63	2000
Korea	0	O	0.39 (1996)	0.48 (1996)	1998
Mexico	55	O	0.72	0.72	-
Netherlands	25	●	1.00 (1996)	1.00 (1996)	1992
New Zealand	0	●	0.44 (1994)	0.85 (1994)	1997
Norway	50	●	1.00	1.00	1995
Portugal	100	O	1.00	1.00	2000
Spain	94	●	0.56	0.99	-
Sweden	50	●	1.00	1.00	1995
Switzerland	7	O	1.00	1.00	1995
Turkey	98	O	0.26	0.68	2000
UK	0	●	0.12	0.19	-
US	0	●	0.12	0.19	-

Note: O no ● yes

Source: Gonenc/ Nicoletti (2000); Open Skies Agreements: U.S. Dept. of State, Bureau of Economic and Business Affaris (http://www.state.gov/www/issues/economic/tra/agrmts_opskies.html)

Parallel to this development, domestic and international markets have been increasingly opened. However, as the columns 3 and 4 in Table 2 indicate, there is great variation: on the one side there are still monopolistic market structures in most of the European countries, on the other hand there is intense market competition in countries such as the US, UK, Canada, Japan and Korea.

During the 1990s, the international aviation markets have also been increasingly liberalized. The US was also playing an active role in this process. The Americans convinced more and more countries to engage into bilateral and multilateral 'Open Skies' agreements (Table 4.2, column 5). These contracts essentially consist of the exchange of traffic rights and the provision of liberal pricing regimes. Whereas the formal liberalization of international aviation markets may be indicated by the existence of open sky agreements, to describe the degree of factual liberalization we can also use the concentration measure (Herfindahl index), too (Table 4.2, column 4). Here it can also be seen that the overwhelming number of countries still have highly concentrated markets.

2.3.3 Electricity

The last infrastructural sector that will be presented here is electricity. Major structural changes of this sector belong to the second wave of privatization. The first transformations began at the end of the 1980s and the beginning of the 1990s. As it is shown in Table 4.3, the 'first movers' in this development are clearly the UK, Norway, New Zealand and Australia. Late comers in contrast are mostly the less developed EU countries such as Greece and Ireland, but also France, Belgium, Canada and Japan.

Table 4.3 Retail electricity market opening in IEA countries

Country	Partial Opening	Full Opening
United Kingdom	1990	2000
Norway	1991	1991
New Zealand	1994	1994
Australia	1994	
Finland	1995	1997
Sweden	1996	1996
Germany	1998	1998
Spain	1998	
United States	1998	
Austria	1999	

Denmark	1999
Italy	1999
Luxembourg	1999
Netherlands	1999
Portugal	1999
Switzerland	1999
Belgium	2000
France	2000
Ireland	2000
Japan	2000
Canada	2001
Greece	2001

Source: International Energy Agency, Electricity Market Reform: California and After. A fact sheet from the International Energy Agency, March 2001.
http://www.iea.org/about/emr.pdf
http://www.iea.org/pubs/reviews/files/italy99/italy.htm

Our preliminary overview of explicit and implicit privatization processes in many countries and various infrastructures has shown, that there are remarkable changes which transform the traditional role of the state in infrastructures significantly. In addition, it has been shown, that these changes are different across countries and across sectors. In the following sections we will discuss relevant literatures dealing with these questions. However, prior to the discussion of the state's stepwise withdrawal from infrastructural functions, we first will discuss the relationship between state and infrastructures at a general level.

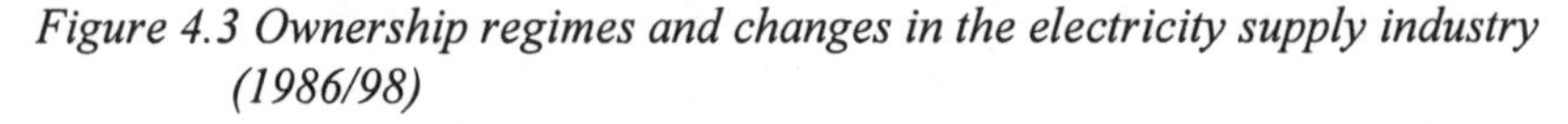

Figure 4.3 Ownership regimes and changes in the electricity supply industry (1986/98)

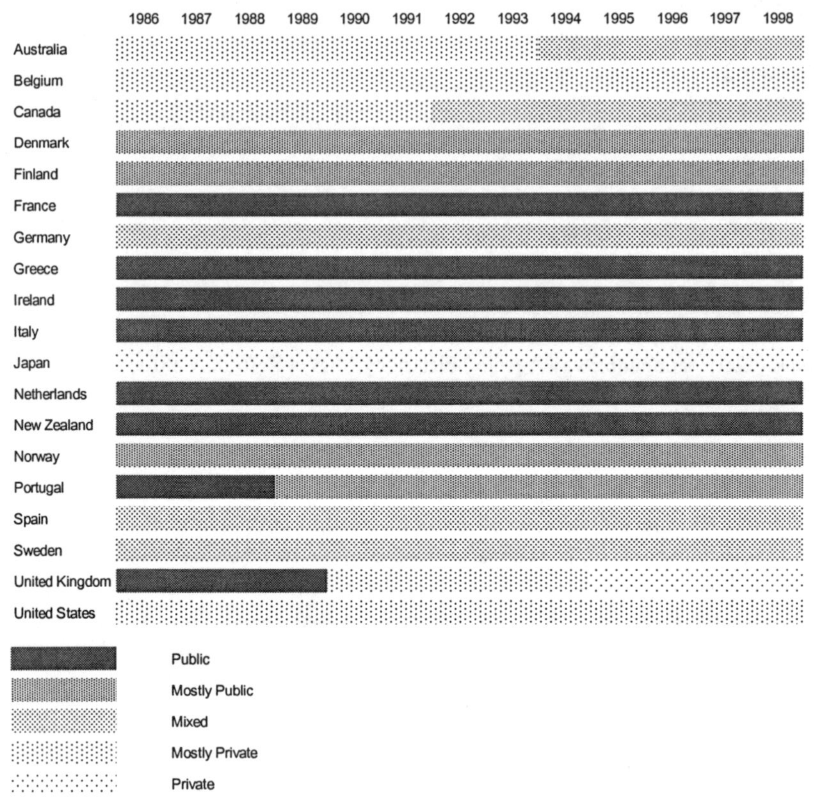

Source: OECD International Regulation Database.

3 THE THEORETICAL 'PROBLEMATIQUE' OF PUBLIC INFRASTRUCTURES: APPROACHES AND EXPLANATIONS

3.1 Infrastructures as Blood Circulation and Nervous System of the State

In state theory the metaphor of the state as 'body' is very common – just think of the famous copper engraving of Hobbes' Leviathan. The network-based infrastructures are often adapted to this body picture, by referring to the blood circulation as structure of transportation (Gudme, 1824, p.1; Ratzel,

1903, pp. 503, 529, 1925, p. 335) or the nervous system as telecommunication (cf. Haubold, 1995, p.8). This picture of transportation and communication routes as lifelines of a federally organized state and a society based on the division of labor (Hermes, 1998, p.334) lets network based infrastructures seem vital for the state. There is no state without infrastructures (cf. Krüger, 1969, p.4). Hence, the basic function of infrastructures is seen in the social, economic and political integration of communities (Hesse, 1979, p.9; Hermes, 1998, p.352; Krüger, 1969, pp.5-6).

3.2 Reasons for Infrastructure Responsibility

The reasons for state commitment within the infrastructure sector can be divided between a) technical efficiency aspects, b) military, state and integrationist motives, c) the demand of state resource 'expropriation rights' and fiscal motives, d) correction of market failure and public control, e) guarantee of extensive supply (socio-political motives) and finally f) democracy-political, legal and environmentalist considerations (see also Hermes, 1998, p. 271).

Technical efficiency aspects can be explained, for instance, by looking at the railway system. Through state engagement into infrastructure provision the parallel building of tracks might be avoided. In addition locomotive and car switching is more tightly coordinated. Economy and society thereby gain full advantages of unified technical standardization, unified tariffs and coordinated timetables. The same is true for telegraph- and telephone systems (Hermes, 1998, p.271; Mayntz/Schneider, 1995, p.96). While organizational centralization might be sufficient for these functions, state commitment is not indispensable. A private monopoly would be equally conceivable.

It is frequently emphasized that the control over transportation, communication and energy systems, and their security as well as quality, is of great importance for military issues (Mayntz/Schneider, 1995, p.96). A fast and reliable communication, just like frictionless transportation of troops has often been a decisive factor for the outcome of war. In addition, the geopolitical interest of a state for social and economical integration of the national territory appears through sufficient possibilities for mobility and communication (railway system, postal service, telegraph system).

Another reason for state involvement in infrastructure provision is the rights of way problem. Network bound infrastructures depend very much on control over geographical scope. In most cases routes cannot be arbitrarily chosen and depend on 'rights of way'. The comparative advantage of state involvement in these situations is that state legislature provides the possibility of expropriation. Finally, in many cases considerable profits have been made by nationalized railways, which played an important role for the state budget (Hermes, 1998, p.277).

In a bourgeois-liberal view of society, which starts from the autonomous and self-interested economy-based citizen, government responsibilities can only be legitimized by the failure of mechanisms of societal self-control. In this respect a central argument among others for state involvement in the development and operation of network based infrastructures, is that the market could not provide them on equally favorable terms. The particular competence of governments to manage these specific systems thus directly results from market failures[2] in this sector.

Adam Smith already includes additional state obligations besides (firstly) defence and (secondly) judiciary: 'The third and last duty of the sovereign or commonwealth is that of erecting and maintaining those public institutions and those public works, which, though they may be in the highest degree advantageous to a great society, are, however, of such a nature, that the profit could never repay the expense to any individual or small number of individuals, and which it therefore cannot be expected that any individual or small number of individuals should erect or maintain' (Smith, 1812 [1776], pp. 570-571) This also includes 'the public works and institutions for facilitating the commerce of the society [...], such as good roads, bridges, navigable canals, harbors, etc.' (Smith, 1812 [1776], p.571).

Because of the significance of infrastructures in the planning for professional and private life (Mayntz, 1988, p.233; Mayntz/Schneider, 1995, p.74), it is often pointed out, that it is the responsibility of the state to provide a wide-spread basis supply on favorably priced terms. Hereby regional as well as social aspects play an important role. Besides the connection and supply of rural areas (even if it does not seem advisable under profitability terms), the critical dependence on all infrastructure based goods, just like a sufficient supply of energy, is interpreted as a welfare function. A core idea is that the state has the responsibility to provide or at least to guarantee the provision of 'means of living'[3] for its people (Bull, 1973, pp. 224, 240; Hermes, 1998, pp.92-93; Wesener, 1986, p.134 ff.).

A link between state and infrastructure can also be established under a *democracy theoretical* perspective. Since modern mass democracies no longer correspond to the small and easily manageable democracy model of the Greek 'polis', they require media and intermediary institutions. Institutions of representative democracy reflect this issue. In addition, space-integrating structures of communications and transportation remain necessary for the development of a democratic public. These structures are supposed to guarantee that the center of power remains easily attainable for citizens.

Certain *fundamental rights* can only be claimed under particular preconditions. There is a link between a democratic state under the rule of law and the existence of network based infrastructures. The German *Grundgesetz* (constitution) explicitly names '*communicative*' basic rights such as the right for freedom of speech (Art. 5 I), freedom of assembly (Art. 8) and freedom of association and to form coalition (Art. 9) as well as privacy of the post, secrecy of the post and of telecommunications (Art. 10). The personal physical freedom of movement (liberté d'aller et de venir) is included in the personal freedom term of Art. 2 II. This means that a state which could not guarantee the provision of infrastructures would also – in some sense – harm the state of law as the 'critical infrastructure for fundamental rights'. As a democratic state, under the rule of law, has to respect and to protect the fundamental right of informational self-determination (data protection) and the right on privacy, it also has to have a vital interest on the constitution of the communicational infrastructures.

3.3 Co-Evolution of Modern Sovereign States and Network Based Infrastructures

Mayntz/Schneider emphasize the co-evolution between modern states and large technical infrastructures. Both were extraordinarily formally organized and hierarchically structured and also mutually stimulated each other's growth and showed increasing degrees of centralization. Through their equally high potential of utility and risk the technical infrastructure systems are supposed to have provoked state regulation and thereby promoted the strong, the intervention-state (Mayntz/Schneider, 1995, p.96). Looking back in history, the development of the modern nation state can be seen as a 'response' to the development of early commercial society and its prerequisites (lowering of transaction costs; abolition of feudal political and legal fragmentation). It is a reaction to the tendencies to spatial and functional removal of boundaries. Hence, the first indications of infrastructural development were already present before the nation state (Ratzel, 1903, pp.500, 502), but only bloomed after its arrival (see also Bernauer, 2000, p.41).

According to Michael Mann the state distinguishes itself as social configuration by its territoriality and centrality: 'Unlike economic, ideological or military groups in civil society, the state elite's resources radiate authoritatively outwards from a center but stop at defined territorial boundaries. The state is, indeed, a *place* – both a central place and a unified territorial reach.' (Mann, 1984, p.198) Only territories that are covered by infrastructures are in the end also ruled territories (Krüger, 1969, pp.6-7). The existence of network based infrastructures, spreading across wide areas with the function to integrate exactly these, is thus the basis (Hermes, 1998, p.341) for this particular power of the state, the form of 'territorial power'. The greater the infrastructural powers of the state are or have become, the greater is the territorialisation of social life (Mann, 1984, p.208). Territorialisation corresponds to a specific model of the state compared to the model of the (Italian) city states and city unions (e.g. South Germany and Hanse) (cf. Bernauer, 2000, p.40 ff.).

3.4 The Market Decides – The State Provides

Different theoretical and ideological perspectives don't see the 'infrastructural power' of contemporary states as an unchallengeable sign of state power to dominate society, but see its role as serving to dominant economic interests. Michael Mann (1984, p.189) writes: 'All infrastructurally powerful states, including the capitalist democracies, are strong in relation to individuals and to the weaker groups in civil society, but the capitalist democratic states are feeble in relation to dominant groups – at least in comparison to most historical states.' The view that state responsibility for infrastructures under advanced capitalist conditions does not necessarily create and support specific action capacities of the state, is shared by neo-Marxist scholars as well as authors from the tradition of the German *Staatsrechtslehre*, who believe it is a problem when the state is driven out of the position of a 'higher third party', and instead becoming a servant and 'accomplice' for the industrial and economic processes, which only has security functions, i.e. to provide for *Ausfallbürgschaft* (Böckenförde, 1991, p.240; Forsthoff, 1971). From this perspective, obviously 'the state is supposed to give without taking anything' (Böckenförde, 1991, p.242). It has to provide important preconditions for economic development in form of infrastructures, however, without having any influence on investment decisions.

Because of this basic function which infrastructures fulfil as a precondition for all other economic activities, an interesting argument has been brought up within the current discussion in globalization. In times of increasing locational competition for mobile capital and human resources, it is argued, the infrastructural function of the state would get more and more important, and might even become its remaining core function (next to the provision of security). According to Wolfgang Streeck under the condition of regime competition public policy must increasingly follow a tendency to limit its substance to a *business-like provision* of an internationally attractive infrastructure supporting the profitability of economic activities. In addition, this policy seems to switch of from the mere use of sovereign state power to the production of incentives and rewards to fairly expected investment (Streeck, 1998, pp.34-35; see also Schulze/ Ursprung, 1998, pp.32-33). The terms of 'provision' and 'limitation' seems to agree with the above mentioned fears of some conservative observers such as, for instance, Ernst-Wolfgang Böckenförde.

3.5 Privatization as Dispersion of Solidarity?

Fears relevant to a state's withdrawal from infrastructure point towards another aspect. It has already been mentioned, that the commitment of the state in infrastructure provision also has a social function, based on the principle of justice. That a society, sets up an integrated network infrastructure through the state as a special form of its self-organization, insinuates to aspects of loyalty and solidarity (Willke, 1992, pp.364-365). In this respect it is emphasized that privatization of infrastructures could indicate a 'dispersion of solidarity'. In this perspective the economically most successful parts of society creep towards a 'secession' from the remainder of society: 'they buy their own superior infrastructure in form of private jets, private security companies, (...) private communication media and, maybe the most serious, private educational system from kindergarten to elite universities.' In this development Willke fears the destruction of a nationally achieved consensus about societal loyalty and solidarity. If there is a parallel development of 'in-official' private infrastructures next to the official public one, not only is the privately invested money lacking, the political pressure needed to keep up high standards of public infrastructures weakens (Willke, 1992, pp. 365-366) Also Habermas (1992, p.425) is referring to the aspect, that different social classes are being selectively affected by the withdrawal of collective goods.

With respect to the state's function for supply or guarantee of infrastructures, Otto Hintze's statement, that only relative, historically contingent and no absolute purposes for a state exist (Hübinger, 1988, p.156; Schneider, 1999, pp.22, 244), also seems relevant. State activities neither can be derived from functional necessities following a technical or economic logic, nor are these functions invariably fixed in 'ultra-stable' institutional forms. Which kind of infrastructures and how much of them the state will provide and operate in which concrete forms is therefore a political question. It is the outcome of political battles and conflicts, of bargaining and deliberation processes, and of institutional arrangements structuring these interactions.

4 THEORIES EXPLAINING STATE WITHDRAWAL FROM THE INFRASTRUCTURE SECTOR

In this section we will discuss the spectrum of theoretical approaches which aim to explain the current developments, that in some countries the state is giving up the functions of provision and management of infrastructures. In order to get a clearer picture of the major theoretical camps, we propose a two-dimensional classification of the current discussion. In a *first* dimension we distinguish *structuralist or functionalist theories of (socio)economical and technological determination* versus *actor-centered and institutionalist theories of political scope of action.* In a *second* dimension *static-comparative versus dynamic-comparative* theories will be distinguished.

4.1 Static-Comparative Theories Versus Dynamic Theories of Diffusion and Contagion

Dynamic-comparative theories stress the correlation between national and international developments and the embeddedness of national policy making into an international environment. Effects of diffusion and contagion are considered. National developments are not looked at as isolated and independent development courses ('cases'), but are, on the other hand, seen as interconnected co-evolutions and interactions and of intertwinings of various kinds (Evans et al. 1993; Gourevitch, 1978; Schneider, 2001; Skocpol, 1979). In this perspective inter-sectoral[4] as well as general country[5] 'infections' are conceivable.

4.2 Structuralist and Functionalist Theories of Economical and Technological Determination

4.2.1 The Structuralist View of Neo-Liberals

Following structuralist and functionalist theories of economical,[6] respectively technological determination, state withdrawal from the infrastructure can be seen as a reaction on a more or less inevitable force to structural adaptation, mainly resulting from global economic integration (globalization) and technological development. From this perspective state activities are increasingly forced to orientate themselves towards efficiency conditions and requirements that are set by techno-economical processes. In this context, a direct supply of infrastructures through the state can no longer be financed. Since mobile production factors gain more and more significance compared to the immobile ones, nation states see themselves more and more exposed to locational competition. This creates pressures to reduce inefficiencies and –

sooner or later – to follow the path of liberalization and privatization (convergence pressure). Modernization processes lead different societies through similar development paths. However, in this perspective liberalization and privatization of infrastructures are not understood as negligence of this sector, but – on the contrary – it is assumed that this sector – on the basis of its critical function – is gaining increasing significance in the competition for mobile factors and thus – in the course of liberalization and privatization – has to be designed more efficiently and more attractive (Schulze/Ursprung, 1998, p.3). In addition to that transportation, communication and energy are all conceived as booming economy sectors, that are able to attract investment capital.

Especially neo-liberal economists, such as Ohmae (1992), Sachs & Warner (1995) and Klaus-Dieter Schmidt (1999), believe that states are exposed to an inevitable convergence pressure through globalization. This, however, is generally welcome, because it is assumed that this would lead to an elimination of inefficiencies and to increase overall welfare.

4.2.2 Critical Structuralism

The thesis of 'economisation' – i.e. the increasing dominance of economic goals and values – is also supported by neo-Marxist and neo-Keynesian authors from the critical camp (Altvater/Mahnkopf, 1996; Gill, 1995; Gill/Law, 1993; Gray, 1998; Hirsch, 1995, 1999; Narr/Schubert, 1994; Scherrer, 2000; Stopford/Strange, 1991; Strange, 1986, 1995, 1996; van der Pijl, 1999). However, the different positions from which the increasing dominance of economic processes is evaluated, vary from skepticism to definite disapproval. It is assumed that state withdrawal endangers solidarity, stability and security. A noticeable increase of social disintegration (indicators are unemployment, social inequality/poverty, criminality etc.) in this perspective goes along with a creeping expansion of repressive state functions, of the police and security apparatus. Hence, disintegration is dealt with in a authoritarian and simultaneously cost-saving manner (Fach/Simonis 2000; Jessop 1996: 373ff.; Junger-Tas 1999; Wacquant 1999). Indications for this development in the Federal Republic of Germany are seen in the so-called 'asylum compromise' or in the '*große Lauschangriff*' (large scale bugging operation) and other technologies of political control.

4.2.3 Techno-Determinism

State dominance in the governance of infrastructural systems over a long period of time often lead to techno-determinist and functionalist perspectives, that infer from (socio-technical) functions to (socio-institutional) form. A classical example is Karl August Wittfogels' '*Orientalische Despotie*'

(1962), in which the main thesis states that large technical irrigation systems in the old orient needed a centralized state as a functional prerequisite (Schneider, 2001, p.32).

In a techno-determinist structuralism perspective in the globalization debate, technology is the motor for the above mentioned convergence. Technological progress is supposed to generate similarly structured problems and solutions for the different nation states (Berger/Dore, 1996; Kerr, 1960). It is assumed that growing interdependence between nation states would accelerate the spread of new technologies around the globe. Growing interdependency across the borders favors the diffusion of technology and thereby reinforces the trend towards convergence (Bernauer, 2000, p.135).

Neo-functionalist integration theories, that have been referred to for the explanation of European Integration since the 1950s (Michelmann/Soldatos, 1994), assume that integration of rather 'technical' sectors, like trade and finances, will spill-over into 'political' sectors (*spill-over effects*). Liberalization of the world economy and the accompanying intensification of international cooperation is thus leading to an increasing convergence of domestic institutions and problem solutions.

4.2.4 Normative Theories of Regulation

Normative theories of regulation (constitutional-economic view of states activities) also belong to the functionalist approaches. Out of this perspective the reduced role of the state in infrastructures can be interpreted as a reaction on the removal of 'objective' conditions. These conditions caused the state to supply material infrastructures until this point. It would be conceivable, that a public good becomes private through technological innovation. For instance, new technology enables the registration of individual consumption and therefore the 'exclusion' of potential free riders. Another possibility would be that technical changes are altering goods in such a way that private actors can produce them more efficiently and more profitably. The state does not have to fill-in this gap any more since the problem of incentive is solved. The conclusion thus is fairly simple and shows a functionalist undertone: the state will only act if the market fails and state withdrawal indicates that market failure no longer exists.

4.3 Actor-Centered and Institutionalist Theories of Political Scope of Action

In contrast to structuralist and functionalist theories of economical and technological determinism many authors (Boyer/Drache, 1996; Busch/Plümper, 1999; Drucker, 1997; Evans et al, 1985; Evans, 1997;

Garrett, 1995, 1998; Garrett/Lange, 1991; Garrett/Mitchell, 1995; Glyn, 1995; (Katzenstein, 1984, 1985); Krasner, 1999; Mann, 1997; (Ruggie, 1983)) express the position that multiple political strategies and thus different national reaction patterns and various development paths are still feasible (persistence of national scope of action). The assumption that convergence pressures exists which force all states onto an identical withdrawal path, is denied. Within these 'political' approaches, which belong to the overall framework of 'actor-centered institutionalism'[7] in the broadest sense, three hypothesis can be further distinguished: a) the partisan approach/ideological factors, b) institutional approaches/factors and c) resource-dependence approaches/factors, which stress the organization and power of societal interests.

4.3.1 Partisan Theory – Do Parties Matter?

'Partisan Theory' says that the state's actions are dependent on who the ruling party(s) is/are and that a difference exists between the parties (cf. the partisan theory of macro policy; Hibbs, 1991). In general it can be said that left oriented parties tend to support the expansion of the public sector and government intervention (Cameron, 1978, p.1246; Davis, Dempster & Wildavsky, 1966, 1974; Downs, 1957, p.116; Hibbs, 1978; Wildavsky 1975; *contrary* Bell, 1960; King, 1969 pp. 136-137; Lipset, 1960, pp. 439-56). New studies in the scope of globalization, namely by Garrett (1995, 1998) and Cusack (1997), concentrate on the significance of *government ideology (partisan approach)* and ask whether or not the strategic space has become tighter due to globalization, or if like earlier new paths around regulations have been found. Garrett thinks so, while Cusack more or less believes the opposite.

It can be shown that in some countries the withdrawal of the state from infrastructure had significance relevance for the ideological orientation of the ruling party. Only under this point of view may the famous radicalism in the privatization and liberalization process in Great Britain or the changeable course of privatization in 1980's France be revealed. Yet the ideological partisan explanations still had its limits. In Sweden, for example, the conservatives parties nationalized troubled industries during the late 1970's, while in Austria the SPÖ-led government began the privatization of state industries in the 1980's (Grande, 1997, p.580). During the 80's it was seen in Australia, and even more so in Labour-ruled New Zealand and socialist Spain, that even leftist parties could cut down on their social spending and encourage liberal market reforms (Castles, 1990; Merkel, 1993; Schmidt, 1993, p.376). Only in the 1990's with election victories by Tony Blair and Gerhard Schroeder in Britain and Germany respectively, has there finally been a wider movement for the adapting of more liberal policies in these two countries.

4.3.2 The Significance of Ideas and the Success of Neo-liberal programs

In this context neo-liberalism is seen as a concept or doctrine of economic policy which is inextricably linked to the privatization and liberalization push of infrastructure during the 1980's (Eising, 2000, pp.30-34; Hall, 1992; Müller, 1994; Nordmann/Plehwe/Walpen, 2000). An Anglo-American phalanx of neo-liberalism was suddenly created by the victory of the elections in 1979 by Margaret Thatcher and Ronald Reagan in 1980. Both governments were highly influenced by the monetarist programmes of the *Chicago School*. During the course of the 80's and 90's Social Democrats were increasingly adapting the new economic paradigm as their own – if not in official party rhetoric, then at least in practice. However it can be seen that each country adopted its own version of reform. The programmatic new-orientation under the label *'Third Way'* in the UK (Giddens, 1997, 1999) and *'New Middle'* in the US at least partially shows this integration of neo-liberalism in the ideology of the Center-Left's (Social Democrats) leadership.

4.3.3 The Institutional Approach: Westminster-Model versus Consensus Democracy

The institutional approaches can be seen as either critique of, or supplement to *Partisan Theory*. The theory states that the maneuvering room of the parties or key players vary according to institutional structures. A paradigmatic comparison in this respect is the Westminster-Model versus Consensus Democracy. An earlier study by Swank (1997) focused on how the political reactions towards globalization are effected by the structure of the country's democratic institutions: 'Is international capital mobility systematically related to retrenchment of the public economy, (or do) democratic institutions and processes shape the ways in which globalization affects national policies?' (Swank, 1997, p.1) Swank uses 'measures for social corporatism (union density, state involvement in wage bargaining, etc.), consensus democracy, and dispersion of authority (federalism, bicameralism, use of referendums)' and concludes that 'capital market integration (maybe with the exception of FDI) does not have a significant influence on government growth, whereas trade integration has a positive rather than negative effect. Capital market integration however does have a significant positive impact on the government share in countries characterized by high corporatism (e.g. Norway, Sweden), high consensus democracy (e.g. Belgium, Netherlands), and low dispersion of authority (e.g. Denmark, Finland). The converse holds for countries with low corporatism, low consensus democracy, and a high dispersion of authority.' (Schulze & Ursprung, 1998, p.30)

As can be seen by our preliminary overview in the initial section, Great Britain – next to the USA – took the leading role in the liberalization and privatization of public infrastructures. The absence of a constitutional entrenchment of public infrastructure provision and operation,[8] along with a highly centralized political decision making process and the popularity of neo-liberalism all contributed in making the passage of conservative privatization policies considerably easier to achieve. The privatization of infrastructure sectors (water, gas, electricity, and telecommunications) were easily achieved through democratic processes (simple parliamentary majorities). The centralization and concentration of the decision-making bodies, shows among other things, the non-existence of a federal participation element and the strong position of the Prime Minister, who is allowed some influence in all departments. During the 1980's the British Conservatives could implement their goals unhindered by cumbersome institutional arrangements (Moon, 1995).

In Germany, on the other hand, vertical (federalism) and horizontal (departmental principle) fragmentation limit the state's capacity. Article 87 GG has created major constitutional hurdles in the privatization of public infrastructure. Because of the required 2/3 majority, privatization was undermined in Germany by the logic of a Consensus Democracy more than by any party-line politics (Grande, 1997, pp.581-582).

Schmidt (1993, p.386) names – mainly based on Arend Lijphart's work (1984; for a most recent version see 1999) – five barriers against majority dominance: a more limited degree of centralization, a stronger second chamber (or equivalent in the form of an institution, which is represented by the executive in member states), an autonomous constitutional jurisdiction and major limitations in the changing of the constitution, proportional voting system and a relatively independent central bank. The barriers against majoritarian decision-making are especially high in Germany (5), Switzerland (4) and the US (4). On the other hand, they are especially low in the Westminster-Model countries – Great Britain and New Zealand[9] – and in France (each 0) (Colomer, 1995, p.20; Huber, Ragin & Stephens, 1993, p.728; Lijphart, 1991, 1994a, 1994b, 1999; Schmidt, 1997, pp. 240-252; in this respect see also Tsebelis' (1995, 1999) concept of 'veto-players').

4.3.4 The Resource Dependence Approach: Classes, Power, Interests and Organization

The theory of power resources is of interest in a context, in which a state's activity does not follow any techno-economical nor institutional logic, but rather when it becomes concrete through political interests (Grande, 1997, p.577). State activity is derived from the interests of social classes, their organizations and ability to deal with conflict, the balance of power between different classes and their organizations, the institutional conditions for governing the distribution of conflicts as well as the strategic maneuvering of the governing elite (Schmidt, 1993, p.377). Both Rent-Seeking Theory and the rather critically oriented class theory approaches belong to this perspective (Cameron, 1984; Esping-Andersen, 1990; Korpi, 1991). Unlike in Normative Theory of Regulation, in which the state is free from considerations of self-interests and is purely focussed on helping out in case of market failure, emphasizing the Positive Theory of Regulation (Public Choice; Analytical Theory of Politics), the state's activities are frequently influenced by self-motives. Furthermore, the state's key-players use egoistic-rationales for the purpose of rent-seeking and extending their domain. This in turn leads to perceptions of the state being inefficient, and inevitably, state denial. In relation to the Rent-Seeking Model, it would be expected that globalization would undermine such coalitions and cartels, and significantly weaken the strength of state bureaucracy in its attempt to achieve its pre-intended goals.

The Power Resource Theory is especially helpful in comparing countries with major class structure differences, where balance of power differences between classes and political parties are especially pronounced, such as Sweden and the US for example (Schmidt, 1993, p.377).

5 CONCLUSION

Our preliminary overview on the situation in key infrastructures in the 26 OECD countries shows that there exists an international diffusion process as well as adaptive pressures from globalization and Europeanization. However, it can also be seen that the countries adapt to these pressures at different rates and manners, according to the respective organization of their institutional systems and actor-constellations.

The two Westminster-Model States, Great Britain and New Zealand,[10] have become the forerunners in the field of privatization and liberalization of infrastructure due to the concentration of their decision-making processes. In the other Anglo-Saxon countries, the US, Australia and to a lesser-degree

Canada, the development is quite similar, despite the more limited action possibilities (esp. in the US) for their respective political systems (governments, parliaments) (Schmidt, 1993, p.386). In the two original neo-liberal countries, Britain and the US, major breakthroughs in privatization and liberalization have been achieved despite their very different political structures. Among the Anglo-Saxon countries in general, there has been widespread acceptance of privatization due simply to their perceived economic benefits, and despite the fragmented institutional conditions prevalent in some of the nations, such as the US (federalism, dived government, etc.). The movement has caught on significantly later in continental Europe, where there is a fundamental difference in how the state's functions are viewed.

The long term goals of the privatization, liberalization, and deregulation movements have until now only partly been achieved (Berger & Dore 1996; Kitschelt et al. 1999). Furthermore, there are major differences, between both different countries and different sectors, in the way in which the changes have evolved. According to Grande/Risse (2000, p.244), in most cases „there is an interaction effect between convergence brought on by globalization pressures, and path dependency created by traditional national structures.' In a kind of 'Luhmannian' tendency of being sensitive to all kinds of paradoxes, they point to a phenomenon of 'divergent convergence' where economic convergence of fundamental goals is combined with institution-based divergence of state's functions. In reality this is not a paradoxical process, but a feature of all processes that are based on 'form constraints'. The degree of convergence always is a function of both, varying pressures to adapt and inherent degrees of internal restrictions for the different 'entities' (i.e. adaptive flexibility) that are forced to adapt to new environments (Schneider & Werle, 1998).

NOTES

1. We are grateful to Carmen Ehni and Ari Pattanayak, who helped us to finish and polish this English-language text.
2. With respect to the problem of market failure we refer to public good (non-exclusiveness) aspects, external effects and natural monopolies.
3. What belongs to infrastructural basic supply is dependent on a given state of technological, economic, and also societal development.
4. Sectoral waves of privatization and liberalization: first of all telecommunication and the aviation sector, then the railway sector, the postal and electricity sectors. That means that the sectoral contagion comes from the telecommunications sector. According to Eising (2000,

p.34) runs out from the liberalization of other net-bound sectors, mainly telecommunication, a demonstration effect, which undermines the hypothesis of the singularity and therefore special position of the line-bound economies.

5. According to Eising (2000, p.33) has also the practice of direct pressure from the USA and international organizations contributed to reform diffusion. So the USA practiced in the relationships to the EU-states direct but limited pressure in the telecommunication and finance sector to improve the chances for market access for the US-companies (see also Woolcock et al. 1991, p.4).
6. These approaches are basically in the tradition of theories that, already saw the increase of states activities as mostly economically determined. Most famous is probably 'Wagner's Law' (1883) of a direct correlation between economic growth and increase of states activities. Broadening of the Wagner-Hypothesis can be found in Abramowitz (1986), Baumol (1986) and Durlauf (1996).
7. From this broad perspective (for a definition of the approach see Mayntz & Scharpf 1995, Scharpf 1997) states activities are explained through specific orientations, goals and strategies of actors as well as their capacities and resources, with consideration of the institutional environment.
8. For the concept of deepness of institutional entrenchment see Schneider (2001, p.262).
9. However, New Zealand has started to move away from the Westminster Model since the introduction of proportional voting rights (Nagel, 1994).
10. See footnote 9.

REFERENCES

Abramowitz, M. (1986), 'Catching Up, Forging Ahead, and Falling Behind', *Journal of Economic History* 46: 2, 385-406.

Altvater, E. and B. Mahnkopf (1996), *Grenzen der Globalisierung. Ökologie, Ökonomie und Politik in der Weltgesellschaft.* Münster: Westfälisches Dampfboot.

Amenta, E. (1993), 'The State of the Art in Welfare State Research on Social Spending Efforts in Capitalist Democracies since 1960', *American Journal of Sociology* 99: 3, 750-763.

Aschauer, D. (1989), 'Is Public Expenditure Productive?', *Journal of Monetary Economics* 23: 177-200.

Baumol, W. (1986), 'Productivity Growth, Convergence, and Welfare. What the Long-Run Data Show', *American Economic Review* 78: 5, 1155-1159.

Bell, D. (1960), *The End of Ideology.* Glencoe: Free Press.

Berger, S. and R. Dore (eds) (1996), *National Diversity and Global Capitalism.* Ithaca NY: Cornell University Press.

Bernauer, T. (2000), *Staaten im Weltmarkt. Zur Handlungsfähigkeit von Staaten trotz wirtschaftlicher Globalisierung.* Opladen: Leske und Budrich.

Böckenförde, E.W. (1991), 'Die Bedeutung der Unterscheidung von Staat und Gesellschaft im demokratischen Sozialstaat der Gegenwart', E.W. Böckenförde (1991), *Recht, Staat, Freiheit.* Frankfurt am Main: Suhrkamp, 209-243.

Boyer, R. and D. Drache (eds) (1996), *States Against Markets: The Limits of Globalization.* London, New York: Routledge.

Brennan, G. and J. Buchanan (1980), *The Power to Tax: Analytical Foundations of a Fiscal Constitution.* Cambridge: Cambridge University Press.

Bull, H.P. (1973), *Die Staatsaufgaben nach dem Grundgesetz.* Frankfurt am Main: Athenäum Verlag.

Busch, A. and T. Plümper (eds) (1999), *Nationaler Staat und internationale Wirtschaft. Anmerkungen zum Thema Globalisierung.* Baden-Baden: Nomos.

Cameron, D.R. (1978), 'The Expansion of the Public Economy. A Comparative Analysis', *American Political Science Review* 72: 1243-1261.

Cameron, D.R. (1984), 'Social Democracy, Corporatism, Labour Quiescence, and the Representation of Economic Interest in Advanced Capitalist Society', in: John Th. Goldthorpe (eds), *The Impact of Parties. Politics and Policies in Democratic Capitalist State.* London u.a., 21-96.

Castles, F.G. (1990), 'The Dynamics of Policy Change. What Happened to the English-Speaking Nations in the 1980's', *European Journal of Political Research* 18: 491-514.

Coleman, J.S. (1990), *Foundations of Social Theory.* Cambridge, MA: Havard University Press.

Colomer, J.M. (1995), 'Introducción, in: Josep Maria Colomer (eds.)', *La política in Europa.* Barcelona, 7-25.

Commons, J.R. (1968), *Legal foundations of capitalism.* Madison: The Univ. of Wisconsin Press.

Cusack, T.R. (1997), 'Partisan Politics and Public Finance. Changes in Public Spending in the Industrialized Democracies 1955-1989', *Public Choice* 91: 375-395.

Davis, O., M.A.H. Dempster and A. Wildavsky (1966), 'A Theory of the Budgetary Process', *American Political Science Review* 60: 529-547.

Davis, O., M.A.H. Dempster and A. Wildavsky (1974), 'Toward a Predictive Theory of the Federal Budgetary Process', *British Journal of Political Science* 4: 419-452.

Deutsch, K.W. (1966), *The Nerves of Government. Models of political communication and control.* New York: The Free Press.

Downs, A. (1957), *An Economic Theory of Democracy.* New York: Harper and Row.

Drucker, P.F. (1997), 'The Global Economy and the Nation-State', *Foreign Affairs* 76: 5, 159-171.

Durlauf, S. (1996), 'On the Convergence and Divergence of Growth Rates. An Introduction', *Economic Journal* 106: 437.

Eising, R. (2000), *Liberalisierung und Europäisierung. Die regulative Reform der Elektrizitätsversorgung in Großbritannien, der Europäischen Gemeinschaft und der Bundesrepublik Deutschland.* Opladen: Leske und Budrich.

Esping-Andersen, G. (1990), *The Three Worlds of Welfare Capitalism.* Cambridge: Polity Press.

Evans, Peter (1997), 'The Eclipse of the State? Reflections on Stateness in an Era of Globalization', *World Politics* 50: 1, 62-87.

Evans, P.B., H.K. Jacobson and R.D. Putnam (eds) (1993), *Double-edged Diplomacy. International Bargaining and Domestic Politics.* Berkeley: University of California Press.

Evans. P.B., T. Skocpol and D. Rueschemeyer (eds) (1985), *Bringing the State Back In.* Cambridge: Cambridge University Press.

Fach, W. and G. Simonis (2000), 'Die Welt des Autors. Eine Polemik', *Zeitschrift für Internationale Beziehungen* 7: 2, 385-398.

Forsthoff, E. (1971), *Der Staat der Industriegesellschaft.* München: Beck.

Friedman, M. (1982) [1962]: *Capitalism and Freedom.* Chicago: Chicago University Press.

Friedman, M. and Rosa (eds) (1984), *Tyranny of the status quo.* San Diego, California: Harcourt Brace Jovanovich.

Garrett, G. (1995), 'Capital Mobility, Trade, and the Domestic Politics of Economic Policy', *International Organization* 49: 657-87.

Garrett, G. (1998), *Partisan Politics in the Global Economy.* Cambridge: Cambridge University Press.

Garrett, G. and D. Mitchell (1995), *Globalization and the Welfare State. Income Transfers in the Industrial Democracies, 1965-1990.* University of Pennsylvania, Australian National University: Unv. Manuskript.

Garrett, G. and P. Lange (1991), 'Political Responses to Interdependence. What's Left for the Left?', *International Organization* 45: 4, 539-564.

Giddens, A. (1997), *Jenseits von Links und Recht. Die Zukunft radikaler Demokratie.* Frankfurt am Main: Suhrkamp.

Giddens, A. (1999), *Der dritte Weg. Die Erneuerung der sozialen Demokratie.* Frankfurt am Main: Suhrkamp.

Gill, S. (1995), 'Globalization, Market Civilization, and Disciplinary Neoliberalism', *Millennium - Journal of International Studies* 24: 3, 399-423.

Gill, S. and D. Law (1993), 'Global Hegemony and the Structural Power of Capital', in S. Gill (ed.)(1993): *Gramsci, Historical Materialism, and International Relations.* Cambridge: Cambridge University Press, 93-124.

Glyn, A. (1995), 'Social Democracy and Full Employment', *New Left Review* 211, 33-55.

Gonenc, R. and G. Nicoletti (2000), 'Regulation, market structure and performance in air passenger transportation OECD'. Economics Dept. Working Papers No. 254, ECO/WKP(2000)27.

Gourevitch, P. (1978), 'The Second Image Reversed: The International Sources of Domestic Politics', *International Organization* 32: 4, 881-912.

Grande, E. (1997), 'Vom produzierenden zum regulierenden Staat. Möglichkeiten und Grenzen von Regulierung und Privatisierung', K. König & A. Benz (eds) (1997), *Privatisierung und staatliche Regulierung. Bahn, Post und Telekommunikation, Rundfunk.* Baden-Baden: Nomos, 576-591.

Grande, E. and T. Risse (2000), 'Bridging the Gap. Konzeptionelle Anforderungen an die politikwissenschaftliche Analyse von Globalisierungsprozessen', *Zeitschrift für Internationale Beziehungen* 7: 2, 235-266.

Gray, J. (1998), *False Dawn. The Delusions of Global Capitalism.* London: Granta.

Gudme, A.C. (1824), *Wie, und auf welche Art und Weise können die Haupt- und Neben-Straßen in den Herzogthümern Schleswig und Holstein radikal verbessert und fortdauernd in gutem, fahrbaren Zustande erhalten werden?* Schleswig.

Habermas, J. (1992), *Faktizität und Geltung. Beiträge zur Diskurstheorie des Rechts und des demokratischen Rechtsstaats.* Frankfurt am Main: Suhrkamp.

Hall, P.A. (1992), 'The Movement from Keynesianism to Monetarism. Institutional analysis and British Economic Policy in the 1970s', in Steinmo, Thelen & Longstreth (eds), *Structuring Politics. Historical Institutionalism in Comparative Perspective.* Cambridge: Cambridge University Press.

Haubold, V. (1995), 'Transeuropäische Verkehrsnetze. Darstellung und Beurteilung der europäischen Verkehrsinfrastrukturpolitik', in H.-J. Ewers (eds), *Verkehrsinfrastrukturpolitik in Europa.* Göttingen, 7-35.

Hermes, G. (1998), *Staatliche Infrastrukturverantwortung. Rechtliche Grundstrukturen netzgebundener Transport- und Übertragungssysteme zwischen Daseinsvorsorge und Wettbewerbsregulierung am Beispiel der leitungsgebundenen Energieversorgung in Europa.* Tübingen: Mohr Siebeck.

Hesse, G. (1979) *Staatsaufgaben. Zur Theorie der Legitimation und Identifikation staatlicher Aufgaben.* Baden-Baden: Nomos.

Hibbs, D.A., Jr. (1978), 'On the Political Economy of Long-Run Trends in Strike Activity', *British Journal of Political Science* 8: 153-175.

Hibbs, D.A., Jr. (1991), *The Partisan Model of Macroeconomic Cycles. More Theory and Evidence for the United States.* Stockholm.

Hirsch, J. (1995), *Der nationale Wettbewerbsstaat.* Berlin.

Hirsch, J. (1999), Was heißt eigentlich »Globalisierung«? Überlegungen zur »neuen Weltordnung« anläßlich des Kosovo-Kriegs, *Das Argument* 232: 691-699.

Huber, E., C. Ragin and J.D. Stephens (1993), 'Social Democracy, Christian Democracy, Constitutional Structure, and the Welfare State', *American Journal of Sociology* 99: 711-749.

Hübinger, G. (1988), *Staatstheorie und Politik als Wissenschaft im Kaiserreich. Georg Jellinek, Otto Hintze, Max Weber.* Stuttgart: Ernst Klett, 143-161.

Jaspers, K. (1965), [1932]: *Die geistige Situation der Zeit.* 5. Auflage. Berlin: Walter de Gruyter & Co.

Jessop, B. (1996), 'Politik in der Ära Thatcher. Die defekte Wirtschaft und der schwache Staat', in Dieter Grimm (eds), *Staatsaufgaben.* Frankfurt am Main, 353-389.

Jochimsen, R. (1966), *Theorie der Infrastruktur.* Tübingen: Mohr Siebeck.

Jochimsen, R. and K. Gustafsson (1977), 'Infrastruktur. Grundlage der marktwirtschaftlichen Entwicklung', in Udo E. Simonis (eds), *Infrastruktur. Theorie und Politik.* Köln: Kiepenheuer & Witsch, 38-53.

Junger-Tas, J. (1999), 'Le «moyennement répressiv» des Pays-Bas', *Le Monde diplomatique.* April 1999.

Katzenstein, P.J. (1984), *Corporatism and Change.* Ithaca, N.Y.

Katzenstein, P.J. (1985), *Small States in World Markets.* Ithaca, N.Y.

Kerr, C., J.T. Dunlop, F. Harbison and C.A. Myers (1960), *Industrialism and Industrial Man.* Cambridge MA: Harvard University Press.

King, A. (1969), 'Political Parties in Western Democracies: Some Skeptical Reflections', *Polity* 2: 111-141.

Kitschelt, H., P. Lange, G. Marks and J.D. Stephens (eds) (1999), *Continuity and Change in Contemporary Capitalism.* Cambridge: Cambridge University Press.

Korpi, W. (1991), 'Political and Economic Explanations for Unemployment. A Cross-National and Long-Term Analysis', *British Journal of Political Science* 21: 315-348.

Krasner, S.D. (1999), *Sovereignity. Organized Hypocrisy.* Princeton, N.J.

Krüger, H. (1969), *Marktwirtschaftliche Ordnung und öffentliche Vorhaltung der Verkehrswege.* Hamburg: Metzner.

Lijphart, A. (1984), *Democracies. Patterns of majoritarian and consensus government in twenty-one countries.* New Haven: Yale University Press.

Lijphart, A. (1991). 'Constitutional Choices for new Democracies', *Journal of Democracy* 2: 1, 72-84.

Lijphart, A. (1994a), 'Presidentialism and Majoritarian Democracy. Theoretical Observations', in Juan J. Linz and Arturo Valenzuela (eds), *The Failure of Presidential Democracy.* Volume 1. Baltimore/London, 91-105.

Lijphart, A. (1994b), 'Democracies. Forms, performance, and constitutional engineering', *European Journal of Political Research* 25: 1-17.

Lijphart, A. (1999), *Patterns of democracy. Government forms and performance in thirty-six countries.* New Haven: Yale University Press.

Lipset, S.M. (1960), *Political Man.* Garden City: Doubleday.

Mann, M. (1984), 'The Autonomous Power of the State. Its Origins, Mechanisms and Results', *Archives européenne de sociologie* 25: 185-213.

Mann, M. (1997), 'Hat die Globalisierung den Siegeszug des Nationalstaats beendet', *Prokla* 27: 1, 113-141.

Mayntz, R. (1988), 'Zur Entwicklung technischer Infrastruktursysteme', Renate Mayntz, Bernd Rosewitz, Uwe Schimank and Rudolf Stichweh (eds), *Differenzierung und Verselbständigung. Zur Entwicklung gesellschaftlicher Teilsysteme.* Frankfurt am Main/New York: Campus, 233-259.

Mayntz, R., and T.P. Hughes (eds) (1988), *The Development of Large Technical Systems.* Frankfurt am Main: Campus.

Mayntz, Renate and F.W. Scharpf (eds) (1995), *Gesellschaftliche Selbstregelung und politische Steuerung.* Frankfurt am Main: Campus.

Mayntz, R. and V. Schneider (1995), 'Die Entwicklung technischer Infrastruktursysteme zwischen Steuerung und Selbstorganization', in Renate Mayntz und Fritz W. Scharpf (eds), *Gesellschaftliche Selbstregelung und politische Steuerung.* Frankfurt am Main: Campus, 73-100.

Merkel, W. (1993), *Ende der Sozialdemokratie? Machtressourcen und Regierungspolitik im westeuropäischen Vergleich.* Frankfurt am Main: Campus.

Michelmann, H. and J.P. Soldatos (1994), *European Integration. Theories and Approaches.* Boston: University Press of America.

Moon, J. (1995), 'Innovative Leadership and Policy Change. Lessons from Thatcher', *Governance* 8: 1-25.

Müller, M.M. and R. Sturm (1998), 'Ein neuer regulativer Staat in Deutschland? Die neuere Theory of the Regulatory State und ihre

Anwendbarkeit in der deutschen Staatswissenschaft', *Staatswissenschaften und Staatspraxis* 4/1998: 507-534.

Müller, W.C. (1994), 'Political Traditions and the Role of the State', *West European Politics* 17: 3, 32-51.

Musgrave, R.A. (1971), 'Infrastruktur und die Theorie der öffentlichen Güter', in Helmut Arndt und Dieter Swatek (eds), *Grundfragen der Infrastrukturplanung für wachsende Wirtschaften.* Berlin: Duncker & Humblot, 43-54.

Nagel, J.H. (1994), 'What Political Scientists Can learn from the 1993 Electoral Reform in New Zealand', *Political Science & Politics* 27: 525-529.

Narr, W.D. and A. Schubert (1994), *Weltökonomie. Die Misere der Politik.* Frankfurt am Main: Suhrkamp.

Niskanen, W. A. (1971), *Bureaucracy and representative government.* Chicago: Aldine Atherton.

Nordmann, J., D. Plehwe and B. Walpen (2000), *Neoliberale Wahrheitspolitik. Neo- bzw. Rechtsliberale Intellektuellen- und Think-Tank- Netzwerke als Säulen einer hegemonialen Konstellation* (Projektgruppe 'Buena Vista Neoliberal?'). Rosa Luxemburg Stiftung (http://www.rosaluxemburgstiftung.de/Aktuell/index.htm).

Offe, C. (1996), 'Die Aufgabe von staatlichen Aufgaben: 'Thatcherismus' und die populistische Kritik der Staatstätigkeit', Dieter Grimm (eds), *Staatsaufgaben*, 317-352.

Ohmae, K. (1992), *Die neue Logik der Weltwirtschaft. Zukunftsstrategien der internationalen Konzerne.* Hamburg: Hoffmann & Campe.

Ostrom, E. (2000), *Understanding the complex linkage between attributes of goods and the effectiveness of property right regimes.* Paper presented at the Conference on "Common Goods and Governance Across Multiple Arenas" at the Max Planck Project Group on Common Goods: Law, Politics, and Economics, Bonn, Germany, June 30-July 1, 2000.

Ostrom, E. and E. Schlager (1996), 'The Formation of Property Rights', in Susan Hanna, Carl Folke and Karl-Göran Mäler (eds) *Rights to Nature.* Washington, D.C.: Island Press, 127-56.

Ratzel, F. (1903), *Politische Geographie oder die Geographie der Staaten, des Verkehres und des Krieges.* 2. Auflage. München/Berlin: R. Oldenbourg.

Ratzel, F. (1925), *Politische Geographie oder die Geographie der Staaten, des Verkehres und des Krieges.* 3. Auflage. München/Berlin: R. Oldenbourg.

Rodrik, D. (1997), *Has Globalization Gone Too Far?* Washington D.C.: Institute for International Economics.

Ruggie, J.G. (1983), 'International Regimes, Transactions, and Change. Embedded Liberalism in the Postwar Economic Order', in Stephen D. Krasner (ed.), *International Regimes.* Ithaca, N.Y., 195-231.

Sachs, J.D. and A. Warner (1995), 'Economic Reform and the Process of Global Integration', *Brookings Papers on Economic Activity* 25: 1-118.

Schäfers, B. (1995), *Gesellschaftlicher Wandel in Deutschland. Ein Studienbuch zur Sozialstruktur und Sozialgeschichte.* 6. Auflage. Stuttgart: Enke.

Scharpf, F. (1997), *Games Real Actors Play. Actor-Centred Institutionalism in Policy Research.* Boulder, Co.: Westview.

Scherrer, C. (2000), 'Global Governance. Vom fordistischen Trilateralismus zum neoliberalen Konstitutionalismus', *Prokla* 30: 1, 13-38.

Schmidt, K.D. (1999), 'Auf dem Weg zum Minimalstaat? Nationale Wirtschaftsordnungen im Wettbewerb', *Bürger im Staat* 49: 4, 212-216.

Schmidt, M.G. (1993), 'Theorien in der international vergleichenden Staatstätigkeitsforschung', in Adrienne Héritier (ed.), *Policy-Analyse. Kritik und Neuorientierung.* Opladen: Westdeutscher Verlag, 371-393.

Schmidt, M.G. (1997), *Demokratietheorien.* 2. Auflage. Opladen: Leske und Budrich.

Schneider, V. (1999), *Staat und technische Kommunikation. Die politische Entwicklung der Telekommunikation in den USA, Japan, Großbritannien, Deutschland, Frankreich und Italien.* Opladen: Westdeutscher Verlag.

Schneider, V. (2001), *Transformation der Telekommunikation. Vom Staatsmonopol zum globalen Markt (1800-2000),* Frankfurt am Main: Campus (forthcoming)

Schneider, V. (2001a), 'Institutional reform in telecommunications: The European Union in transnational policy diffusion', in Maria Green-Cowles, Jim Caporaso and Thomas Risse (eds) *Transforming Europe. Europeanization and Domestic Change,* Ithaca: Cornell University Press.

Schneider, V. and R. Werle (1998), 'Co-Evolution and Development Constraints. The Development of Large Technical Systems in Evolutionary Perspective', in Clara E. García and Sanz-Menédez (eds.): *Management and Technology.* Luxembourg: European Commission, Vol. 5, 1998, 12-29.

Schulze, G.G. and H.W. Ursprung (1998), *Globalization of the Economy and the Nation State.* Konstanz: Unpublished paper (in German: Schulze, Günther G. and Heinrich W. Ursprung (1999): Globalisierung contra Nationalstaat? Ein Überblick über die empirische Evidenz, in Andreas Busch und Thomas Plümper (eds), *Nationaler Staat und internationale Wirtschaft. Anmerkungen zum Thema Globalisierung.* Baden-Baden: Nomos, 41-89.)

Skocpol, T. (1979), *States and Social Revolutions. A Comparative Analysis of France, Russia and China.* Cambridge: Cambridge University Press.

Smith, A. (1812) [1776], *Wealth of Nations.* London: Ward, Lock & Co.

Steiner, F. (2000), 'Regulation, industry structure and performance in the electricity supply industry', OECD Economics Dept, Working Papers No. 238, ECO/WKP(2000)11.

Stopford, J. and S. Strange (1991), *Rival States, Rival Firms. Competition for World Market Shares.* Cambridge: Cambridge University Press.

Strange, S. (1986), *Casino Capitalism.* Oxford: Blackwell.

Strange, S. (1995), The Limits of Politics, *Government and Opposition* 30: 291-311.

Strange, S. (1996), *The Retreat of the State. The Diffusion of Power in the World Economy.* New York: Cambridge University Press.

Streeck, W. (1998), 'Einleitung: Internationale Wirtschaft, nationale Demokratie?', in *Internationale Wirtschaft, nationale Demokratie: Herausforderungen für die Demokratietheorie.* Frankfurt am Main: Campus, 11-58.

Swank, D. (1997), *Global Markets, Democratic Institutions, and the Public Economy in Advanced Industrial Societies.* mimeo (Marquette University).

Tsebelis, G. (1995), 'Decision Making in Political Systems. Veto Players in Presidentialism, Parliamentarism, Multicameralism and Multipartyism', *British Journal of Political Science* 25: 3, 289-325.

Tsebelis, G. (1999), 'Veto Players and Law Production in Parliamentary Democracies. An Empirical Analysis', *American Political Science Review* 93: 591-608.

Van der Pijl, K. (1999), *Transnational Classes and International Relations.* London: Routledge.

Wacquant, L. (1999), 'Ce vent punitif qui vient d'Amérique', *Le Monde diplomatique,* April 1999.

Wagner, A. (1883), 'The Nature of the Fiscal Economy', in Richard A. Musgrave and Alan R. Peacock (eds) (1958), *Classics in the Theory of Public Finance.* London: Macmillan, 1-8.

Wesener, W. (1986), *Energieversorgung und Energieversorgungskonzepte.* Münster: Selbstverlag d. Inst. für Siedlungs- u. Wohnungswesen.

Wildavsky, A. (1975), *Budgeting. A Comparative Theory of Budgetary Processes.* Boston: Little, Brown.

Wille, E. (1993), 'Die Bedeutung der öffentlichen Infrastruktur für die wirtschaftliche Entwicklung – Notwendigkeiten in den neuen Bundesländern', in Peter Eichhorn (ed.), *Finanzierung und Organization der Infrastruktur in den neuen Bundesländern.* Baden-Baden: Nomos, 11-36.

Willke, H. (1992), *Ironie des Staates.* Frankfurt am Main: Suhrkamp.

Wittfogel, K.A. (1962), *Die orientalische Despotie. Eine vergleichende Untersuchung totaler Macht.* Köln: Kiepenheuer & Witsch.

Woolcock, S., M. Hodges and K. Schreiber (1991), *Britain, Germany and 1992 – The Limits of Deregulation.* London: Royal Institute of International Affairs and Pinter.

PART THREE

Country/Sector Studies

5. Policies for Open Network Access

Jens Arnbak[1]

1 INTRODUCTION: THE FOURTH INFORMATION REVOLUTION

The last century of the second millennium was the era of the global telephone network. A steadily growing number of member states of the International Telecommunication Union (ITU) knit their national infrastructures together into one fully connected international utility for their citizens. Despite two world wars and the fall of mighty empires, the 20th century drew to a close with a network reaching all but a billion phone users. This number is not enough to speak of a truly universal service, but is certainly a unique score for a new technology and for international standardization benefiting the welfare of citizens in all member states. Here, I intend to discuss the future role of regulation of two related revolutions, one in the specific sector of (electronic) technology, media and telecommunications (TMT), and the other in general economic thinking.

Past inventions in the area of information and communication technologies (ICT) teach us that they can change more than just consumer welfare. Only little is known about the societal impact of the initial invention in Mesopotamia, *writing*. We do know how revolutionary the combined Greek inventions of written *books* and the attached *protocols* for co-ordinated reading became in both government, education and culture: When documented on paper, practical experience soon developed into civil engineering and Roman law, and the muses also learned to write in order to entertain more people.[2] What happens today using programmable computers, bit coding and data communications, should remind us of the third information revolution five hundred years ago: the revolution caused by the *printing press with movable type*, combined with *merchant shipping*. Gutenberg's invention reduced the cost of reproduction and spreading of texts and pictures by orders of magnitude. Within half a century, the thousands of skilled monks meticulously cutting complete pages in wood by hand, had been displaced by a much smaller number of lay craftsmen working in teams to run several hundred copies of books, selling at a price which a peasant could pay. Dutch and Italian merchant cities brought their liberal governance of shipping to bear on the handling of information and so prospered immensely, at the expense of competitors from countries that were less open or simply land-locked[3]. Soon, the information doctrines celebrated in traditional institutions such as the Church and its universities were to be challenged fundamentally, too.[4]

Now it is classical telephony-based regulation and the traditional inter-governmental status of the ITU that face similar challenges by the entrepreneurial governance of modern ICT, notably because of the advent of the Internet and electronic commerce. What are the symptoms of this fourth information revolution?

2 THE WINDS OF CHANGE

First of all, the two global markets for telecommunications equipment and for telecommunication services grew considerably faster recently than the average world economy in general, and the plain old telephone system (POTS) in particular. Chances are that within the next few years there will be just as many users of the Internet and of digital mobile phones as of fixed telephony, i.e., about one billion users for each of the three! There is convergence of these markets, with considerable overlap of user communities. The telephone network is already (too) heavily used for access to the Internet, which has grown by some 80% per year and accounts for more than half of the 'call minutes' in some European countries. Mobile users will soon be able to access the Internet by broadband third-generation (3G) networks. In short, data communications is now taking the lead from voice traffic, in terms of both innovation, volume and turnover.

Second, the main technology drivers during the past two decades will continue to act for some time ahead. Think of:[5]

- the continuing improvement of the price/performance ratio of Very Large Scale Integrated (VLSI) circuits, important in network infrastructures as well as in customer equipment, including PCs
- optical techniques for *bulk* long-distance transmission and switching of information
- radio techniques for *individual* user access over short distances (cellular networks, 'wireless local loop')

- the introduction of new computer platforms and network overlays in POTS, in order to create and manage more advance services ('intelligent networking').

Third, basic telecommunication services are front-runners in the international harmonization and liberalization of national markets agreed by the member states of, first, the European Union (EU) and, soon after, of the World Trade Organisation (WTO). There are structural reasons for this leading position of the telecommunications sector, far ahead of other network utilities. New information and communications technologies offer the unique combination of economic features[6] shown in Table 5.1.

Table 5.1 Features of information and communication technologies

1. transport with the speed of light (unlike airlines, rails, roads, pipelines, etc.)
2. massive transport at vanishing unit cost, without loss of quality (unlike electric power)
3. instant copying/broadcasting, bundling and re-routing/refilling of information (unlike mail, printing and publishing)
4. diverse options for customer access: choice between wired access (with strong economies of scale, scope and/or density) and wireless access (with lower costs of area coverage, e.g. cellular networks; broadcasting).
5. lightweight/portable terminal devices (unlike sea, air and rail networks).

Last but not least, government's role in controlling the national economy is visibly changing. During most of the 20th century, the *distribution* of welfare across society and - somewhat later - the *stabilization* of the national economy (e.g., by maximizing employment or by controlling inflation and balance of payments) overshadowed the classical financial function of government, namely, *allocation* of limited public resources. Over the last two decades, however, this balance appears to be changing back towards classical economic thinking. The demand for better services and new public investment has induced most governments to give priority to two closely related questions of optimum economic allocation:

- Which tasks can national government do better than the private sector? and

- How should government find the necessary funds to execute such tasks?

The global wave of privatization of public telecommunication operators (PTO's) clearly illustrates the reappraisal of the economic priorities of governments, when facing the policy issue of whether allocation of scarce state assets to PTO's is (still) needed.

I experienced the shortcomings of the traditional financial arrangements of a state-owned network operator when moving from Denmark with its private regional phone companies to the Netherlands in mid-1972. The Dutch PTT had already exhausted its annual appropriation on the government budget, so I had to wait for about 8 months to get a phone connection – an example of the fortuitous and unproductive denial of access which still prevails in many countries adhering to a state-owned PTO.

3 OPEN ACCESS TO ALL FOR ALL: CHALLENGES FOR PUBLIC POLICY

Private financing and operation of critical networks ('utilities') does not remove the need for stating and realizing public goals. Two key questions in this context can be distinguished:

- Under which conditions are private enterprises able to perform better in the communications services sector than a state-owned operator, given the high investments needed in ICT-based infrastructure and the public-policy goals to be met?
- What kind of regulation is appropriate to enforce the public-policy goals and give consumers a choice, where possible, by promoting fair competition?

Answering these questions presents governments with a dilemma: On the one hand, the majority of users and their elected politicians focus on the *national* market as the most relevant for regulation. On the other hand, telecom firms increasingly operate in the open *international* ICT-sector, pay more attention to competitive developments beyond the national borders and may try to keep competitors out of their home market. This may even happen with government blessing, if a state monopoly is merely privatized without being simultaneously exposed to the disciplining forces of competition on a liberalized national market. Only the latter development will give national consumers an open choice between alternatives. The strong network economies of scale and scope make entry in a previous monopoly market difficult enough, even if government does not protect the former state monopoly.

This dilemma requires that a judicious mix of public policies be chosen and enforced. On the one hand, classical competition policy may control abuse of dominant market power in order to *maintain* competition where it already exists. On the other hand, new proactive rules ensuring network interconnection and third-party access are needed to *create* competition where it was banned by statute: Lifting the ban on market entry ('deregulation') is not enough, since *users* will not shift to small new competitors unless these can offer 'any-to-any' (inter)connections. The appropriate national policy mix depends on economic, social and political constraints for opening up the new market, but has to deal with at least the following five issues of public interest, namely how to,

1. *control mergers, acquisitions and leverage of network dominance into downstream service markets*, to avoid re-instatement of monopoly power hindering market entry of new competitors;
2. *promote competition and non-discrimination in access networks*, the most costly[7] but least used part of a public communications infrastructure;
3. *ensure availability and reliability of high-capacity trunk networks ('electronic highways')*, to cope with the explosive growth of mobile and internet traffic;
4. *provide consumers with transparency of prices, conditions, directories and conditional-access systems*, both for basic services and for content delivered via – at least the dominant - networks. Fair competition equires informed buyers;
5. *define and deploy truly universal service*, to bridge physical distances and lower the access and information thresholds, for needy citizens and defined public institutions at home, and to all countries abroad - *but without distorting competition!*

Convergence of technologies suggests that no network should be *a priori* excluded for delivery of any service. Governments may wish to use the price mechanism (*e.g.* in spectrum auctions) to promote efficient use of scarce network resources. However, segmentation of services should occur for business reasons, not by imposing regulation related to particular divisions of technology, such as wired or wireless, analogue or digital, circuit or packet switching, etc. Open access *to* all and *for* all should be the leading principle of choice in the communications sector, not only to maximize the positive economic externalities of networks, but also as a matter of social fairness and cultural equity.

4 RULES AND REGULATORS

It is sometimes claimed that sector-specific rules and regulators to address the above five challenges will only be needed for a short period of transition, say, for opening up a national telephone monopoly to competition. Frequently, this viewpoint is based on either *laissez-faire* ideology or vested interests, rather than analysis of, let alone experience with, the need for proactive regulation to improve competition in networked markets.

Incumbent network operators carry heavy extra burdens during the present transition to competition on national markets. Understandably, this makes these organizations the most vocal lobbyists for early abolishment of sector-specific regulation, and for complete reliance on general competition law, which they experience as less disturbing to their business.[8] However, the present dynamics of networked markets and the innovative speed of the TMT sector prevent timely resolution of all public concerns by competition law. This works *ex-post*, after the alleged abuse took place. The lengthy Microsoft court case in the USA has become a sad illustration of the time, resources and uncertainty in resolving the issue of tying of a Web browser, *Explorer*, to a former generation of the dominant operating system for personal computers, *Windows 95.* Moreover, the 'essential facilities' doctrine, a key concept in US competition law for obtaining access to bottleneck facilities of dominant players and also invoked as a useful concept in the European Commission's Access Notice[9] from 1998, does not guarantee success before the European Court of Justice. In the subsequent Bronner case[10], the Court laid down virtually forbidding economic conditions for imposing third-party access obligations on dominant players.

Public policy must provide better predictability for investors and market players, especially where first-mover advantages are as compelling as in networked markets. Ultimately, the Commission accepted the need to provide a binding EU-wide regulation[11] mandating timely unbundling of the local loop in the incumbent phone network, in order to foster more rapid provision of digital broadband access[12] for European citizens by competitive pressure. Thus, the necessary predictability could be matched to the flexibility and dynamics of the ICT- and TMT-sectors.

Clearly, future regulations have to be neutral in terms of technology, as distinct from most present regulations so specifically focused upon classical (circuit-switched) voice telephony. Predictability and flexibility can be merged in a generic regulatory framework, which should be a seamless extension of general competition law, but specifically designed to resolve *ex-ante* the five issues of open access stated in the previous section. The appropriate national authority would make determinations and settle disputes within a prescribed time and in accordance with the general framework. However, the regulator should withdraw or forgo a rule, when market forces satisfy the policy objective. Such 'sunset clauses' or other regulatory forbearance reflect the evolving nature of ICT markets better than incorporating detailed supranational legal provisions meticulously in domestic law.

This brings me to the position of the 'independent' regulator required by European community law and the 'impartial' regulator prescribed by the WTO agreement on basic telecommunication services. An immediate question is: Independent from what, from operators and their shareholders, from ministries or from daily politics in general? Where are the countervailing checks and balances? Could independent regulators become unaccountable? Or conversely, are they perhaps more likely to become captured by narrow industry interests, if given inadequate resources to perform their duties in a disinterested and timely manner? Adequate attention should be given to all these important questions. Democratic monitoring of the performance of independent regulators might help, for instance using public parliamentary hearings of regulators and sector players. This tradition has proven itself well in some countries.

The rule of general competition law is necessary to avoid undue extension or abuse of dominant market power in new, possibly unregulated downstream markets such as internet service provision. Accordingly, the decisions of sector-specific communication regulators must be seen not to run counter to general competition law. This can be ensured by close formal and/or practical co-operation with the national competition authority, such as in France, Denmark and the Netherlands. Alternatively, the communications regulator can be granted 'concurrent power' to also apply competition law, as in the U.K. The latter option contributes to a smooth retreat from sector-specific rules where justified, without losing the sector expertise.

Appeal courts should be able to annul decisions taken by the authorities in violation of the basic principles in the regulatory framework. National judges may hesitate to consider complicated network issues without disinterested guidance to this framework. Because of the TMT market dynamics, it is more important to develop international guidelines and principles of best implementation practice for regulators and judiciaries, than to write a very detailed and rigid framework. Such a body of guidelines, or 'soft law', would need to be developed by appropriate international co-operation in organisations like the WTO, the European Commission, the ITU, and their specialized agencies. Finally, national regulatory authorities in a region should work together in order to ensure consistent behaviour in individual markets of that region[13] and to resolve cross-border disputes.

To illustrate this dynamic process, consider the recipe in Table 5.2 for developing a light(er) and broader regulatory regime. In order to reduce public intervention in modern communication markets to the level which is strictly necessary, an escalation of questions should be answered.

Table 5.2 Procedure towards less interventionist regulation of communications markets

1. Is there a public interest to be satisfied? If yes,
2. Does that public interest call for a specific service or access facility to be offered? If yes,
3. Does the (market) sector provide that service or facility without public intervention? If no,
4. Can the market failure be discovered and adequately repaired by the general rule of (inter alia, competition) law? If no,
5. Can the market failure be removed by imposing appropriate ex-ante sector-specific rules and regulations on relevant players? If no,
6. Can (and should) government itself provide the desired public service or essential facility, e.g. through a state monopoly or by subsidies?

Clearly, the answers to the questions in Table 5.2 would become less far-reaching when liberalized communications markets effectively give customers sufficient choice. Only in a few future cases would the final question (6) be reached and positively answered. Legislators and regulators will still have to answer the two penultimate questions (i.e., 4 & 5), and thus determine the appropriate balance between reliance on general competition law and the need for specific regulations.

5 THE LEGAL FRAMEWORK: STRUCTURAL OR BEHAVIORAL?

The flow diagram in Figure 5.1 indicates some of the regulatory and competitive differences between the key network sectors ('public utilities'). Their economic and technological characteristics result in different regulatory regimes in order to address specific market failures (Table 5.2, step 4) or more generic policy requirements such as safety, integrity, or plurality of information. Despite the fact that general competition law spans all of these sectors, it is seldom able to address all specific issues of a utility, particularly not where targeted regulations are required *ex-ante* to ensure appropriate (co-) operation of the network(s) or economic and other societal policy goals.

The growing dynamics of TMT costs require special attention in the communications sector. Novel approaches to transmission and switching, such as the suite of Internet Protocols (TCP/IP), change network economies radically from inside. Where sufficient economies of scale can be achieved with optical cables, the marginal cost of *long-distance transmission* tends to zero. This 'death of distance' reveals the increasingly dominant cost of the *local networks* providing access to individual customers.

Figure 5.1 Regulatory challenges in different network sectors

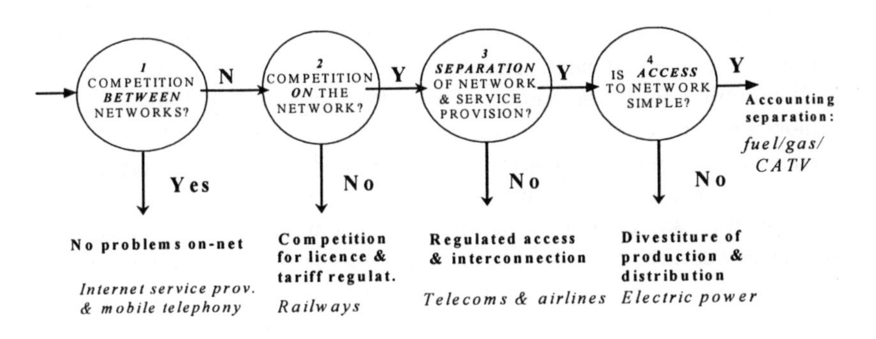

But where traditional benefits and costs are shifted to different user communities or to other parts of communication networks, demands for modifications of the framework for public control of tariffs and access obligations will soon arise. In the terminology of competition law, the relevant product market and/or geographical markets may need frequent investigation and, if necessary, adjustment. Such regulatory re-alignments of relevant markets from time to time are catered for in the 1999 Review of the EU Open Network Provisions (ONP). Clearly, this requires a novel combination of the skills of empirical market analysts familiar with competition law and rapid, but measured responses of regulators. Such responses range from market interventions where new bottlenecks emerge, to forbearance from previously imposed obligations where new technologies offer satisfactory alternatives.

An example of such a new alternative is prepaid (subscription-free) mobile telephony. This may remedy the universal service issues raised by full re-balancing of fixed-telephony tariffs, a controversial EU requirement[14] not yet implemented in most national markets. Re-balancing is necessary in order to remove barriers to market entry for both,

(1) new network operators, raised by the incumbent's line pricing deficit (i.e., below cost), and
(2) service operators, raised by a corresponding mark-up ('access deficit charges') to the incumbent's interconnection fees.

By removing the access deficit charge from the regulated interconnection tariffs, OPTA induced the incumbent to rebalance its retail rates by July 1, 1998 - a time when prepaid mobile telephony with 'free' handheld terminals already promised to offer reduced overall phone costs at the lowest usage levels. In the Netherlands the 'life-line' fixed phone subscription ('Belbudget') is chosen by only a small fraction of those residential consumers who would, in principle, benefit.

The current ONP directives were drafted in the mid-1990s (or even earlier) and thus focussed only on the conventional markets of fixed voice telephony and low-speed leased lines. They do not address some key challenges for national regulators now, just a few years later. Thus, regulators are generally not empowered to resolve new market problems, such as pricing of internet access or calls from fixed phones to mobile terminals at home and abroad, let alone the exorbitant - or at best intransparent - roaming prices confronting GSM-users outside their home country.

So why have these new market issues not been resolved by the general competition authorities in EU/EEA member states or in Brussels? Certainly not because antitrust experts were unable to define the relevant markets, using the well-established general principles in case law. But because most intervention instruments of classical competition law are binary: they require the difficult choice of the antitrust authority between complete *laissez faire* and imposing a structural break-up or heavy fines on companies for abuse of a dominant position, determined *ex post.* Thus, general competition law and jurisprudence can establish only rather wide outer boundaries of acceptable behavior by any dominant player. The inherent uncertainties and delays of this approach are not conducive to new entry into unregulated networked markets with powerful incumbents.

A *structural* liberalization of telecommunications in the USA was imposed by the antitrust authorities. It involved the (horizontal) breaking up of AT&T into a long-distance operator disciplined by new competitors, plus seven regional Bell Operating Companies without room for vertical integration of 'enhanced' services or horizontal integration with mobile phone networks in the same area. While the regional Bell companies have later been allowed to re-merge gradually as local network competition slowly grew, vigorous competition between long-distance networks and on 'enhanced' (*i.e.*, computer-based) services developed rapidly.

Presumably for reasons of political feasibility, Europe adopted a 'softer' approach than the USA to telecom liberalization by allowing the (state-owned) incumbents to continue their vertical integration of network operation and service provision as practiced in the good old days of state monopoly. However, this approach was made subject to *behavioral* rules for granting interconnection and third-party access, now enshrined in the ONP directives and enforced by national regulatory authorities which must be independent from (state) ownership of incumbents. With adequate competition from the new GSM networks, the fixed-phone incumbents were generally allowed to continue national mobile phone operations, at least of their (analogue) mobile networks.

As experienced with independent regulation of national and international financial markets by Central Banks, an approach based on timely *ex-ante* interventions and instant publication of decisions by regulators contribute to more transparent and stable markets. Maximum predictability is a vital factor for investments, business decisions and sustainability of companies as capital-intensive as those operating in TMT markets. Competition authorities only deliver speedy *ex-ante* decisions in the event of intended mergers or acquisitions of a substantial nature (in terms of market share, such as concentrations involving incumbents). Hence smaller players and new entrants turn to the telecom regulator for pro-competitive dispute rulings in cases of interconnection and third-party access.

Regulatory interventions turn out to be particularly crucial for competition involving two-way networks: where end-users can also *transmit* traffic, rather than merely receive networked deliveries as in cable television (CATV) or power distribution, the network operator's turn-over is proportional to the *square* of the number of end-users.[15] The rule explains why access agreements with larger operators are more difficult to negotiate on reasonable terms for small network operators than in utility sectors with purely distributive networks (see Fig. 6.1): the commercial bargaining power is related to the square of the subscriber numbers on each network. Clearly, the major operator loses a smaller proportion of his traffic revenues on interconnection costs than any minor operator, whose subscribers are more likely to communicate *off-net* than *on-net*.

This extra imbalance between unequal players also indicates why the traditional peering (based on reciprocal 'Bill & Keep' arrangements) between internet providers are increasingly being replaced by interconnection charges imposed unilaterally by the larger provider on smaller competitors. The rapid shake-out of ISPs not affiliated with incumbent phone companies is a related phenomenon, which reinforces the vertically integrated dominant companies. In this context, a recent conclusion of an OECD Working Party may be quoted:

> An integrated firm has a strong incentive to discriminate against its downstream rivals. Behavioural regulation to overcome this incentive faces an uphill task and is unlikely to be fully effective. Experience shows that the level and quality of competition is higher under a policy of vertical separation or operational unbundling.[16]

In the European arena, such a structural separation between an incumbent operator and its internet service provider(s) could be based on an *ex-post* ruling by the antitrust authority against proven abuse of a dominant *economic* position. Alternatively, specific *ex-ante* legislation to avoid dominance of internet provision for other reasons of *public policy* would be required, for instance to avoid discrimination in information provision and/or to maintain cultural plurality. The recent EU regulation on local-loop unbundling[17] is an example of the latter avenue.

6 SERVICE OR NETWORK COMPETITION – A REGULATORY CHOICE IN EU TELECOMMUNICATIONS?

While telecom-regulators in EU/EEA countries generally do not have the choice between structural or behavioral market interventions, they often seem confronted with another important choice – that between facilities-based (network) competition and service competition ('make or buy?'). OPTA has sometimes been accused of favoring service competition by its rulings on wholesale and retail prices of networks with significant market power, thereby ostensibly causing undue delays in the roll out of alternative infrastructure. However, the real point of issue here is not the choice between two ultimate options for sustainable competition in the long term. The problem concerns the timely choice of interventions to open up a market, so that market players can themselves make the appropriate 'make or buy' decisions under competitive forces.

The dynamically changing market balance between these two generic types of competition is inherent in the EU's simple pricing rules: non-discriminating, cost-oriented objective wholesale pricing of interconnection and access to the incumbent's network. This implicitly precludes a national political or regulatory preference. That is in my opinion the appropriate European approach. Access to (scarce) network capacity is essential for *any* type of competition to emerge in the short term, given the accepted presence in the EU internal market of vertically integrated (ex-) monopolists - and the prohibitive initial costs of deploying alternative fixed networks to the majority of consumers. Moreover, the introduction of new service platforms by competitors will facilitate their own individual determination of where to roll-out alternative networks in the longer term. It should be borne in mind that competition on an open market is a discovery procedure for the market players, and so by definition cannot be designed or constructed in detail by the regulator – let alone the government.

Despite OPTA's strict enforcement of cost-orientation in the Netherlands and the downwards pressure on national and international retail prices through vigorous service competition by new carrier-select companies, there has indeed been a rapid growth in network investments after market liberalization in 1997. Independent research[18] shows that these investments are driven by long-term plans of network operators. The researchers recommend initial services competition, combined with gradual increases of access prices as a long-term incentive to 'make, rather than buy' decisions. This was the pricing policy adopted by OPTA for unbundled local loops in 1999. A key precondition was the re-balancing of the retail phone rates[19] discussed in Sect. 5, without which the unbundled local loop cannot be correctly priced on a competitive market.

To conclude, given the political acceptance of vertically integrated dominant players in the European setting of open network provision, regulators cannot seek a permanent structural solution right from the outset of liberalization. Telecom regulators and market players do not have recourse to the simpler and more radical approach to deregulation adopted on the wilder shores of the Atlantic. They must live together, joined by permanent reciprocal critique, and humbly accept Karl Popper's piecemeal approach to the discovery of knowledge - in this case of telecom market developments and consumer satisfaction.

NOTES

1. TU Delft & OPTA, P.O.Box 90420, 2509 LK The Hague, Netherlands (www.opta.nl). This paper is an update of an invited keynote delivered to the ITU Regulatory Summit, *Telecom '99*, Geneva.
2. Eric A. Havelock, *The Muse learns to Write*, 1986.
3. J. C. Arnbak, J. J. Van Cuilenburg, E. J. Dommering c.s., *Verbinding en Ontvlechting in de Communicatie*, ('Connection and Unbundling in Communications', in Dutch), 1991, ISBN 90 71894 15.
4. Peter F. Drucker, *Management Challenges for the 21st Century*, Butterworth-Heinemann, 1999, ISBN 0 7506 44567.
5. Jens C. Arnbak, 'Technology Trends and their Implications for Telecom Regulation', in William H. Melody (ed.), *Telecom Reform Principles, Policies and Regulatory Practices,* 1997, ISBN 87-7381-071-1.
6. Jens Arnbak, 'On the Dynamics of Access, Entry and Costs in Electronic Communications Markets', in *Regulating Communications Markets* (Claus Dieter Ehlermann & Louisa Gosling, eds.) , European Competition Law Annual 1998, Hart Publishing, Oxford, 2000, ISBN 1 84113 099 00.
7. In a conventional fixed phone network, two-thirds of the capital costs may relate to local access.
8. Arguably, the most successful case of invoking the doctrine of misuse of power in the European telecommunications sector is the Commission's telex-case *versus* British Telecom two decades ago - not exactly in a market of great economic importance at the time, nor with much future dynamics.
9. Commission Notice of 31 March 1998 on the Application of the Competition Rules to Access Agreements in the Telecommunications Sector, 1998 O.J. (C 265/02).
10. European Court of Justice: Oscar Bronner case, (C-7/97, 26 Nov. 1998). See, in particular, Advocate-General Jacobs, 28 May 1998.
11. O.J. L336, 30 December 2000.
12. By digital subscriber loops (xDSL). The policy objective is EU-wide promotion of the information society and *e-commerce*, as proclaimed by the European Summit in Lisbon in March, 2000. The regulation was adopted by the European Parliament and Council with exceptional speed.
13. In the EU/EEA, the Independent Regulators Group (IRG) agree on *Principles of Implementation and Best Practices.*
14. Rebalancing removes the (incumbent's) classical bundling/cross-subsidy between fixed and variable telephone rates by raising the phone

subscription to a cost-oriented level, in return for lower call rates. While clearly benefitting business users and competing operators, this does raise the monthly phone bill of *small* residential users.

15. This rule of thumb, while named 'Metcalfe's law' after an American internet guru, has been used by phone engineers since the early part of the 20th century.
16. *"When should regulated companies be vertically separated?"*, revised report by the secretariat, OECD Working Party on Competition and Regulation, DAFFE/CLP/WP2(99)6, June 2000.
17. See notes 11 and 12.
18. M. Cave et al., *"The Relationship between Access Pricing Regulation and Infrastructure Competition"*, Report to OPTA and DG Telecommunications & Post by Brunel University, March 2001 (available on www.opta.nl).
19. See note 14.

6. Liberalization and Technical Change in Finland

Tom Björkroth and Johan Willner

1 INTRODUCTION

Technical progress and low prices in telecommunications are often described as essential conditions for economic development and competitiveness in general, and in Europe also as preconditions for the single market project (see, for example, Advanced Communications Technology and Services, Workplan, 1994, p. 3). Cheap and rapid interchange of information is necessary in large and/or transnational companies or in vertically and geographically separated production chains, and is thus an essential part in what we call globalization.

On balance, studies on the possible connection between expansion in the telecommunications infrastructure and economic growth, such as Madden and Savage (1998) and Röller and Waverman (1998), tend to suggest a positive relationship, which is also consistent with the observation that expansion of the public infrastructure in Finland has tended to precede improvements in private sector performance (Björkroth and Kjellman, 2000).

Privatization and liberalization in telecommunications are usually seen as integral parts of a process of globalization and technical progress. Private companies are believed to be more efficient and innovative than old-style public monopolies, at least if there is competition. Technical change has meant that competing providers of telephone services can now coexist, thus transforming a market that was once seen as a natural monopoly.

Both theoretical and empirical research on the impact on (static) efficiency of public and private ownership are inconclusive (see, for example, Martin and Parker, 1997, and Willner, 2001), and even less is known about how privatization affects technical progress. It is often argued that competition may be a more important determinant of efficiency than ownership, and it is more or less taken for granted that liberalization is the main cause of reduced prices in telecommunications. However, the usual mechanism by which competition reduces prices applies for profit maximizing firms; the outcome is less certain if the incumbent is a monopoly with a public service commitment, as was often the case earlier in Europe. Liberalization would then reduce prices only insofar the monopoly position has meant slow technical progress, or if the incumbent has been transformed to a commercial enterprise as part of the process.

Some evidence, like Brunekreeft and Gross (1999) in the case of long-distance calls in Germany, suggests that entry leads to reduced prices. However, in the US the incumbent monopoly AT&T was a profit maximizing company, but the research on its break-up is inconclusive. Potential entry may have reduced incumbent toll prices, and the break-up may have lead to cheaper long-distance calls (Blank et al., 1998; Hausman et al., 1993). However, the market is still an oligopoly with tacit collusion (MacAvoy, 1998); there might have been no reduction in long-distance prices without intervention from the Federal Communications Commission (Taylor and Taylor, 1993). When it comes to local carriers, it seems that competition explains less than improvements in human and physical capital (Sung, 1998).

This contribution focuses on Finland, where long-distance telecommunications have recently been digitalized and reorganized through corporatization and liberalization. The country is now well known for advances in electronics and biotechnology (in addition to its traditional and now highly developed technology in pulp and paper), and was also a pioneer in digital switching and digitalization, even when telecommunications were organized as public and/or non-profit maximizing enterprises.[1] Telecommunications are not yet privatized, but Finland is a forerunner in liberalizing, as reflected in the Green Paper and the Telecommunications Act of 1987. We shall present an overview, together with a statistical analysis of the relative impact of digitalization and liberalization on prices and a discussion on the conditions for welfare to increase.

2 TELECOMMUNICATIONS IN FINLAND – AN OVERVIEW

2.1 Historical Background

The ground was prepared for the telecommunications industry in Finland in 1886, when The Imperial Telephone Decree laid down the terms for operation and installation of telephone cables in Finland, which was then a Grand Duchy within the Russian Empire. Independence in 1917 meant that the network became the property of the Finnish state.

In the beginning of the 20th century, telephone companies were usually established by national but also to some extent foreign providers of equipment. Their number peaked at 815 in the 1930s, by which time the state-owned network Valtionpuhelin (VP) began to take over unprofitable private operators. New license applications from potential private operators were often rejected, and VP was consciously undercutting its rivals. Unsuccessful attempts were made in 1931 and 1948 to nationalize the entire network and create an integrated organization based on the telecommunications service Posti- ja Lennätinlaitos (PLL). Opponents interpreted this activity as based on ideology or an attempt to raise revenues rather than as an ambition to harmonize a heterogeneous network.

VP's strategy of acquisitions and expropriation caused in 1921 local companies to create the Association of Telephone Companies (ATC), whose members intensified their efforts towards technical development. While encouraging mergers among smaller units, ATC campaigned against centralization and expropriations, thus making further implementation of VP's strategy difficult. All this meant that the private carriers operated in cities where new technology could be made profitable, while VP had to concentrate on rural areas (Ministry of Transport and Communications, 1995, p. 12).

The private and commercial company Etelä-Suomen Kaukopuhelinyhtiö (ESK) dominated the market for long-distance telecommunications. The cream-skimming made possible by such a near-monopoly became apparent when it refused to apply for a concession for the line between Helsinki and St. Petersburg, despite pressure from the Senate, and declined to extend its network from Helsinki to Kuopio and to the south-west archipelago, despite substantial demand. Moreover, ESK did not meet the demand for increased connections in southern Finland despite a good financial position. This resulted in congestion and dissatisfaction, in particular within the business community.

An attempt by ESK to introduce a more expensive form of call with higher priority failed to ease congestion, and attempts by VP to offer cheaper late evening calls were of little help. The state controlled long-distance network was in the early 1920s not developed enough to provide an alternative to ESK (Risberg, 1959, pp.422-423, 444). However, VP supported a much more extensive state-sponsored operation, knowing that telecommunications were nationalized in most European countries for the same reasons as the telegraph networks. It was easy to get support among politicians and the media for state participation in an industry where the return on investments in equipment was more than 7%, in particular when intrusions from multinational companies (L. M. Ericsson and Siemens & Halske) were perceived as threats (Moisala et al., 1977, pp.348, 359).

However, while there was general agreement on the need to expand the state-owned network, nationalization of the industry as a whole met resistance, for example among leading newspapers. Therefore, a committee suggested in 1931 that only long-distance telecommunications were to be nationalized (with full compensation), while local networks were to remain as private (but often non-commercial) or municipal monopolies. This resulted in a take-over of ESK in November 1934 and a subsequent merger with VP (Risberg, 1959, pp.538/41).

Further pressures towards expansion were also caused by the decision to hold the 1940 Olympic Games in Helsinki. Thus, despite funding obstacles, the state-controlled network grew by an annual average of 16500 connection kilometers in 1934/40, which was impressive as compared to previous years (Risberg, 1959, pp.541/42). The games were cancelled by the outbreak of war, but the expanded infrastructure then turned out to be of vital importance.[2]

2.2 Recent Developments

The monopolistic structure in telecommunications remained unchallenged until the 1980s. While the long-distance network has been owned by the state, most local operators have until quite recently been non-profit maximizing consumer-owned shareholding companies or municipal enterprises. Call charges have been harmonized through political pressures making large geographical differentials unsustainable.

The national network was completely automatized in 1980. The subsequent digitalization made open and profitable competition between public and private operators possible by eliminating the characteristics of a natural monopoly (see for example, The Ministry of Transport and Communications, 1995, p. 12). The management saw it necessary therefore to transform the organizational structure of VP. The changes that were implemented during the 1980s represented the most radical reforms in any public sector organization in Finland during the decade.

Further rationalization was seen to be needed in order to reduce staff in administration, management, and installation, but civil servant status and other administrative restrictions prevented this. Therefore, the organization was transformed from a state agency to a so-called state-owned business enterprise that was separated from the state budget in 1991. This did not yet mean full corporatization, but made more radical restructuring possible. Initially, staff were mainly reduced through retirement, and later on by firing older employees and replacing them by younger persons which were employed in sales, marketing, and computer departments (Alasoini et al., 1991, pp.18/24). The number of employees declined by 47% between 1985 and 1993. Figure 6.1 illustrates the number of employees in the state-owned enterprise (Telecom Finland) and in the telephone companies (TC).[3]

Figure 6.1 Number of employees among telecommunications operators,[4] 1980/94

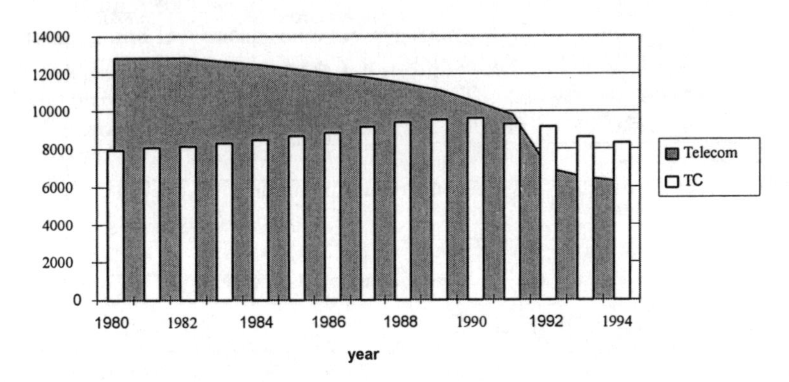

Source: Telecommunication statistics, 1995, p.34.

There was also a perception that legislation had to be changed. The decree of 1887 did not provide an adequate licensing framework for modern network services such as telefax and data transmission, and was altered so as to allow for free development. This made it possible for private telephone companies and a group of their business customers to establish a new data service provider in 1985, Datatie Ltd, whose optic cable trunk network with digital exchanges was the first to be built to compete with the public network.

The statutory monopoly rights were finally invalidated in 1987 by the new Telecommunications Act, with amendments in 1988, 1990, and 1992. This piece of legislation made telecommunications operation subject to a license granted by the government, the first license being granted to the new independent state-owned business enterprise of 1991. The regulation of the industry was separated from the business activities through a new Telecommunications Administration Centre, which was subordinated to the Ministry of Transports and Communications (MTC). The new administrative structure is illustrated in Figure 6.2.

Figure 6.2 Administration of telecommunications

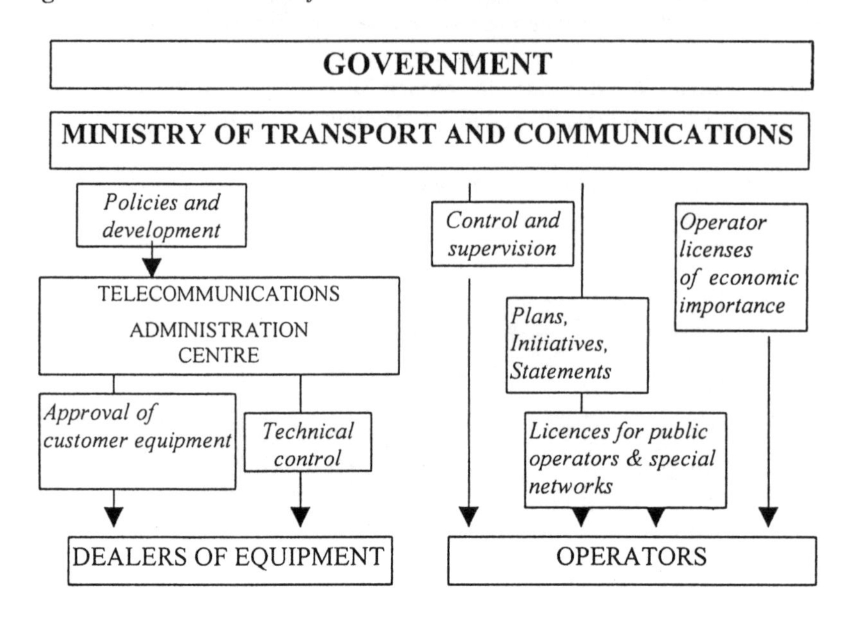

Source: MTC, 1995, p.14.

The importance of a successful telecommunications policy is recognized to have far reaching effects on the growth of the Finnish economy (MTC, 2000). In the long run, the policy behind liberalization has emphasized the importance of well-designed legislation on competition, to avoid abuse of market power and to prohibit cross subsidies (MTC Telecommunication Statistics 1993, p.8). Full privatization is likely in the near future, in the sense that the state will abstain from majority ownership in Sonera (formerly Telecom Finland). The main intent has been to create a sound framework for the telecommunications, with minimal regulation as long as the outcome conforms to the objectives of the authorities (MTC, 1999). It is also emphasized that the industry shall be an example for other countries in the future as well (MTC, 2000), with increasing international co-operation between both manufacturers, like Nokia, and operators, like Sonera.

Another important reform was the introduction of teletraffic areas in 1994. These replaced the earlier local area netgroups, and meant about a fivefold increase in the number of subscribers that can be reached by a local call, but hence also a decline in the market for long-distance calls.

Competition in long-distance and international calls began with the entry of Telivo, initially a subsidiary of the state-owned energy company IVO, but subsequently acquired by the Swedish state-owned telecom operator Telia. The authorities wanted a 'controlled reform', and therefore limited Telivo's market share to 5% during the first year. The Finnet group, which consists of former local operators, entered in 1994 and captured a market share of about 52%. Despite additional entry, the market is essentially a duopoly. Figure 6.3 illustrates market shares for domestic long-distance calls. The market for international calls was opened in 1994; the market structure is otherwise similar, but Sonera has a somewhat stronger position.

Figure 6.3 Market shares (in terms of minutes) of the main operators

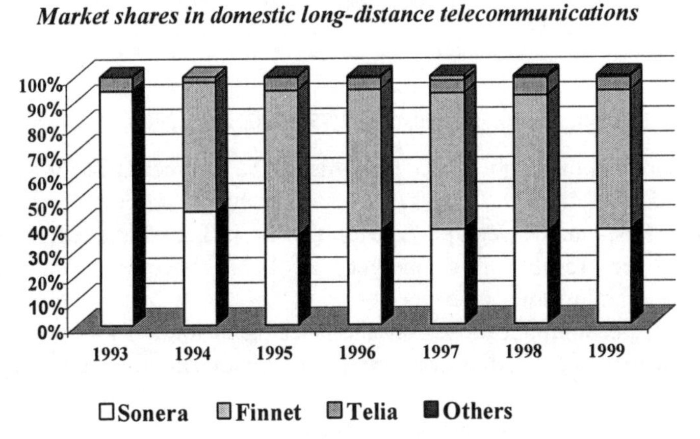

It is obvious that prices have been reduced during this period. Figure 6.4 shows the index for the cost of a Finnish household-profile user, as compared to the average cost for a similar user basket in all OECD-countries (from 1991 to 1994) and to the average cost in European Union (from 1995 to 1999) for the same user basket. Variations in the user profile across the years are ignored.

However, the strong impact of digitalization means that we cannot know for certain that this development is mainly caused by liberalization. Moreover, the incumbent has been transformed from a typical public-sector utility to a not yet privatized commercial plc. In the next sections we make an attempt to distinguish between the effects.

Figure 6.4 The indexed cost of domestic calls for a household user with OECD and EU averages =100

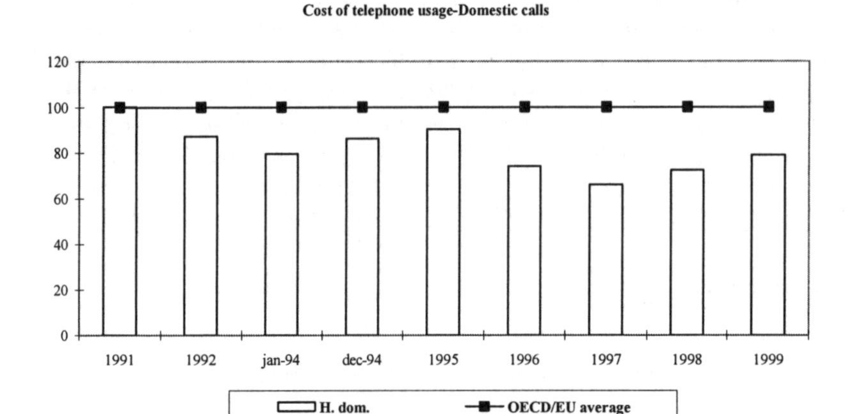

Source: MTC Telecommunication Statistics, 1995, 1996, 1999, 2000.

The development from the 1980s onwards can be summarized as follows:

1981 The Post- and Telegraph Service (Posti- ja Lennätinlaitos), which was the result of a merger in 1927, becomes Post- and Telecommunications Service.

1987 The Telecommunications Act abolishes the statutory monopoly. The Ministry of Transport and Communications administers telecommunications.

1988 Competition in corporate networks and data transmission.

1990 Amendments of the telecommunications Act of 1987 abolishes the special rights of National Board of Post and Telecommunications. Free competition in data- and GSM networks is established.

1990-1991 Telecommunications become a state-owned business enterprise (Tele). Corporate networks subject to free competition. Licenses for regional radio telecommunication networks.

1992 New licenses ensure entry in long-distance and local telecommunications.

1993 Limited competition in markets for long-distance and international calls.

1994 Full corporatization of the state-owned business enterprise into PT Finland Ltd; separation of subsidiaries in telecommunications (Telecom Finland) and postal services. Full scale competition in local, long-distance and international telecommunications. Teletraffic areas replace local area netgroups.

1995 New licenses ensure competition in local digital cellular systems (DCS) networks.

1996 Amendments to the Telecommunications Act implying i) obligations to lease telecommunications connections to other operators; ii) an end to discretionary licensing; iii) deregulation of customer charges.

1997 The Telecommunications Market Act replaces the old Telecommunications Act, which results in i) no licenses needed except for in the construction of mobile networks; ii) operators being required to have separate network and service operations; iii) improved possibilities for operators to lease each others lines; iv) control of telephone companies with 'significant market power'. Decision on partial privatization by Parliament.

1998 Telecom Finland Ltd becomes completely separated from the postal services, changes name to Sonera Plc and is listed on the Helsinki Stock Exchange. Partial privatization (22.2%).

1999 Free licenses ensure competition in third generation mobile networks. Subscription operators obliged set local network charges lower than local call charges, thus making end-to-end pricing possible.[5]

2000 State ownership in Sonera is reduced to 52.9% and the government is given the authorization to full divestiture.

2.3 An International Comparison of Importance and Density

During the period 1980/97, telecommunications have constituted a fairly large proportion of GDP in both the US and Britain, and their role have increased in Finland, Sweden, and in particular Italy during the period 1980/97. The relative importance of telecommunications for the total value added is illustrated by Figure 6.5.

Digitalization was initiated in Finland in 1980, as soon as automatization was complete. A fairly good measure of technical standard is provided the number of subscriptions that are connected to a digital network, i.e. the direct access of a subscriber to a digital network, as shown for selected countries in Figure 6.6. France was the first and Finland second to achieve full digitalization in 1995, while Germany provides an example of late adoption.

Figure 6.5 Contribution of telecommunications to GDP (%)

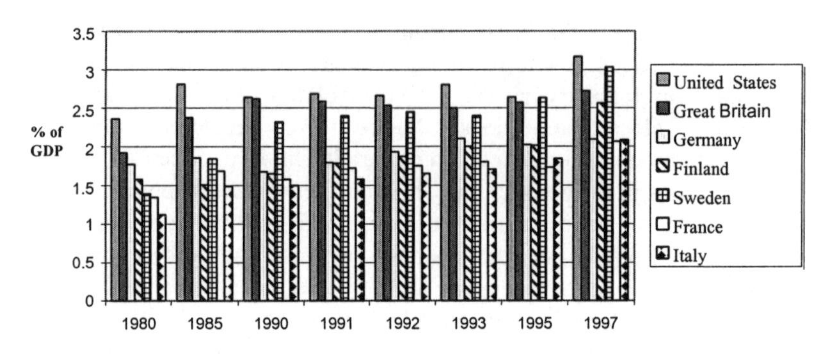

Source: MTC Telecommunication Statistics.

Finland, together with many other European countries had by 1998 reached a density of about 55 main connections per one hundred inhabitants. This figure has been reduced during the recent years, not least because of the rather dramatic increase in the number of mobile subscriptions, which have become more popular as equipment, subscription fees, and call charges have become cheaper. This development has in many cases reduced the market value of telephone company shares (MTC, 1996). The total number of subscriptions has grown fairly rapidly from 1970 to 1998, at an average annual rate of 6.9%, but with an average annual growth rate of 31.1% for mobile subscriptions in 1980/98.

The number of subscribers in the fixed network has decreased in 1997/98, as follows from Figure 6.7, and may decrease further, because high mobile penetration rates mean that a mobile subscription is a substitute rather than a complement. Finland has reached a higher density in mobile subscriptions than the rest of Europe, followed by Sweden and Italy. Figure 6.8 highlights this development and illustrates the significant scope for future expansion elsewhere. This, together with the emergence of new services, may partly explain the present tendency to restructure the market for mobile communications in Europe.

Figure 6.6 The percentage of digitalized main subscriptions in the fixed network

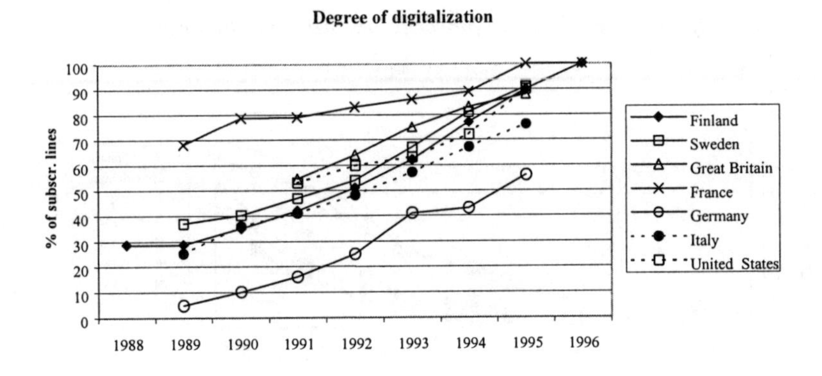

Degree of digitalization
% of subscr. lines
100
90
80
70
60
50
40
30
20
10
0
1988
1989
1990
1991
1992
1993
1994
1995
1996
Finland
Sweden
Great Britain
France
Germany
Italy
United States

Source: MTC Telecommunication Statistics.

Figure 6.7 The number of main subscriptions in the fixed network per 100 inhabitants[6]

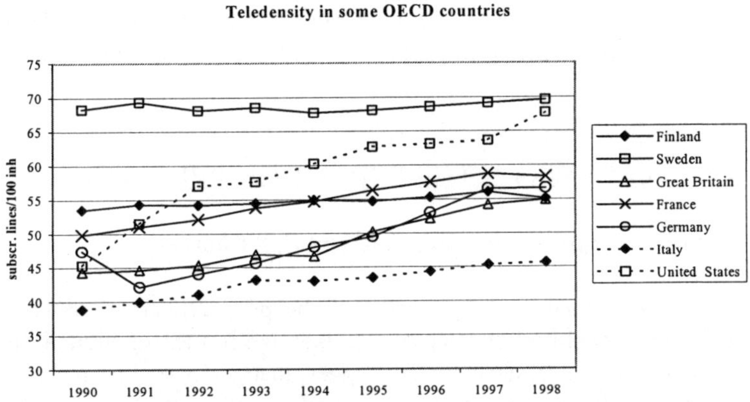

Teledensity in some OECD countries
subscr. lines/100 inh
75
70
65
60
55
50
45
40
35
30
1990
1991
1992
1993
1994
1995
1996
1997
1998
Finland
Sweden
Great Britain
France
Germany
Italy
United States

Source: MTC Telecommunication Statistics.

Liberalization, partly made possible by the long tradition of co-existence between different ownership forms, and early adoption of new technology, are the main reasons for the high mobile phone penetration in Finland (Åkermarck, 2000; Grüber and Verboven, 2000). An analogue Nordic mobile telephone system (NMT) was introduced as early as 1982. Ten years later, Finland was first in the world to adopt the GSM-standard, and is now a forerunner in mobile phone technology in supplementary services, such as text messages and data services.

Figure 6.8 The number of mobile subscriptions per 100 inhabitants[7]

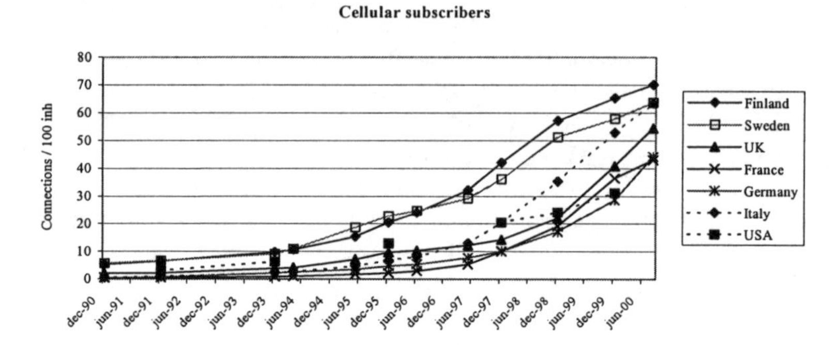

Source: MTC Telecommunication Statistics.

Mobile telecommunications have provided a similar near-duopolistic structure as the markets described in 2.2 above, despite the presence of a third network operator. This is hardly altered by the subsequent granting of a national GSM license to the network operator Suomen 2G-group in January 2000, and by the presence of the service providers RSL Com and Saunalahti Plc.

3 AN ANALYSIS OF THE IMPACT ON PRICES

3.1 Technical Progress, Liberalization, and Call Charges

It is more or less taken for granted that the price reductions in Finland depend mainly on liberalization, despite the significance of digitalization. But models of technical development suggest that prices will decrease in an oligopolistic industry also with the adoption of new and cost-saving technology (Reinganum, 1989, Jensen, 1982, Stoneman 1987, Banker et al. 1996, Grout, 1996). To assess the relative importance of digitalization and liberalization for explaining the development in Finland we therefore use a so called intervention analysis (see McCleary and Hay, 1980, and Box and Tiao, 1975).[8]

Figure 6.9 Real cost of 70 off-peak long-distance calls during 1918/94

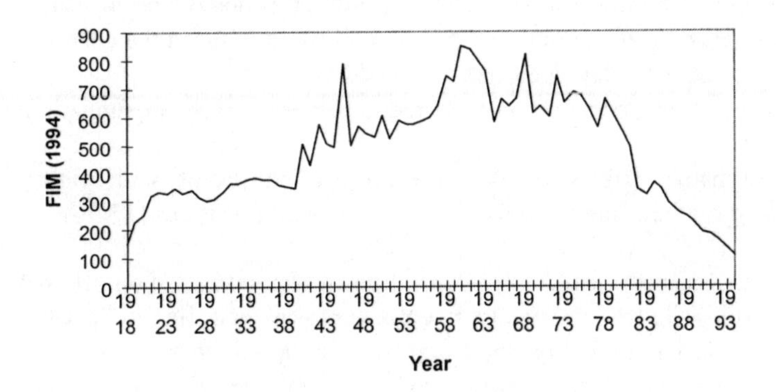

It is obvious from Figure 6.9 that prices have been reduced after digitalization. To check whether there is significant evidence for the impact of another intervention as well on daytime charges, we first modeled the impact of the onset of digitalization 1980 with a single, downward sloping 'ramp'-effect. Among several alternatives, the following model provided best fit when including a similar ramp-effect for liberalization in 1987:

$$(1-B)LnY_t = \varpi_1 I_{1980} + \omega_2 I_{1987} + C - \phi_1 (1-B)LnY_{t-1} + a_t \qquad (1)$$

The parameter estimates are presented in Table 6.1. It can be interpreted as follows:

Table 6.1 Estimates for a model with two interventions in the log transformed daytime trunk call charges series

Model	Parameter estimates	t ratio	RMS	LBQ (k = 15)	
Whole period with interventions in 1980 and in 1987 as "ramps"					
(1,1,0)	AR (1) –0.4337	-4.31***	0.015249	21.12	(14)
	Constant 0.03449	2.13**			
	ω_1 -0.07878	-2.36**			
	ω_2 -0.1048	-2.24**			

This can be interpreted as follows:

(a) The onset of digitalization in 1980 has lowered the daytime trunk call charges by 12% annually.
(b) Allowing for an intervention in 1987 improves the model's performance.
(c) When analyzing the period 1980/87, digitalization reduced the cost for a 4-minute domestic daytime trunk call by 47%.
(d) The first step of liberalization 1987 reduced these cost by an annual rate of about 10%.
(e) The estimated effects of deregulation are consistent with figures presented by the Ministry of Transport and Communications (17/96).[9]

We tried to assess the effect of digitalization and liberalization on off-peak charges as well. The first intervention component was identified to be a first order transfer function. Following from the assumption that allowing for competition would reduce tariffs gradually, the second intervention component was chosen as a ramp. This does not necessarily rule out tariffs that approach any particular level asymptotically, but the post-intervention segment is too short to verify this. We estimated the following model for the whole period with two interventions:[10]

$$(1-B)LnY_t = \frac{\omega_1}{(1-B\delta_1)}(1-B)I_{1980} + \omega_2 I_{1987} + C - \phi_1(1-B)LnY_{t-1} + a_t \qquad (2)$$

Our results are summarized in Table 6.2. The results may successfully be interpreted in terms of the ratio of the post- and pre-intervention levels, which enables us to determine the percentage change in equilibrium level. Doing this, applying the theory of a first order transfer function, yields the following results:

(a) The total percentage change in the equilibrium level because of digitalization is –73%. But since δ_1 has quite a large value, the new level would be reached very slowly.
(b) At 1987 (i.e. observation 70), the level of the series, as determined by the first intervention, is 65% lower than the pre-intervention level.
(c) The effect of liberalization on the post-1987 part of the series is an annual decrease in tariffs of 11%. The residual mean square (RMS) statistic is lowered from the pre-intervention model (0.017915) to 0.017677. This supports the hypothesis that this model version really improves the performance of pre-intervention model on the entire series. However, the model for the whole period has parameter estimates

slightly different from the pre-intervention model. The AR(1) parameter changed from -0.4250 to -0.3822. The t-ratio for this parameter changed from -3.81 to -3.64.[11]

Table 6.2 Estimates for a model with two interventions in the log transformed night-time trunk call charges series

Model	Estimate		t-ratio	RMS	LBQ
I_{1980} as a first order transfer function and I_{1987} as a 'ramp'					
(1,1,0)	AR(1)	-0.3822	-3.64***	0.017677	17.94
	C	0.02528	1.46		
	$\omega 1$	-0.2022	-2.44**		
	δ_1	0.8444	6.97***		
	ω_2	-0.1116	-1.90*		
Obs./Df= 7/70					

The analysis suggest that the first intervention component is a first order transfer function. However, while the first step towards liberalization can be modeled as a 'ramp' effect, the t-value of the ω_2 parameter (-1.90) casts some doubt on significance. However, a similar pattern is suggested by the backcasting method, which yields significant parameter estimates,[12] and thus implies that the assumed effects are correctly specified. This suggests that the main development of the night-time tariff series was started very early in the 1980s. At that point the first step towards liberalizing the market significantly affected the series, causing an additional downward slope.

Price competition may have been suppressed in practice because of the threat of government intervention in case of a price war, in order to ensure that operators remained able to maintain and develop their networks.[13] *Finnet* refers to Kaukoverkko Ysi, which is owned by the Finnet group that was established by local operators, *Sonera* is the state-owned former monopolist, and *Telia* refers to the Telia Finland (former Telivo Ltd) in Figure 6.10. It seems obvious that the incumbent lowered daytime charges substantially prior to the entry of Telivo in 1993, thus suggesting that the most important price reductions took place before actual competition.

Figure 6.10 Nominal charges (pennies per minute) by operator and by type of call. (Charges during working hours are indexed by 1, evening and weekend charges by 2, night-time charges by 3.)

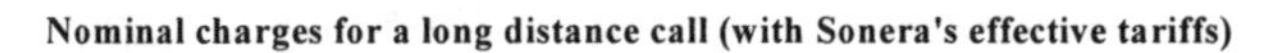

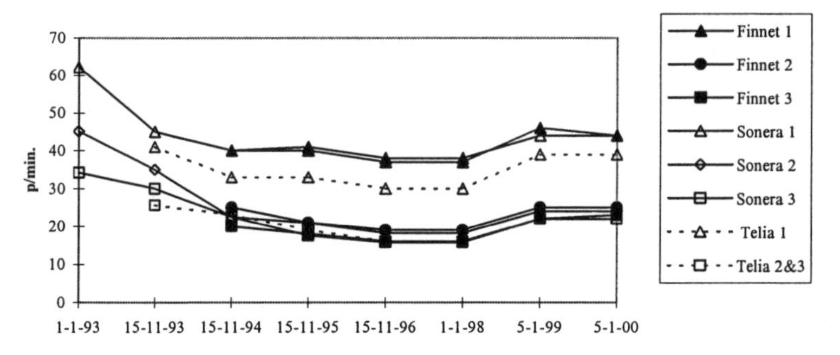

3.2 Changes in Tariff Structure

Competition, technical progress, and privatization may affect not only the level but also the structure of charges, as for example suggested by evidence from Germany (Brunekreeft and Gross, 1999). This section focuses on evidence for structural breaks in the tariff structure, thus providing complementary insights on the effects of liberalization and technical progress. This does not require sophisticated econometric tests, because a superficial analysis of the ratio between daytime and off-peak charges for both domestic long-distance calls and calls to Sweden can reveal the presence of some rate rebalancing. Prices are obtained from telephone directories (1LOU, 1963/95) and from Ilmonen (1994/97).[14] Figure 6.11 shows the relation between daytime tariffs and off-peak tariffs for both domestic long-distance calls and for calls to Sweden.

There are several abrupt changes in the ratio of domestic daytime and reduced-rate tariffs.[15] The first occurs in 1975, as off-peak charges were introduced for the first time. The sharp reduction in the off-peak tariff in 1982 represents a more dramatic change. There is a decrease after 1987 and an increase 1993/96. The development is more stable in the case of calls to Sweden, but the introduction of reduced-rate charges in 1986 led to a change. Further increases were experienced in 1995 and 1996, as night-time tariffs were reduced proportionately more. Thus, it is possible that digitalization (1980/94), decisions on liberalization in 1987 and full-scale competition in 1992, and subsequent entry in 1993 have affected the rate structure.

Figure 6.11 The ratio of daytime to reduced-rate tariffs for domestic long-distance calls and for calls to Sweden

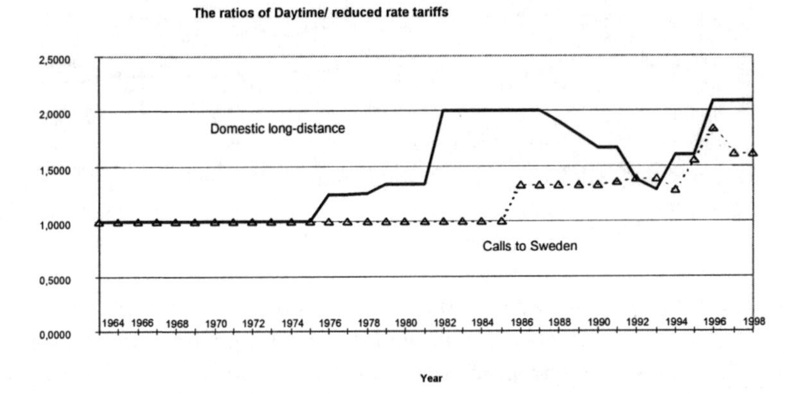

An analysis of how tariffs on long-distance calls relate to international calls may also reveal the presence of cross-subsidies to compensate for tariff reductions and rate balancing elsewhere. Operators do not have full control of this ratio, because they cannot determine the prices of network access set by the foreign operators, but their mark-up is endogenous. Figure 6.12 presents the ratio of domestic and international (i.e. Sweden) long-distance tariffs, suggesting that the digitalization period is associated with substantial change, in particular in the case of the off-peak tariffs in 1982. The early 1990s seem to produce a sharp reduction in both cases, this has to be tested formally.

However, Figure 6.12 has little to say on causation. A visual inspection of the nominal tariffs may therefore be a valuable complement. In Figure 6.13 we have plotted the indexed nominal tariffs for domestic daytime (Dom1) and reduced rate (Dom2) calls, and tariffs indexes for calls to Sweden during working hours (Swe1) and off-peak (Swe2), with 1970 as base year. First, the years when reduced rates were actually applied follows from the divergence of Dom2 from Dom1 (1975) and of Swe2 from Swe1 (1986). Second, it is also obvious that the dramatic fluctuation in the nominal charges for domestic long distance calls is responsible for most of the fluctuation in ratios A and B, since charges for calls to Sweden have been more stable.

Figure 6.12 The ratios of domestic long-distance to international tariffs: Daytime (A) and reduced rate (B)

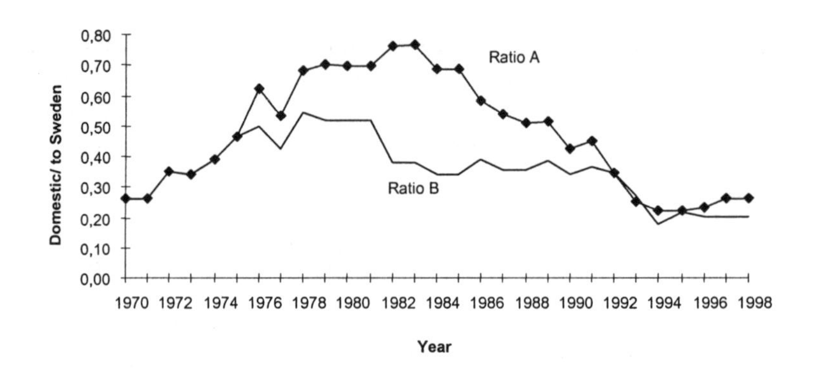

Figure 6.13 The indexed nominal tariffs for domestic daytime (Dom1) and off-peak(Dom2) long-distance calls and for calls to Sweden during daytime (Swe1) and off-peak (Swe2)

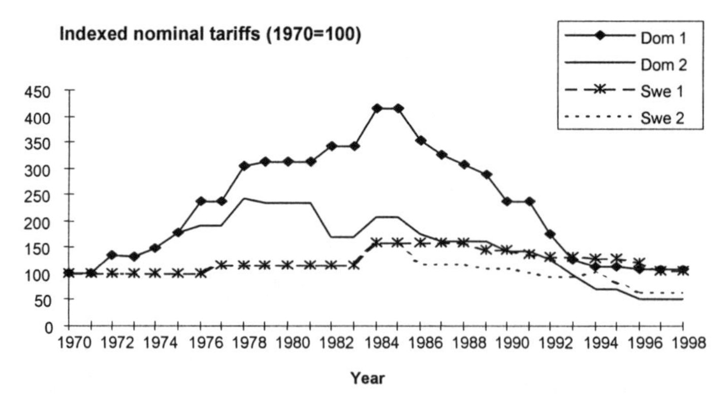

One reason for the difference in volatility may be that domestic charges reflect the costs of operating, expanding and modernizing the long distance network. It may also be the case that the domestic incumbent reduces its mark-up on domestic calls in order to delay entry after liberalization, but such a dramatic reduction would on the other hand not have been possible without the new switching technology.

We used a sequential Chow test to determine the timing of structural breaks in the tariff structure for the domestic long distance calls formally.[16] When applying this approach on ratios A and B, it turns out that changes in tariff structures do not have to be associated only with market reorganization, because of the importance of technical change. However, the results do not contradict the finding that there is some connection between liberalization and changes in the tariff structure.

A check for bias due to serially correlated errors in the analysis of structural breaks suggests that it is not appropriate to assume that the pattern of residual autocorrelation is equal for two sub-periods, contrary to some earlier studies. We prefer an approach of rolling together the tests of variations in structural parameters and autocorrelation.

3.3 A Summary of the Empirical Findings

To conclude, this analysis suggests that digitalization and liberalization have affected both the level and structure of tariffs, but it also appears that the most important explanation for reduced tariffs is digitalization. The empirical analysis has not captured the fact that the corporate objectives of the incumbent may have changed from a public service commitment to a greater emphasis on profits, thus strengthening the impact of liberalization. Next section provides a theoretical framework for evaluating a development, which includes changed corporate objectives as well as a change in the market structure.

4 A DISCUSSION OF ALLOCATIVE EFFICIENCY

4.1 When Will Liberalization Increase Allocative Efficiency?

Concentration in telecommunications has been reduced by liberalization almost everywhere. More competition would increase the total surplus and benefit consumers on a conventional market, but the outcome is less certain if the incumbent is a public agency with wider objectives than profit maximization. This may have been the case in Finland, because estimates of the (absolute value of the) price elasticity of demand for the relevant period are too low for being consistent with profit maximization under monopoly (see Sullström, 1995, Granfelt and Torniainen, 1993). In this section we ask how fragmented the liberalized market must be in order to outperform a public monopoly and whether such a fragmentation is feasible, given the presence of fixed costs.

Suppose that the incumbent has maximized a weighted sum of welfare (total surplus) and profits, with the weights λ and $1-\lambda$ respectively. Let p and q represent price and quantity, let 'competition' and (public) monopoly be indexed by c and m, and let F represent the fixed costs of each operator. The post-liberalization market has usually been oligopolistic rather than perfectly competitive. 'Competition' therefore means an n-firm oligopoly where the incumbent is privatized or, like in Finland, transformed to a commercial state-owned plc. The change in total surplus can then be approximated as follows:

$$\Delta W = \frac{1}{2}(q_c - q_m)(p_c - p_m) - (n-1)F \qquad (3)$$

For example, deregulation can lead to a higher price and a lower output than under the public monopoly, as when λ is high and n is low. The effect of privatization and deregulation on allocative efficiency is then unambiguously negative, and this is reinforced by duplication, as reflected in the term $(n\text{-}1)F$.

On the other hand, if entry leads to a lower price, this positive effect is to some extent offset by the increase in fixed costs associated with the duplication of networks. The operators have not agreed to reveal data that would have provided a rough figure for F, but our estimates suggest that the component $(q_c - q_m)(p_c - p_m)/2$ is about 48 (in millions of FIM) on the market for domestic long-distance telecommunications.[17] This amounts to 6% of turnover in 1993.[18]

However, we can get an indirect insight on the significance of F as follows. Suppose that liberalization will ultimately lead to the presence of as many operators as can break even. A simple model with somewhat more structure then allows us to identify the extent of fragmentation that is required for liberalization to improve welfare, without having to know F. Suppose that inverse demand is $p = a\text{-}x$, and that deregulation means a symmetric Cournot-oligopoly. We ignore changes in marginal costs c because of liberalization; this seems justified in light of, for example, Martin and Parker (1997) or Willner (2001). Suppose that n operators can break even. Their gross profits are then approximately equal to their fixed costs:

$$F \approx \frac{(a-c)^2}{(n+1)^2} \qquad (4)$$

Maximizing a weighted sum of profits and welfare would yield $x_m = (a\text{-}c)/(2\text{-}\lambda)$, while the Cournot solution would yield $x_c = n(a\text{-}c)/(n+1)$. Insert into inverse demand, use (4) and rearrange:

$$\Delta W = \frac{(a-c)^2}{(n+1)^2}\{\frac{[(n-1)(1-\lambda)-\lambda]^2}{2(2-\lambda)^2} - (n-1)\} \quad (5)$$

Solving for n gives the number of firms that must be able to break even for a given value of λ.

If the incumbent has been highly commercial, as when λ is for example 0.1, liberalization improves welfare if it is possible for 10 operators to break even. By contrast, if the public service commitment has played a crucial role, as when λ is for example 0.9, we get a welfare improvement only if the technology allows for an extremely fragmented market structure (n = 261). Values of λ of, say, 0.3, 0.5, and 0.7 would require that at least 14, 21, and 43 of the 261 firms can break even. If the incumbent has been completely commercial (λ = 0), liberalization does not improve welfare unless 9 operators can break even. This means that the market is still in one sense a natural monopoly if, say, only 8 firms can make profits.[19]

The model expresses the conditions for maximum competition to increase allocative efficiency and is of course not applicable if there are other entry barriers as well. The market then remains oligopolistic. The welfare gains of liberalization may turn out to be fairly modest if operators in addition tend to merge, or if markets become more concentrated for other reasons. Figure 6.4 suggests that domestic charges may again be increasing.

It follows from the model that liberalization cannot increase allocative efficiency unless it is possible to get a significantly more fragmented market structure than at present in Finland. This result should be interpreted with caution, because of the strong assumptions, but it suggests directions for further research (which should ideally take place before radical changes such as privatization and liberalization are made). An extended analysis might for example allow for different types of demand functions and/or oligopoly solutions. A Bertrand solution would yield lower prices, but might also more easily lead to collusion. The presence of a Stackelberg-leader would mean lower mark-ups after liberalization. Slow switching should also be incorporated.

4.2 Other Aspects of Competition

The telecommunications industry is no longer a natural monopoly in the sense that competing operators cannot co-exist, but it may still be the case that the costs of competition exceeds its benefits. Moreover, the alternative to competition between profit maximizing operators is not necessary a commercial monopoly.

There are other reasons than fixed costs for why there is not a complete consensus on liberalization. It is possible to make cheaper calls, but not always without substantial efforts. To obtain the full benefits from liberalization in Finland requires a comparison of complicated pricing schedules. Moreover, a customer who refuses to insert a code (3/5 digits) for a given operator is charged according to the most expensive option. Most public telephones are now card operated, with no compatibility between the operators.

Some extent of 'confusion marketing' (as defined in Guardian, Jobs & Money, 14.10.2000) seems to be a characteristic of newly deregulated public utilities. This lead to an early criticism by Willner (1996) of so called 'artificial competition'. It remains to be seen whether these side effects represent a temporary problem of information and/or coordination, or whether they reflect some persistent market failure.

5 CONCLUDING REMARKS

The still state-owned telecommunications company Sonera has been highly innovative and belongs to the forefront in the industry in Europe. The foundations for its present achievements were laid when it was still an integral part of the public sector in Finland, thus providing a counter example to the notion that privatization is a necessary condition for innovativeness.

It may be difficult to know the precise extent to which Sonera's predecessors emphasized non-commercial objectives, but we know that the commercial emphasis has gradually been strengthened during the transformation from a public-sector agency. Profit maximization in a monopoly or in an oligopoly may be associated with potentially large welfare losses, as compared to the first-best solution. Competition can therefore increase allocative efficiency, provided that the number of operators that can break even is sufficiently large. Otherwise, a similar analysis would associate large welfare gains with a change from an oligopoly to a welfare maximizing public or third-sector monopoly.

The intervention analysis suggests that digitalization has been crucial for the price reductions that we have observed, but it seems that the effect of liberalization is also significant. Note also that it may be difficult to distinguish between a remaining public service commitment and strategies to deal with the threat of future competition, and that we do not yet know the extent to which profit margins have been reduced by competition. Thus, it remains possible that costs have been reduced to such extent that lower prices are consistent with higher profit margins, as in the US according to MacAvoy

(1998). It remains for further research to analyze this interesting possibility, given that we already know that competition in telecommunications also bring some disadvantages, such as 'confusing marketing'.

Finlands development has been impressive, and includes both innovativity within public sector organizations and commercial enterprises. This suggests that technical progress may be more dependent on the ability to create dynamism in a given type of organization, such as Telecom Finland/Sonera (which is still owned by the state) or Nokia, rather than by easy solutions, such as changes in ownership and market structure.

It is also worth noting that opinions are divided on Finland's response to a couple of recent challenges. The process in which third generation telecommunications were granted has been described as a 'beauty contest', in striking contrast to the auctions in Britain and Germany. Licenses were not tied to any particular network standard, because the authorities wanted a competition between technologies as well. Criticism that this might mean subsidies and an encouragement of efficiency is dismissed by the authorities. A decision to rely on private initiatives rather than public investments in broadband communications has also met criticism.

NOTES

1. Finland is sparsely populated, and the impact of business restructuring and globalization has been stronger than in most countries during the last decade, which highlights the importance of telephony as a substitute to physical mobility.
2. However, a proper expansion of the network would have required the use of cables instead of adding new overhead wires to an already crowded network, which was vulnerable to damage by ice and snow.
3. Of the 11,100 made redundant in the whole state-owned group (renamed Post and Telecommunications), 26% were employed in other industries, 26% became unemployed, 28% were retired, while 5% were re-employed by the group. The fixed term contract expired for 14% of the total.
4. Number of permanent staff, part of the personnel working part-time. Excludes other operators (121 employees in 1994)
5. Local network charges refer to the local part of a long-distance or mobile call.
6. From 1991, the values for Germany include the network of former East-Germany.
7. The figures for August 2000 are estimates.

8. Prices have been obtained from telephone directories (1LOU, 1963/95), from Ilmonen (1994/98), and from Kangas (2000). Older data are obtained from Berg (1939), Törnqvist (1952, 1971 and 1977), Risberg (1959), and Jutikkala (1977).
9. MTC compared the prices of day-time trunk-call charges, focusing on *de facto* competition. It turns out that the price of the cheapest alternative (of three operators) was reduced by 19.5%. Note however that MTC focuses on the trunk-call component only, while the user has to pay for the whole trunk call.
10. I_{1980} refers to the intervention in 1980 (i.e. observation 63) and I_{1987} refers to the intervention of year 1987 (i.e. observation 70).
11. If we interpret this without taking into account the second intervention, the result implies that the night-time charges seem to have decreased all through the 1980s and even in the early 1990s. This suggests that there is not much effect left for the second intervention. Based on the data of 70 night-time domestic trunk calls, this result implies that these costs would have been lowered from 613.2 in 1979 (measured in FIM, 1994) to 167.40. This asymptotic level lies somewhere between the 1991 and 1992-year levels.
12. $\phi_1 = 0.42$ (-4.29), C=0.03 (1.74), $\omega_1 = 0.2068$ (-2.56) $\delta_1 = 0.845$ (7.31), $\omega_2 = -0.113$ (-1.98), t-values in parenthesis.
13. Competition in telecommunications, OCDE/GD(96)114, Competition policy Roundtables No. 6.
14. Studying the ratios of these charges allows for the use of nominal charges of the former state-sponsored monopoly (Tele).
15. 'Off-peak' and 'reduced rate' are used to define the first reduced charge following the tariff for calls made during working hours.
16. This approach does not exactly conform to the spirit of a Chow test, but a complementary analysis with the more appropriate Cusum test did not alter the conclusions.
17. This positive effect may also be offset rate re-balancing, but this effect does not seem to be strong in the light of 3.2 above. Note also that the time period (1992/94) is so short that we may safely ignore the impact of technical change on marginal costs.
18. Björkroth (2001) provides a slightly different approach which yields higher estimates of the welfare change, by focusing on averages rather than on a distinction between day-time and off-peak calls, thus making it possible to include all calls in the analysis.
19. It is also possible to reformulate the model so as to get conditions in terms of the Herfindahl index of concentration.

REFERENCES

'Advanced Communications Technology and Services' 1994, Workplan, DGXIII-B-RA946043-WP, August.

Åkermarck, M. (2000), 'History of Mobile Phone Subscriptions in Finland', mimeo.

Alasoini, T., P. Järviniemi and J. Pekkola (1990), 'Organisaatiomuutokset PTL-Telessä. Henkilöstön käsityksiä muutoksesta ja työnsä ehdoista', *Työpoliittinen tutkimus*, 4, Työministeriö, Helsinki.

Banker, R.D., H.-H. Chang, and S. K. Majumdar (1996), 'Profitability, Productivity and Price Recovery Patterns in the U.S. Telecommunications Industry', *Review of Industrial Organization*, 11, 1-17.

Berg, E.A. (1935), *Södra Finlands Interurbana Telefonaktiebolag*, Helsinki: Etelä-Suomen Kaukopuhelinosakeyhtiö.

Björkroth, T. (1998), 'The Impact of Technical Change and Competition on Telecommunication Tariffs in Finland', unpublished licentiate thesis, Department of Economics and Statistics, Åbo Akademi University.

Björkroth, T. (2001), 'Market Structure and Welfare Effects in the Finnish Market of Long-Distance Telecommunications', mimeo, Department of Economics and Statistics, Åbo Akademi University.

Björkroth, Tom and Anders Kjellman (2000), 'Public Capital and Private Sector Productivity - A Finnish Perspective', *Finnish Economic Papers*, 13 (1), 28-44.

Blank, L., David L. Kaserman and John W. Mayo (1998), 'Dominant Firm Pricing with Competitive Entry and Regulation: The Case of IntraLATA Toll', *Journal of Regulatory Economics*, 14 (1), 35-53.

Box, G.E.P. and G.C. Tiao (1975), 'Intervention Analysis with Applications to Economic and Environmental Problems', *Journal of American Statistical Association*, 70 (349), March.

Brunekreeft, G. and W. Gross (1999), 'Price Structures in the Liberalized Market for Long-Distance Telecommunications', mimeo, University of Freiburg.

'Competition in Telecommunications Competition Policy Roundtables' 1996, OCDE/GD(96)114 No.6, Finland.

Granfelt, J. and J. Torniainen (1993), 'Teletoiminnan verotuksen kokonaistaloudelliset vaikutukset', Liikenneministeriön julkaisuja, 59/93, Helsinki.

Guardian, Jobs & Money (14.10.2000) 'Ringing up the right numbers'.

Grout, P. (1996), 'Promoting the Superhighway: Telecommunications Regulation in Europe', *Economic Policy*, 11 (22), 109-154.

Grüber, H. and F. Verboven (2000), 'The diffusion of telecommunications services in the European Union', mimeo, European Investment Bank and University of Antwerpen.

Hausman, J., T. Tardiff and A. Belinfante (1993), 'The Effects of the Breakup of AT&T on Telephone Penetration in the United States', *American Economic Review*, 83, 178-184.

Ilmonen, J. (1994), 'Suomen telemaksujen hintataso 1993', Helsinki: Liikenneministeriön julkaisuja 2/94.

Ilmonen, J. (1995), 'Suomen telemaksujen hintataso 1994', Helsinki: Liikenneministeriön julkaisuja V 9/95.

Ilmonen, J. (1996), 'Suomen telemaksujen hintataso 1995', Helsinki: Liikenneministeriön julkaisuja V 6/96.

Ilmonen, J (1997), 'Suomen telemaksujen hintataso 1996', Helsinki: Liikenneministeriön julkaisuja 4/97.

Ilmonen, J (1998), 'Suomen telemaksujen hintataso 1997', Helsinki: Liikenneministeriön julkaisuja 17/98.

Jensen, R. (1982), 'Adoption and Diffusion of an Innovation of Uncertain Profitability', *Journal of Economic Theory*, 27, 182-193.

Jutikkala, Eino (1977), *Puhelin ja puhelinlaitokset Suomessa 1877-1977*, Helsinki/Turku: Puhelinlaitosten Liitto.

Kangas, Pertti (2000), 'Suomen telemaksujen hintataso 1999', Helsinki: Liikenneministeriön julkaisuja 14/2000.

Liikenneministeriö Televiestintätilasto (MTC, Telecommunications Statistics), Issues 1992-2000, Helsinki.

MacAvoy, Paul W. (1998), 'Testing for Competitiveness of Markets for Long Distance Telephone Services: Competition Finally?', *Review of Industrial Organization*, 13 (3), 295-319.

McCleary, R.C. and R.A. Hay (1980), *Applied Time Series Analysis for the Social Sciences*, London: Sage.

Madden, G. and S.J. Savage (1998), 'CEE Telecommunications Investment and Economic Growth', *Information Economics and Policy*, 10, 173-195.

Martin, Stephen and David Parker (1997), *The Impact of Privatization. Ownership, Efficiency, and Corporate Performance in the UK*, London, UK and New York, US: Routledge.

Ministry of Transport and Communications (1995), 'The effects of Competition on Employment in the telecommunications Industry: Case Finland', Publications V29/95, Helsinki.

Ministry of Transport and Communications (1996), 'Puhelintoiminnan kehitys kilpailutilanteessa Iso-britanniassa, Ruotsissa ja Suomessa', Liikenneministeriön julkaisuja V17/96, Helsinki.

Ministry of Transport and Communications (1999), 'Verkkoviestinnän haasteita ja tavoitteita', Press release.

Ministry of Transport and Communications (2000), Telemarkkinoiden toimintaympäristö 2000-2003, Press release.

Moisala, U.E., K. Rahko, and O. Turpeinen (1977), *Puhelin ja puhelinlaitokset suomessa 1877-1977*, Edited by Jutikkala, E., Puhelinlaitosten Liitto r.y, Helsinki.

Piekkala, H. (1999), 'Televerkkojen vuokrausvelvollisuus ja hinnoittelu kilpailuoikeuden näkökulmasta', Turun Yliopiston Oikeustieteellisen tiedekunnan julkaisuja, Yksityisoikeuden julkaisusarja B:42, Turku.

Reinganum, J.F. (1989), 'The Timing of Innovation', in R. Schmalensee and R.D. Willig (eds), *Handbook of Industrial Organisation*, Volume I, Amsterdam: North-Holland.

Risberg, E. (1959), *Suomen lennätinlaitoksen historia*, Helsinki.

Röller, L.H. and L. Waverman (1998), 'Telecommunications Infrastructure and Economic Development: A Simultaneous Approach', working paper.

Stigler, G.J. (1964), 'A Theory of Oligopoly', *Journal of Political Economy*, 72, 44-61.

Stoneman, P. (1987), *The Economic Analysis of Technology Policy*, New York: Oxford University Press.

Sullström, R. (1995), 'Liikenteen tulo- ja hintajoustot-kotitaloustiedustelujen aineistosovellus', Liikenneministeriön mietintöjä ja muistioita B: 3/95. Liikenneministeriö, Helsinki.

Sung, Nakil (1998), 'The Embodiment Hypothesis Revisited: Evidence From the Local U.S. Local Exchange Carriers', *Information Economics and Policy*, 10 (2), 219-236.

Taylor, William E. and Lester D. Taylor (1993), 'Postdivestiture Long-Distance Competition in the United States', *American Economic Review*, 83, Papers and Proceedings, May, 185-190.

Telephone Directories, 1LOU, 1963-1995.

Tirole, J. (1988), *The Theory of Industrial Organization*, Cambridge, Mass., US and London, UK: MIT Press.

Törnqvist, Leo (1952), *Post- och Telegrafverkets tariffer under åren 1926-1950 i belysning av indexberäkningar. Bilaga till Post- och Telegrafstyrelsens berättelse för år 1950*, Helsinki: Posti- ja Lennätinhallitus.

Törnqvist, Leo (1971), *Post- och Telegrafverkets ekonomiska utveckling till år 1970*, Helsinki: Posti- ja Lennätinhallitus.

Törnqvist, Leo (1977), *Post- och Telegrafverkets ekonomiska utveckling till år 1975*, Helsinki: Posti- ja Lennätinhallitus.

Varian, H.R. (1992), *Microeconomic Analysis*, New York, US and London, UK: Norton.

Willner, Johan (1996), 'Social Objectives, Market Rule and Public Policy: The case of ownership', in P. Devine, Y. Katsoulacos and R. Sugden (eds), *Competitiveness, Subsidiarity and Industrial Policy*, London, UK and New York, US: Routledge, pp. 12-41.

Willner, Johan (2001), 'Ownership, Efficiency, and Political Intervention', *European Journal of Political Economy* (forthcoming).

7. A Waterloo of Utility Liberalization? How Great Deregulation Expectations were Dashed by the Dutch Water Industry in the 1990s

Emiel F.M. Wubben and Willem Hulsink

1 INTRODUCTION

One of the most original (and longest) titles in the social sciences literature is the one chosen by Pressman and Wildavsky for their policy analysis of a federal urban regeneration programme: *Implementation: How great expectations in Washington are dashed in Oakland; Or, why it's amazing that federal programs work at all, This being a saga of the Economic Development Administration as told by two sympathetic observers who seek to build morals on a foundation of ruined hopes* (1973/1984). Their implementation study is a classic example of a top-down policy process based on apparently sound economic and political ideas, developed in the administrative center, which encountered serious difficulties in their practical applications and implementation at the grass-roots levels. The recent developments in the Dutch water supply industry may resemble Pressman & Wildavsky's ambiguous findings. Also in this case, a grounded, ambitious program to deregulate the water industry was unfolded by the government in the mid-1990s, but the proposals of the two subsequent coalition cabinets of liberal-conservatives, social democrats and liberal-democrats basically came to nothing. Was the Dutch water monopoly so sticky, impeding major changes institutional, or is this case indicative of the turning pendulum of liberalization?

For a long time, the Dutch drinking water industry, with its history of incremental changes, seemed impervious to liberalization and new entry, privatization, and regulatory reform. In 1997, the Dutch water industry became the third major utility placed into the liberalization and privatization spotlights, following the telecommunications and energy sectors. The Pro-Competition, Deregulation and Quality of Legislation (PCD&QL)-project group of the Ministry of Economic Affairs (Ministerie van Economische

Zaken, 1998) had become actively involved in the opening up of utility markets, and started seriously considering privatization and deregulation of the water industry (i.e. divestments and partial private ownership, competitive tendering, selective liberalization) the question for the Dutch drinking water industry became pregnant: how to respond to such a potentially hostile and turbulent program? Could they remain master of their own destiny by a pro-active industrial and corporate restructuring, or would they be confronted with radical proposals opening their sector to private ownership and competition?

For an assessment of the water industry, its companies, and its management, the outsider has to know some of the typical features of the water industry. First of all, one has to take into account that water is an 'essential', affordable, regional product, heavy and hard to store, quality-sensitive, and entailing health and safety risks. Secondly, the liberalization process of the water industry in Western Europe and the Netherlands in particular does not accord to standard EU deregulation practices. Basically, the liberalization of the telecommunications and energy markets was driven by the European Commission, who implemented the so-called European agenda for establishing internal (network & utility) markets (see chapter 2, Van Miert).

The European liberalization directives typically function as a crowbar and/or scapegoat to force the opening of the national utility markets and get deregulation going. In contrast, there exists no such thing as a European Water Liberalization Directive. Largely, because there is hardly any cross-border trade in the water industry, and hence no legal basis for the Commission to intervene. The European Union (EU) does not come any further than publishing the Water Framework Directive (2000/60/EC), and the Drinking Water Directive (98/83/EU), fostering river-basin water protection policies and enforcing certain quality controls and provisions to provide consumers with relevant information, respectively.

Finally, with regard to the organization of the water industry there is no common standard. In Europe there is no predominant paradigm, nor a trend towards some ideal form by the member states. In the EU the dominant governance form varies between direct public management (e.g. Denmark, Spain), direct supra-municipal management (e.g. Germany, Italy and Scotland), delegated public management (e.g. Belgium, The Netherlands), delegated private or mixed management (e.g. France), and direct private management (England and Wales) (Eureau, 1997; Wubben, et al, 1998b).

We will typify the evolution of the public debate in the Dutch drinking water sector and analyze the positioning of the key market players over time in this respect. This policy process of (re-)structuring the water sector will be reconstructed by a presentation of the evolution of ideas over time, the facts and statistics relevant for understanding the discussion in particular stages and any available alternatives put forward within the policy arena. First, the initial positions are depicted of the industry and its players around 1996. Next, the forces challenging the relatively insulated water industry will be the focus of attention, over a five-year period till 2001. That section of the study will alternate, a series of policy exercises and quantitative studies on the situation. The prospects for and performance of the Dutch drinking water industry are depicted via a series of scenario-studies. A scenario is a rich and detailed portrait of possible future conditions; it helps to identify and understand signals, problems, prospects, options, and returns. A scenario-study simplifies the avalanche of data into a limited number of possible states (Wack, 1985; Godet, 1987; Schoemaker, 1995).

2 SETTING THE SCENE: INITIAL POSITIONS AND ROLES

The public task entrusted to the Dutch water companies is 'ensuring that the distribution of reliable drinking water to the users in a distribution area is guaranteed in the quantity and with the pressure demanded by the public interest' (1957-Water Act, art.4.). By 1996, the popular opinion on the water industry seemed to be positive. According to a representative consumer poll, by the industry association VEWIN, the Dutch were rather satisfied with their water supply companies, with the exception of the hardness of water and complaint settlements. Around 88 percent is (very) satisfied with the execution of the prime task of water companies, that is, taking care of reliable tapwater (VEWIN, 1997).

Dutch consumers take it for granted that at any given moment they may expect clean and cheap water to run from the tap. The high quality of drinking water is appreciated and consumers do not seem to bother about the price of water. Finally, also the government promotes a high quality of drinking water, because the positive external effect on the collective well being is considered essential. Until the mid-1990s, the performance of the Dutch water companies was rated as 'good' to 'very good': the quality of the infrastructure, technical expertise, density, environmental performance, guaranteed delivery and water quality (NUS, 1995; ISW, 1997; VEWIN, 1996). For a brief industry analysis, organizational, technological, economic and legal aspects will be presented.

2.1 Organizational Aspects

The Dutch water industry has some unique characteristics. Broadly defined the Dutch water sector includes the activities and organizations involved in the supply of drinking water and the drainage and purification of waste water, also referred to as the water chain (see figure 7.1). The industry executes a number of water-related tasks, both in operational terms (collection, distribution, damming, drainage and purification), and in support activities (maintenance, supervision and planning). See figure 7.1.

One can distinguish between water companies, municipalities (collecting sewage), purification boards (water treatment and disposal) and District Water Councils (*Waterschappen:* effluent disposal and water source protection). Two ministeries (i.e. Public Health & the Environment and Public Works), twelve provinces (for regional environmental policy and partial shareholders of the drinking water companies), municipalities (as shareholders of the drinking water and the local sewage companies), and the semi-governmental entity *Rijkswaterstaat* (i.e. public engineering company for infrastructural works) are politically responsible for the development and implementation of water policy. VEWIN, the umbrella organization for the drinking water industry, is the liaison between the water companies and the national policy community, and also seeks to promote the collective interest of the drinking water sector as such (quality of service, promoting sectoral efficiency, sharing best practices, public education etc. The other two trade associations are the Union of District Water Councils (water management) and RIONED (sewage).

Our research focuses on the water supply companies in the Netherlands: those organizations directly involved in the raw water collection, water treatment and distribution of water in the Netherlands. The market structure of this water supply industry can be described as a system of regional public monopolies, holding long term concessions on behalf of the provinces, monitored through the ownership structure, be it provinces and/or municipalities. Internally most of the companies are organized like a classic public utility company with divisions organized along functional lines. Only a small minority of the companies had adopted a more consumer-oriented divisional structure in the mid-1990s.

Figure 7.1 The Dutch water system: upstream-downstream

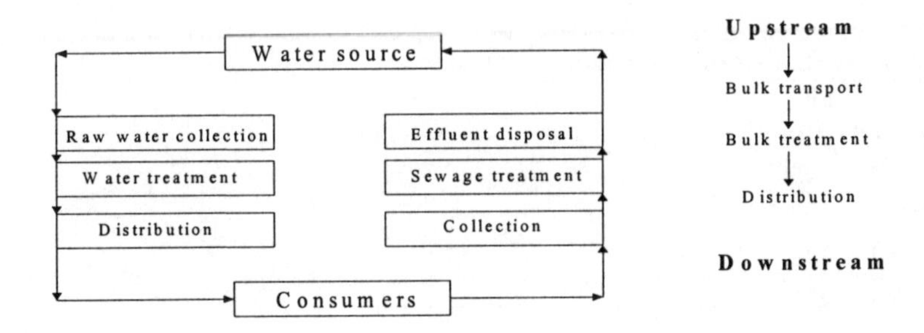

Around the turn of the 20th century, the water industry comprised of a very small number of public companies (see table 7.1). From the earliest concessions for Amsterdam and Den Helder onwards, in the mid 19th century, the Netherlands have had private companies with concessions for constructing and operating water networks. Nowadays, we speak of distribution areas, allotted on the basis of the Water Act. The system of concessions was the result of both a lack of sufficient expertise and an unwillingness to take financial risks on the side of the municipalities (ABN AMRO, 1996, p.8). In those days the private companies entering the market were often forwardly integrating steel companies providing the network, making large one-off investments (high sunk costs) and running operational risks. Still, the concessions did yield handsome rewards for all the parties involved. The number of water companies grew fast in the late 19th and the first half of the 20th century, from 68 companies in 1900 to 229 in 1938. The growth in the number of companies took place especially by running small networks. Until World War II a considerable number of companies stayed in private hands.

Since World War II, drinking water is supplied by a consistently decreasing number of municipal water companies, indicating a slow but persistent consolidation/concentration trend, that is orchestrated through legislation and sometimes enforced in courts (e.g. on Doorn, Maastricht and Groningen).

Between 1960 and 1980 (102 companies) the number of companies was halved, just like between 1980 and 1990 (53 companies).

Table 7.1 The number of water supply companies over the years

Year	Number of water supply companies
1900	68
1938	229
1967	146
1980	102
1990	53
2000	24

Source: www.vewin.nl, 2001.

By 2000 the number halved again. By 1997 we have 3 companies (of a different kind) who focus exclusively on water production; 3 (smaller) companies who focus on distributing externally supplied water; and 20 companies that are vertically integrated (see table 7.2), combining water production and supply. Of the 26 companies in total, 24 plc's are owned and controlled by local and regional authorities, with only one pure municipal service and one ltd.

There used to be huge size differences between the Dutch drinking water companies, but these differences decrease due to the effect of ongoing consolidation (see table 7.2). Most municipal networks have merged into bigger (sub-)regional networks. As their names suggest each company has its own geographic area. The concessions provided a water company exclusive rights for the distribution of water within the specified area. This geographic division of markets usually ran parallel with municipal or (sometimes) provincial boundaries, but the consolidation leaves only provincial water companies. Some expect the number of water supply companies to halve again to a dozen water companies in another decade.

Table 7.2 Overview of companies active in the water supply sector, 31/12/2000

Name	**Water**	**Delivery drinking water (million m3)**	**Empl. (fte)**	**Customers x 1000 connections**	**Labor intensity (FTE/ x 1000)**
WGr	G, S	47	226	267	0.85
Nuon WF a)	G	47	235	278	0.85
WMD	G	31	173	189	0.90
WMO a)	G, S, R	74	439	487	0.90
Hydron F	G	18	95	108	0.88
WGd a)	G	80	411	511	0.80
Nuon WG a)	G	51	73	290	0.25
Hydron MN	G	80	519	509	1.02
GWA b)	S, D	93	655	420	1.56
PWN	G, S, D	90	824	683	1.21
WBE	G	146	475	725	0.66
DZH	S	79	577	550	1.05
Hydron ZH	G, E	46	281	313	0.90
Delta	G, S	40	221	202	1.09
WMOB c)	G	104	548	586	0.94
WNWB c)	G	64	260	322	0.81
TWM	G	13	88	71	1.24
WML	G, E	68	471	456	1.03
NA	S	-	27	42	0.64
NM	G	6	30	34	0.88
Doorn	G	2.5			
WBB	S	-	62	-	
WRK	S	-	133	-	

Notes: Type of water used: G = ground; E = embankment; S = surface; D = dune; R = river. a) recently merged into Vitens; b) municipal service; c) merged into Water Brabant in 2001; d) WBB and WRK service other supply companies.

Source: Water Supply Statistics 2000 (VEWIN, 2002).

2.2 Technological Aspects

Drinking water is an amorphous bulk product, which comes into being when collected ground and/or surface water meets certain quality standards. Table 7.3 presents relevant data with regards to the relation between collection and consumption. Despite economic cycles and some price fluctuations the total distribution of water supplied via the water network has been relatively stable since 1989, at roughly 1.2 billion cubic meters per year. Of the total use of water 90 percent is collected by the companies themselves, in particular for industrial cooling, agriculture, and chemical treatments, and as base material for production beverages (see table 7.3). With regard to constructing and/of managing their installations or in the purification of the water, the water companies are hardly active. In line with the general tendency towards outsourcing non-core activities, industrial customers that are for their key operations dependent on collecting water (e.g. chemical companies) and owners of properties with large water networks (e.g. holiday resorts) seek to engage external parties, such as the drinking water companies but also specialized water service companies such as Vivendi, for their water sourcing and management demands.

It is noteworthy that, of the average domestic consumption of 130 liters per person per day, a mere 4 percent or 5 liters is used as drinking water (Water statistics 1996, p. 11); elsewhere, similar quota are reported (WSA, 1996). Domestic customers or simply put, households, dominate the demand for drinking water. The average Dutch household uses about 122.5 cubic meters per year, which means that some 60 percent of all drinking water is consumed by small-scale consumers (Consumer Association, 1997). Over the period 1995-2001 the average demand per person per day decreases by 1 percent per year to 126 liters. Around 95 percent of the water supplied by water companies is drinking water, with some 5 percent ‘other qualities’, mainly water of inferior quality used for industrial purposes (for instance rinsing) or in agriculture.

Nonetheless, the growth of the sales of this category of ‘other water’ is remarkable: VEWIN (2002) predicts a further growth to 100 million cubic meters, after a 6 percent growth per annum over the period 1996-2000. Some large-scale industrial and many small-scale agricultural consumers provide their own ‘other water’. In view of a lack of transparency of the ‘self-supply’ market of direct company intake and of the objectives of our research, we have limited ourselves to the water supply companies, i.e. the market for drinking water.

Table 7.3 The use of water in the Netherlands (total mln m^3 in 2000; in Euros)

	m^3 per connection per year	total demand	
Domestic consumers	< 300	741	(63%)
Intermediate users	300< ..< 10.000	214	(18%)
Large scale users	>10.000	172	(14.5%)
Various: leakage, firewater, measurement losses		54	(4.5%)
		------- +	
Subtotal drinking water quality		1181	(100%)
Other qualities		85	

Total delivered by water companies		1.266	(11%)
Direct company intake		11.300	(89%)*

Total water supplies		12.566	(100%)
Other statistics:			
Drinking water connections		7.042.000	
- of which metered		96%	
Turnover		Meuro 3.209	
Number of employees		6.803 fte	
Investments		Meuro 397	

*: Of which approximately 11.000 for cooling

Source: Water supply statistics 2000 (VEWIN, 2002).

The Dutch water suppliers use as their raw material either ground or surface water. Ground water by its nature is fairly pure and therefore requires limited treatment before it can be delivered to customers. The main sources of water are surface water taken from both large and small rivers. The take-in of water is organized efficiently, i.e. at large scale. Surface water is subjected to extensive treatment and it is directly passed on or subjected to dune and embankment infiltration. The result of these raw material characteristics and the greater distances in terms of transportation is that a more expensive purification treatment is required when compared to the use of ground water. Water quality is controlled directly after purification or, as with companies, at the point of delivery. Just as sourcing and purification, delivery is organized regionally. For delivery one created fine-grained networks with hardly any connections between regional networks.

To conclude, the water industry is organized primarily at a regional scale, oriented at full coverage, the highest possible quality and guaranteed delivery. The industry created an effective but rigid, capital intensive infrastructure, i.e. large scale vertically integrated systems.

2.3 Economic Aspects

In principle water is not a public but an individual good or a merit good. Public goods are defined as products where exclusive rights cannot be organized, and the use of a product by one does not exclude the use of that very product by the other. In various countries water is typically supplied as bottled water which is traded as an individual good in regular markets. Thus, exclusive ownership rights can be established. However, water may be called a merit good: in the Netherlands local authorities own the water companies, and the government prescribes, via the Water Act, that water rates have to be moderated for public health reasons (Hancher *et al.* 1997). Historical contingencies have made the Dutch water industry a quasi-collective good: water is supplied via public bodies, which have built a fine-grained natural monopoly infrastructure for the high-quality standard product.

The Dutch water companies provide just a few products. The standard product is drinking water for consumption, at a quality-standard much higher than prescribed. Prices are formally determined by the shareholders on proposition by the executive directors. Second, industrial water is delivered by water companies and consists primarily of drinking water quality (160 million m^3). Here, in principle prices, qualities, delivery schedules, etc., result from bilateral negotiations. Third, water of other qualities comprises primarily of some 'grey'-water for households and SME. Collection and delivery of basic water and drinking water requires very costly parallel systems. Fourth, water companies also provide water services, like laboratory services, billing for third parties, and environmental protection. In the Netherlands, the water supply companies are typically not involved in the purification of waste water.

In economic terms water is a so-called necessary product. Water is price inelastic and income inelastic: Demand hardly fluctuates as a result of a (modest) price fluctuation or changes in the economic climate. Various studies have shown that the so-called price elasticity is nearly zero, especially for households, with a best guess estimate of -0.4 (Kooreman, 1993; Wubben et al, 1998a). In economic theory, such a price elasticity is incompatible with either profit or turnover maximization (Wubben, et al, 1997): if they were, profits and turnover respectively could still grow significantly through (huge) price increases. Considering that the water industry shows an average profitability of 3 percent (Achttienribbe, 1997, 547), the companies appear to ignore the extra 'room' for extra profits or turnover: consumers, pumping up their own ground water (not subject to taxation), as well as by a growing number of the large customers (taxed at 0.08 Euro). Thus, we may conclude that water companies do not aim for maximization of profit or turnover. Industrial and agricultural demand is more sensitive to price changes. In these markets it is possible to influence demand through price policies. Their higher price elasticity is effective due to the room for maneuver offered by current legislation. An increase of the water price, due to ground water taxation of 0.15 Euro per cubic meter water, drawn from a well by water companies, resulted in evasive behavior by agricultural customers. This has resulted in an increase in such undesired phenomena as settlement, well exhaustion and land dehydration.

The water market is a mature, allegedly saturated mass market. Tap water is fully competitive with bottled water. In 2000 an average household uses almost 1,800 liters drinking water per year. When supplied by tap water it costs approximately 3 Euro. An equal amount of bottled water costs 1200 Euro: it is 400 times (sic!) more expensive than tap water. Over 2000, the average Dutch person still continues to consume 17 liters of mineral or bottled water (VEWIN 2001, p.23). Consumer tests did not indicate any significant taste differences between the two. To illustrate, near Utrecht the groundwater source for regular tap water is exactly the same as the source for the bottled A-brand Sourcy, located at the other side of the highway.

The water supply industry in the Netherlands is characterized by regional monopolies, that use capital-intensive vertically integrated infrastructures oriented at water intake and purification with the aim of guaranteed delivery of high quality water to households. The companies are typically public companies owned by provinces and municipalities, being regulated primarily at national and provincial level. So the supply of drinking water is a network utility with a natural monopoly. The minimally efficient scale (MES) of purification and transportation makes large-scale supplies in a geographically connected area desirable.

Furthermore, a single water supply-network is substantially cheaper than a system consisting of parallel networks. In this respect the water industry is a natural monopoly different from, for instance, mobile telephony. The market for large customers is open for in set competition. In fact one witnesses (international) competition on tenders for water supply and the purification of waste water only in large industrial areas, like the Rotterdam harbor. Finally, regarding economies of scale above MES, several publications conclude the following: "This implies an absence of scale economies at the level of the total appointed business." (OFWAT 1993, 10; OCFEB, 1997, 38). No calculations could be found on the advantages of exchange relationships. It is in contrast with the economies of scale arguments backing the growing list of mergers. In make or buy-decisions autonomy in sourcing seems to prevail. Merger is preferred over establishing exchange relations. Explanations for the ongoing consolidation in the Dutch water industry may be improving (vertically) public governance, fostering (horizontally) sectoral policies, and the strategic ambitions of top-managers.

The water industry is hindered by the *Tragedy of the Commons*: general resources are being used in excess, as those benefiting from it do not have to pay the cost. The reason is essentially that there is no owner sending the users a bill (Wubben, 2000). Especially land consolidation, drainage and water level maintenance is responsible for the relatively limited surface water supplies in the Netherlands. Water companies, farmers and industrial enterprises extract water from (usually non-durable) sources. As a consequence, the environment, especially water sources, are being damaged by fertilizers, pesticides, and water becoming brackish and bacteriologically contaminated.

Funding of the Dutch water industry is characterized by the total absence of government subsidies, a stable turnover, a high capital intensity and a domination of local and historical circumstances. Prices in principal are set to cover costs with write-offs based on the historical cost price. According to those involved the characteristics of public ownership and stable cash flows ensure that water companies get around 1.0 percent-point discount on capital loans when compared to companies in other sectors. We have established that in some cases profit shares transferred to the owners, provinces and municipalities are substantial. These transfers are a veiled taxation, often included in the political decision-making on local tax rates.

With regard to market entrance and substitution products the incumbents have a strong position. The predominant small and medium size water users are so-called protected customers; they are obliged to buy from their regional, public monopolist. As discussed above, there is evasive behavior on the side of large industrial customers and small agricultural customers. Law, not de jure but de facto, reduces even the potential amount of market entrants to the existing parties: market entrance is only allowed via mergers and acquisitions by other public companies. The natural monopoly situation makes new entry or third party access (so called in-set competition) unfeasible.

2.4 Political and Legal Aspects

The water industry is subject to no less than six, overlapping laws. The policy and governance framework of the Dutch water industry comprises several layers: self-regulation within the VEWIN-framework is combined with governmental regulation at various levels, especially concerning quality and public health aspects, mid-term infrastructural planning and guaranteed delivery. Legally speaking we can distinguish between national, regional and local levels of supervision (i.e. government and parliament, provinces, and municipalities). Because of local and regional ownership structures, monitoring and screening is more detailed at lower administrative levels.

One may distinguish between the water system and the water chain. At the national level the structure of the water chain is primarily determined by the Groundwater Act, and the following three pieces of legislation: the Water Management Act (WMA), which concerns surrounding water supplies; the Water Pollution Act (WPA) which concerns the collection, purification and drainage of (waste) water; and the Drinking Water Act (DWA), which concerns the collection, processing and distribution of (tap)water. The district Water Councils and the of DHPW are primarily involved with the WMA; the WPA is aimed at the district water and purification boards. This study is mainly concerned with the 1985 Drinking Water Act and its successor, comprising of the entire water chain from collection, via processing to distribution. Connected to or even at the basis of the water chain is the water system, to which above all the Drinking Water Act and the WMA are relevant. The provinces regulate all public and private water collection concessions. Water supply to households is regulated in contracts concerning the connection and supply conditions (Twynstra and Gudde, 1997).

At the ministerial level, two departments oversee and organize the sector. The DHPW is responsible for: (1) formulating policy regarding water-quality and a lasting water supply, through integral quality monitoring, water chain cooperation, and tackling dehydration and pollution issues; (2) monitoring adherence to environmental legislation, as defined in the Water Act, more specifically the quality of the (drinking) water, as well as monitoring the implementation of quality systems and certification. Second, the Department of Agriculture, Nature, and Fisheries is concerned with managing excess manure and fertilizers contaminating ground water. The Department for Economic Affairs, and the Competition Commission (NMa), primarily concerned with promoting economic dynamics in general, has increasingly become more powerful in the protected utility sectors thus far by proposing pro-market and private ownership policy alternatives.

Tasks converge at the provincial level. In addition to formulating policy with regards to the environment, traffic and transport, and water works, provincial authorities, by virtue of the Groundwater Act, have the following responsibilities: giving out licenses for groundwater collection and water management (for example, the reinforcement of river dikes). The provinces are also involved in executing and supervising policies. This concerns the supervision of the water industry (based on the Water Act and concessions that are not used any longer) and the supervision of the District Water Councils and regional water management. Finally, a number of provinces has a major stake in regional water companies: from an ownership point of view they are responsible for the 'micro-supervision' of the economic performance of the companies and the execution of their social and responsibilities.

At the municipal level, individual and/or collective supervision takes place on the basis of direct ownership. This micro-level supervision of the company's economic performance and the execution of its social task are especially concerned with the following points: the price of water, the level and quality of services, and the investment level of the company. Within the Netherlands, the regulation of the water industry is radically different from the other public utilities: it is the only one without direct price or profit regulation. Formally, the water tariffs are set in consultation with the Board of Commissioners (BoC), representing the shareholders (i.e. provinces and municipalities). But the members of the BoC, formally serve both the interests of the general public, and, as local authorities, also their own shareholders interests (e.g. concern for dividends and any other proceeds).

The following conclusions can be drawn from the sketch industry analysis. First, the popular positive opinion on the water companies is backed up by high ratings on quality and technological parameters. Second, the number of companies, almost all with shares in the hands of the local or regional authorities, is falling systematically from over 200 to 26 in a 50 years period. There are no economies of scale explanations for the (recent) consolidations. Third, there is neither direct competition nor market entry apart from in-set competition for large company customers. However, there is evasive behavior to pump up water for own use by small farmers and large companies. Fourth, domestic, price-inelastic consumers take some 60 percent of the rather stable turnover of drinking water quality. Fifth, water production and distribution is typically vertically integrated. Sixth, self-regulation and direct-ownership supervision are combined with selective governmental regulation at various levels, especially concerning quality aspects, mid-term planning and guaranteed delivery. The water companies are players in a complex network. In 1996, in a thorough industry analysis, the ABN AMRO concludes that for the time being there are no serious threats for the Dutch water supply industry; neither privatization, liberalization, market entrance, nor a serious change in governmental policies (ABN AMRO, 1996, pp.67/69). In strong contrast, however, already within one year the water industry was prioritized for a deregulation trajectory.

3A TIPPING THE WATER (DHPW-SCENARIO STUDY, 1997)

In 1996, preparations have begun with the formulation of the new Drinking Water Act. To facilitate that stakeholder-oriented revision process the DHPW published a scenario document, written by the Dutch consultant Twynstra Gudde (1997). The aim of that document is to clarify the discussion and the final decision making process with regard to the scope and form of the DWA so as to foster the preferred developments. This scenario trajectory is based on an open dialogue on the one hand, but, on the other, conditioned by statements issued by government and Lower House. It includes, e.g. the 1996-statement by the Dutch Lower House that vertically specializing on water collection, purification or delivery is out of order. This is in strong contrast to developments in other utilities.

The research trajectory arrived at five normative scenarios, that is, constructed possibilities which can be emulated: (1) Reference-scenario: the current situation. (2) All products and services are produced and delivered by Organizations with Exclusive Market rights (OEMRs) owned by (local) governments. In the scenarios three, four and five, respectively, industrial water, water of 'other qualities', and water services. Scenarios three, four and five may be combined. The scenarios are detailed for the operational delivery of water (quality, delivery, and price) and the sustainability of water resources (quality, delivery, returns, and protection of sources). The scenarios are compared on the costs and feasibility of the scenario-related organizational forms.

The detailed scenarios reveal interesting insights. With regard to the reference scenario the report emphasizes the lack of transparency, but without addressing the complexity of the sector and its relation with excessive investments (gold plating). The second scenario is elaborated in two directions. First, given an OEMR with a permanent concession, the scenario focuses on the question how to guarantee low prices under a monopoly. It is derived that the initial costs for the required expansion of surveillance will be much lower than the long run advantages of this scenario. An authority directing prices is advised. Second, presuming an OEMR with a limited concession period necessitates the separation of water companies into two companies, i.e. the infrastructure ltd. and the management ltd., consisting of personnel and managers running the business. The infrastructure ltd. is a public organization and made available to the winner of the tender for the management ltd. The sheer size of the maintenance costs (including re-investments) fundamentally hinders private ownership of infrastructure under this limited concession system. Nevertheless, it is concluded that the benefits of tendering will be higher than the sum of extra initial and periodic costs. With regard to the scenarios three, four, and five, it is emphasized that, due to the Cohen-committee, the water companies will have to reduce their stakes in the products/services to a minority position.

The scenario study is telling in that the aspect price is not brought into question, and technological system innovations are excluded from consideration. It is remarkable to find that the report concludes that under all scenarios the aspects price and business are amongst the undisputed items. In contrast, the researchers cast doubts on all other items, like safeguarding quality and certainty of delivery. The focus of attention of almost everyone in the industry was on exactly these items, in shrill contrast to prices and commercial returns. Wubben et al. (1998a) have put forward the opposite opinion: quality and delivery are far from problematic, in contrast to prices. Price was the derived variable, dependent on exogenous variables like quality.

There is not the least idea about regulatory capture, market entry by foreign companies, market power, productivity, or cost prices. This view is confirmed by the naivety regarding the dynamics of the sector after concessions have been tendered. Furthermore, the scenario-study, with a time horizon of 15 to 20 years, excludes technical developments from serious consideration. This is remarkable, because around 1997 ICT and membrane technologies are introduced at large scale. Surprisingly, at this point, the writers of the report warn against the narrow-mindedness of those active in this field (Twynstra & Gudde, 1997). Finally, evaluating this scenario-study, it may be concluded that the acknowledged window of opportunities was rather small.

3B NAVIGATING TO OPEN WATERS, 1996/97

In 1997, politicians, media, and the public at large were confronted with the publication of an exploration into the possibilities for introducing market elements in this somewhat inconspicuous sector. This econometric research into the water industry was conducted at the behest of the Department for Economic Affairs (OCFEB, 1997). See figure 7.2. As it is extracted, water is free of costs. Because of the *Tragedy of the Commons*-problem, groundwater collection is taxed. Still, three quarters of the companies (almost) exclusively uses perishable groundwater. A mere fifth of all the companies uses surface water only (see table 7.2). They are slightly more expensive on average. The share of small-scale users varies between 50 percent and 80 percent of sales, with an average of 63 percent. According to the OCFEB-rapport, annual wage costs per employee vary considerably from Euro 32.100 to Euro 48.300 with an average of Euro 39.073. The cost price of water per cubic meter varies between Euro 0.68 and Euro 1.68 at an average of Euro 1.08.

The rapport holds the opinion that the only legitimate reasons for a company to be expensive are variables over which the company has no control. Differences in cost prices that may not be attributed to such variables are understood as misuse of means, and therefore inefficiency. So we understand that, e.g., cost differences due to the conservation of nature in sourcing areas, important for quite a few companies, are not acceptable. The study uses the data enveloping method and 1991-95 data.

The researchers calculated potential gains by detailing cost-inefficiencies (corrected for client base, sourcing, number of connections), welfare losses (related to price elasticity), and profits. Cost-inefficiencies account for only one-third of all cost differences, adding up to 15.2 percent of total costs on average, or 158 MEuro (Dfl 350 million) in 1995. Welfare losses are rather small, i.e. 0.7 percent of total costs, which is due to the low price elasticity. Surprisingly, over the period 1991-95, profits grow from zero till over 5 percent of total costs. The soaring profits are disturbing as water companies used to be typically not-for-profit companies and captive users cannot switch to alternative suppliers.

Figure 7.2 Costs of drinking water for the average household in the Netherlands (total costs in DFl. per annum)

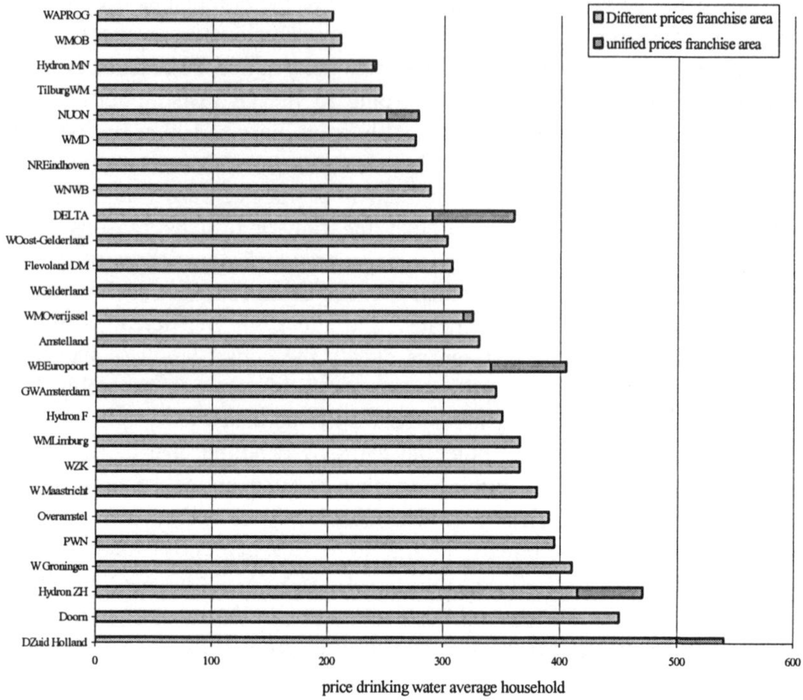

Source: Consumer Association, 1997.

The report derives results for a benchmark industry, i.e. the water companies of England and Wales. Over the period 1989 and 1996, under competition, standardized total costs fell by 12 percent in total. For the period 1991-1995 the standardized costs vary by 29 percent, with a spread of 12.9, both significantly better than the respectively 41 percent and 17.4 for the Netherlands. In England and Wales, competition, privatization, regulation, market dynamics and enforced cost cuts resulted in lower inefficiencies (average 9 percent), higher welfare losses (average 3.2 percent) and high, so-called 'fat cat', profits (average 30.9 percent). In this comparison, on two out of three items the Dutch companies perform better.

The potential gains for the Netherlands are primarily in reducing the cost-inefficiencies: a par position with British water companies regarding reducing inefficiencies boils down to 15.2 percent, derived above, minus 9.0 percent is

6.2 percent of total costs, or at least 63 MEuro (at an annual basis, prices 1995). The report suggests that considerable cost reductions could be achieved in both water supply and purification by a phased introduction of a mix of market mechanisms. It concludes that an efficiency gain of 6 percent to 15 percent was feasible through a number of policy measures, such as the establishment of a supervisory body, regular benchmarking and outsourcing.

The research turned out to be a good crowbar, but it had several serious detriments. The following drawbacks can be listed: (1) the company that is to serve as a yardstick could be different each year; (2) given the depreciation method used companies that have had to make recent investments immediately fall way back in such a comparison; (3) as long as the core activities of the water companies are not specified clearly and for a longer period of time it is impossible to make a proper comparison of the costs, precisely because all the useful/agreed-upon non-core activities will emerge from the calculations as purely inefficient users of resources; (4) finally, a reliable econometric comparison for the time being is too crude to produce any valid conclusions that are not already clichés to the parties involved. Nevertheless, at least the research succeeded in stirring up the sector. The Department for Economic Affairs used these data as ammunition for a more liberal Water Act.

4A WINDSTORM WARNING VEWIN-SCENARIO STUDY, 1997-98

In 1997, the widespread commotion that resulted upon the OCFEB-publication made the representatives of the industry decide in favor of a new and radical scenario study for the Dutch water supply companies (Wubben, et al, 1998a). Specific combinations of driving forces in the Dutch political economy were generated by collecting experiences with privatization, releasing market forces, and alternative regulatory regimes prevalent in other countries and/or other utilities. They give rise to logically distinct scenarios by combining sets of driving forces with predetermined elements, trends and uncertainties. The decision-making variables are regulation, differentiation/integration, cooperation, investments, chain integration, water quality, price, and delivery guarantees. Three possible scenarios were generated for the Dutch water industry and its institutional foundation.

With regard to predetermined elements, trends and uncertainties this research contrasted the earlier scenario study. Regarding predetermined elements, emerging trends and insecurities specific assumptions were made. The most important predetermined elements are (1) investments already made, and (2) the limited growth in demand for tap water. The latter is crucial for it reduces the potential market dynamics to a redistribution game between suppliers. The principal trends seem to be: a growing emphasis on surface water as a resource; ongoing concentration; the emergence of new techniques fostering decentralized water collection or denitrificatrion (e.g. membrane and filtering technologies); the emergence of new products (closed circuits, rain collection); allocative and dynamic efficiency are becoming more important to central authorities; the problems of resource management in relation to the long-term safeguarding of supplies. The key insecurities are the following: (1) the distance between the authorities (privatization) and water companies; (2) third-party access (TPA) or in-set competition; (3) applying new insights and rules regarding competition policy, corporate governance, the EU-transparency directive; (4) lowering of the access threshold through technical developments; (5) the principal orientation in a revised Water Act.

The three scenarios differ radically from one another[1]: The first scenario, entitled 'free navigation', places market forces on center stage: just let the water companies compete. The driving forces are the following: customer-driven; market forces take precedence over privatization; some deregulation; and, consolidation of capacity. A market-oriented public-private coalition will drive this scenario, resulting in a quickly transforming, industry-oriented cluster. There is also a group of cost-oriented ground water based companies, and the rest lacks a clear vision and strategy (market development or cost minimalization). The second scenario is based on private activities, with the government playing a defining role in relation to the water market with regard to both the market structure (licensing systems, subsidies, mobility thresholds, etc.) and the conditions to certain behavior (e.g. investment planning).

At crucial moments control would be in the hands of an external party, the supervisor. The driving forces are the following: privatization of the water companies; process-innovative companies; regional monopolies ('fringe' competition: inset appointments); interventionist government with regard to investments; 'level playing field' and consumer protection. The companies remain monopolists but through yardstick regulation efficiency is systematically improved. The burden of proof lies with the companies that are performing less well. The third scenario, emphasizes the advantages of cooperation and can be understood as self-regulation by the sector, reducing or preventing government intervention. The driving forces are cooperation, self-regulation, mutual adjustment, and limited government influence. This scenario can be described as an evolutionary adjustment, with a timely anticipation of environmental dynamics. The sector's umbrella organization is promoting local best practices at the national level. This can be the start of a further vertical integration along the water chain. It is especially the 'self-cleansing' quality of self-regulation within the water industry that here prevents government intervention.

The conclusions from this scenario-study are diverse. First, the attention paid towards legislation, technology, governance, economics, and business signals the liberalization of water industry to be complex, multi-facetted. Second, the research acknowledges the potential for pro-active strategic behavior by corporations and coalitions of public and private stakeholders. Finally, the object of this research is primarily the water industry and individual corporations, and much less public policy.

4B CHARTING NEW WATERS: BENCHMARK 1997

The pro-actively initiated benchmark study for the VEWIN was executed by Accenture Consulting, in 1998 on the basis of 1997-data (VEWIN, 1999). No less than 80 volume-percent of the delivered drinking water, was represented in this voluntary study. The aim of the study was to provide substantial insights into the performance of the water supply companies and to formulate Best Practices to improve business processes.

The following four perspectives were covered: Water quality (quality index figure); environment (LCA-index); services (report grade by client poll); and, finance and efficiency (closed model at company level and standardized operational costs at process level). As was to be expected, the results regarding water quality and environment were very positive: The quality-index of water was at 98 points out of a maximum of 100, radically exceeding the legal standard (60 points) and the VEWIN recommendations (81.5 points). The Environmental score of the water supply companies varies enormously between 5 and 69 points [hereafter denoted as: var.5-69]. Yet, the environmental impact of water per household is just a laughable 2,3 or 0,9 percent of the environmental impact of the production, distribution and consumption of respectively gas and electricity.

Thus, environment is a non-issue. Service levels are graded at 7.7 out of 10 [var.7.3-7.9], lower than a Dutch energy company (7.9) but higher than a retailer (7.0). However, only 15 percent of the companies enforce consumer standards and hardly any translates these standards into service guarantees. With regard to finance and efficiency the spread in drinking water tariffs is seriously discomforting. The tariffs per cubic meter for an average household vary no less than a factor 2.5. It implicates that anywhere between 0.4 percent to 1.2 percent of the family budget is spent on water. Total costs are determined by taxes, capital costs, operational costs, and depreciation costs. See table 7.4. Of operational costs 46 percent is related to labor, 33 percent to services by third parties, just 5 percent to purchasing water sourcing, and 16 percent to miscellaneous.

The research refers, respectively, to the following explanations of the cost differences: water sources; solvency targets; purification and transport costs, related to different sources; and sourcing, labor intensity, and client size. A value chain has also been detailed, comprising of the following activities: planning process; production process; distribution process; sales process; and, supporting activities. Production costs are largely determined by water sources. Client contact via paper is expensive, as is a relatively high number of distributive regional units, and the small size of production units. To conclude, the major savings are to be found in the cost categories operations and investments.

Table 7.4 Costs components in Dutch Guilders per cubic meter (1Dfl. = 0.4525 Euro.) Pooled stands for the top three companies versus the lowest three companies

Category	average	variance	multiplication factor
Total costs	2.54 (100%)	1.52-3.83	2.5
Taxes	0.30 (12%)	0.06-0.42	4 All groundwater vs. Surface water companies
Capital costs	0.44 (17%)	-0.05-1.28	5 (pooled)
Depreciation	0.43 (17%)	0.12-0.73	3 (pooled)
Operational	1.37 (54%)	0.95-1.88	2 (pooled)
Production	0.34	0.21-0.48	2.3 (pooled)
Distribution	0.47	0.34-0.67	1.5 (pooled)
Sales	0.14	0.09-0.18	2 (pooled)
Support	0.42	0.26-0.62	2.5 (pooled)

Source: VEWIN, 1999; Andersen Consulting, 1999.

The water industry was applauded for its unprecedented openness to this name-fame-and-blame benchmarking research. As long as market competition is absent administrative (benchmark) competition may work as well. It all depends on the social pressure managers feel when their company performance is sub-optimal. The results may be as good as market pressure, without the detrimental effects of exploiting and curbing monopoly rents. Serious criticism was also raised. Especially the absence of dehydration (local impact) in the environmental impact score, the delivery guarantees in the evaluation of services, and any labor intensity yardstick is criticized.

On the other hand, the evidently good water quality and environmental performance hardly justify a substantial attention in this benchmark. Also the discussion on core activities continues: is environmental protection of dunes and forests (related to water sourcing and water purification) a core activity? The most severe criticism relates to the non-participation of especially the industry-oriented water companies, Delta and Europoort. Thereby, the representativeness of the data set is seriously jeopardized. Finally, the monitoring of mid-and longer-term infrastructural investments was also brought into the debate (Pont, 1999, p.14).

By 1998, the water industry successfully integrated criticism. But despite the Benchmark initiative and lobbying, liberalization was again proposed in the 1998 Policy letter Revision Water Act, the so-called 'Policy Guidelines (*Hoofdlijnennotitie*)'. Due to intensive lobbying by the water industry through their VEWIN association, a public health scare caused by a number of legionella infection, and a fundamental disagreement between a pro-competition Cabinet and a more conservative Parliament supporting the public service monopolies, a Policy Letter was sent to the House instead of a Water Act. This Policy letter presented a kind of balancing act between liberalizing industry water provision on the one hand, and direct ownership supervision, and imposed governmental regulation.

By April 1998, still somewhat surprisingly, and in the wake of the election period, the Lower House voted against any of the proposed pro-market experiments. The members of the House referred to the potential negative consequences for tariffs, public health and the environment (Lower House, 1997/98, 25869, nr.2). In the motion Feenstra, supported by a large majority in Parliament, the social-democrats pushed forwards some precautionary principle, namely; 'No liberalization, unless.. .' The burden of proof regarding liberalization is on the proponents. The result was the initial policy guidelines became watered down and now the central government had to support and promote sector-wide self regulatory initiatives in the area of water economies, water companies' development towards a 'greener' management, the creation of user councils, integral quality provision and internal benchmarking. The water industry successfully lobbied against liberalization and administrative ring fencing and pro-actively initiated a major benchmark study.

By 1999, the benchmark led to a major increase in cost-cutting consultancy work in the water sector, further improvement of corporate control-mechanisms, and a loss of direction in related public policies. The companies preferred slow incremental change, without firing any employees. The industry even signed an agreement not to fire any employee for the unacceptably long period of a whole decade. With regard to corporate control, the DHPW decided to re-assess the Water Act proposals: the newly appointed responsible minister Pronk announced a ban on privatization, and market experiments. It was unclear, however, how much of this agenda he could realize in the political arena. The public at large was still in the hands of the market adepts, but criticism against liberalization was raised more and more often. It is indicative that the coalition party social-democrats openly moved the burden of proof to the proponents of further liberalization in any industry. At the same time, new mergers took place amongst the publicly owned water companies. The only remaining Ltd amongst water companies, that is Doorn, was de facto nationalized, i.e. taken over by another water supply company. As a widely appreciated result, all companies started initiatives to improve their own performance.

5A IN THE RAPIDS: A.D.LITTLE-SCENARIO STUDY 3, 1999

By 1999, the future prospects of the water supply companies were undecided and the debate continued. The consultancy A.D. Little (1999) published another scenario-study for the members of the industry association VEWIN. The object of this study is primarily the individual corporation, and much less the future organization of the water industry and/or public policy. Many companies remained hesitant: How revolutionary would the transformation be in the end? Is a multi-utility more suitable, better acceptable and feasible than an integrated water-chain company; etc? This study tried to provide a clear picture of the possible strategic choices open to the companies and their consequences.

First, the research distinguished between five business models, each one specified along three dimensions: (1) functions, e.g. infra-management; (2) products, e.g. tapwater, and bottled water; and, (3) processes, e.g. purification, and sewerage. The five business models are the following: Mono-water supply company; Waterchain company; Integrated multi-utility; Multi-utility service provider; and, Multi-utility infrastructure manager.

The prime uncertainties taken into consideration for the scenarios are, first, market-restructuring and speed of implementation, and, second, the impact of innovation and product differentiation. The first uncertainty is determined by the indistinct policy guidelines by the EU and Dutch government. The second uncertainty is determined by unknown technological learning curves and diffusion patterns. With regard to a radical reduction of the minimal efficient scale, much is expected from membrane technology. ICT-induced innovations in metering technologies facilitate liberalization.

The two axes of uncertainties stretch out in two directions defining four scenarios. The first scenario, called valuable water, combines strong innovation and product differentiation with gradual market restructuring: Infrastructure remains public business, but trade and delivery of water is privatized. Law clusters ownership and management of infrastructure. The second scenario, the rapids, combines strong innovation with radical market restructuring: private companies partake in concessions; advancement of decentralized water supply; increase in number of players and product differentiation. Pressure is towards specialization, resulting in debundling of functions and processes.

The third scenario, named waterway, unites limited innovation with radical market restructuring: private participation via concessions; regulated network company to stimulate Third Party Access. This scenario stimulates bundling along all dimensions, offering substantial cost advantages. It will result in capitalization of the power position of the asset owner. Finally, customer loyalty may be enhanced. The fourth scenario, headed watership down, joins the limited innovation with gradual market restructuring: water supply companies integrate with sewerage and waste water purification; billing is outsourced; liberalization and privatization forbidden by law. Due to a lack of incentives most probably all functions will remain bundled. Water will be distinguished from other more 'commercial' products, and the water chain will be realized.

Next, the study concentrates on the best strategic fit of water supply business models with the different scenarios. Note, however, that the researchers do not detail the yardstick of strategic fit or success of a modality. The still predominant mono-water supply company turns out to be second best to the waterchain company in all circumstances; this mono-company modality seems to be useful when any commitment to a specific scenario is rationally impossible. The waterchain company is superior to all in the scenarios with limited innovation. The integrated multi-utility is to be preferred when the market does not enforce specialization, that is in less innovative environments. The multi-utility service provider holds the by far most interesting position merely in the rapids-scenario. However, it is not the radical restructuring that is crucial here, but the potential for innovation and product differentiation. It is noteworthy to mention that the multi-utility infrastructure manager seems to be the more successful modality in a radically restructuring industry. Nevertheless, it is at best the second best modality in all four scenarios. The study details also the potential for expansion under the different modalities.

5B FALLING TIDE, SECOND BENCHMARK, 2000

The second Benchmark study is executed in 2001, using data of the financial year 2000. The structure of the research is almost identical to the first Benchmark study on 1997-data: the four perspectives remain identical, and the presented 1997-data were adjusted for changes in definitions and participants. This second benchmark takes account of several of the deficiencies of the first study, like dehydration and labor intensity data. However, no extra data are available on investments or consumers. This time, the researchers managed to collect data for 90 volume-percent of the delivered drinking water (Accenture, 2001). Especially, the inclusion of the industry-oriented, Rotterdam-based WaterBedrijf Europoort (WBE) raised participation by 10 percent points. See table 7.5 for the results. The 1997-data are represented in between brackets.

For the year 2000, the results on most items are not substantially at odds with the 1997 benchmark. The results regarding water quality and environment are again very positive. The quality-index of water comes to a halt at 97.2 points ['97: 96.5] out of a maximum of 100, again dramatically exceeding the legal standard (60 points) and the VEWIN recommendations (currently 76.2 points). The water supply companies themselves seem to take the precautionary principle to the extreme. The environmental impact score improves nicely to 25 index points per cubic meter [var.13.5-38.3]['97: 26.8]. That variable is very sensitive to minor improvements, as for one company already the full switch to green electricity has an impact of some 50 percent regarding the environmental impact score. Service levels are graded at 7.6 ['97: 7.7] which is higher than the retailer (7.3)['97: 7.0].

Criticism has increased on billing and written contacts. Surprisingly though, over the three-year period since 1997 the number of companies enforcing consumer standards has risen strongly from 15 percent to 60 percent. The evaluation of the water industry by clients in comparison to the retailer is, however, not so positive now and less pronounced.

Over the three-year period, overarching the two benchmarks, drinking water tariffs have risen more than both the Consumer Price Index (CPI) and costs (see table 7.5). Tariffs have risen on average by 11 percent to 1.34 Euro per cubic meter. For an average household the tariffs differ by a factor 2, similar to 1997. Tariff-increases amount to 4.1 percentage points above aggregated CPI, which is 6.9 percent. Total costs have risen by 5.0 percent on average since 1997. Especially for the industry-oriented companies, like Europoort, different measurements result in rank-differences up to six places in a list of 15 companies. The company specific cost differences over the years are explained primarily by higher depreciation costs and capital costs. Compared to 1997, a substantially larger share of operational costs is related to outsourcing to third parties, i.e. from 33 percent in 1997 to 40 percent in 2000. The share of costs related to labor has fallen from 46 percent in 1997 to 42 percent in 2000. The operational costs per connection have increased by 3.4 percent.

Table 7.5 Costs and growth for various components by 2000, in Euros

Category	average per liter (a)	Average per connection (b)	dispersion factor costs per connection (c)
Total costs	1.28 +11%	205 +5%	1.64 [1.75]
Taxes	0.13 +5%	20 +3%	4.9 [4.5] (ground- vs. surface water corp.)
Capital costs	0.29	46 +4%	4.2 [5.6] (pooled)
Depreciation	0.26	42 +12%	2.2 [2.7] (pooled)
Operational	0.66	97 +3.4%	1.7 [1.5] (pooled)
Production		21 +3%	1.8 [2.1] (best ground- vs. surface water corp.)
Distribution		29 –22%	1.6 [1.9] (pooled)
Process-support		8.9+ 8%	2.6 [2.7] (best ground- vs. surface water corp.)
Sales		12 + 13%	2.6 [2.1] (pooled)
General process		28 +20%	2.0 [1.9] (ground- vs. surface water corp.)

(a) the average costs for the cost-components for 2000 per cubic meter, and the total increase;
(b) average costs per connection in 2000 plus total increase since 1997, when available;
(c) the multiplication factor between the highest and lowest cost scores per connection for 1997 and 2000 (data on 1997 between brackets). Here, for 1997, the authors derive some data. Pooled stands for the top three vs. the worst three companies.

Source: VEWIN, 2001; Accenture, 2001.

Over the period under scrutiny, substantial cost cuts have been realized at operational costs, especially in the distribution process. In sharp contrast with these findings, the costs for capital, depreciation, sales and the general process have risen substantially. Operational costs per connection have risen by 3.4 percent in total. Nevertheless, total operational costs have risen by 10 percent over this period (Accenture, 2001b, p. 18).

Further information as to the performance may be provided by labor productivity (FTE per 1000 connection) and the weighed average capital costs (WACC). In 2000, the average labor intensity is 1.13, between a minimum and maximum of respectively 83 and 144 (both pooled), differing by a factor 1.73. (Vewin, 2001, p.64; Vewin, 2002b, p.17). Some professionals claim an efficient utility company has to realize a labor intensity of 1.0 fte per 1000 connections for a mono-water company and 1.0 fte per 1500 connections for a multi-utility, like NUON. In that respect it is remarkable that both the top- and worst performers comprise of multi-utilities and mono-water companies. Taking the yardstick of 1.0 as standard, the worst performers still have a potential for productivity improvements of no less than 40 percent! Strangely enough this Benchmark information is at odds with the Water Supply Statistics 2000. Two-thirds of the companies perform better than the yardstick, pushing average labor intensity below 1.0. It is acknowledged in the report that the costs differences of sales, distribution, and the general process are to be explained primarily by labor intensity (Vewin, 2001b, p.13).

Next, the WACC was high and has risen by approximately 5 percent, on average per connection. One may question the rise in capital costs and depreciation. Capital costs are related to solvability targets on the one-hand and on the other hand dividend policies. The costs for equity represent no less than 42 percent of total costs of capital, or twice the solvency ratio. Dividend did not increase much. As a result, the solvency ratio has risen on average from 15 percent to 19 percent, i.e. 1 billion Euro [var.1 percent-42 percent]. None of the companies accords to standard practices to improve solvency ratios by issuing new shares. One may conclude that the labor intensity, and the WACC are at least not impressive.

Do we see the emergence of gradually more efficient so called *fat cats* in the Netherlands? The parties involved in the benchmark are positive about the instrument and the results (VEWIN, 2001b). However, Accenture (2001b) noticed that top managers in the water companies set the potential for improvement at a maximum 10 percent for their own companies, being at the same moment much more optimistic for the industry in total: the potential and ambition is with the neighbors (Accenture, 2001a, p.21), not in their own backyard? The report itself indicates cost cutting potential in operations, investment rationalization, and tax-reduction. Those involved in the Economic Affairs department criticize the freedom not to participate in the study as well as the resulting selectivity of the data basis (VEWIN, 2001b). In this three-year period both the operational costs, total costs and the tariffs have risen by around 11 percent per liter, which is 4 percent in excess of the inflation rate. There has not been any real cost cutting. Also the variance of various cost categories has not improved much. The enthusiasm for the benchmark study is amazing, considering the development over time of tariffs, costs, labor intensity, and WACC, consumer satisfaction and the opinions of management. Although the results have not been impressive so far and the sense of urgency seems to be lost, most stakeholders have already become convinced about the benchmark.

6 NAVIGATING WITHOUT COMPASS? 2 SCENARIO-STUDIES, 2000-01

From 2000-01, two additional scenario studies are worth mentioning. These publications confirm that the trend in orientation shifts to the internal organization. The consultancy Twynstra Gudde published the results of extensive research, in winter 2001 (Twynstra Gudde, 2001). The emphasis is on the organizational consequences of alternative scenarios: what are the consequences for the strategy, structure, systems, labor, management style, and culture of future water supply companies? Structural forces shaping the prospective water industry are: sustainability (integrated water chain management), technological innovation, increasing (pan-European) deregulation and liberalization, and further efficiency concerns. The companies can evolve into a regional provider of drinking water, a (specialized) participant in the water chain (drinking water, waste water treatment, sewage treatment), a subsidiary of a multi-utility, and an international water services company. In an intermediate series of meetings with top-managers it became evident that the managers still do not seem to know what development trajectory to take. Everything can become crucial, and thus no priorities can be set.

Furthermore, in 2001, Accenture publishes a brochure, with the meaningful title ‘Who takes the lead?’ (Accenture, 2001a). It presents the results from a survey amongst top managers of Dutch water companies. It does not present scenarios but business models. It becomes evident with this report that the ambitions of top managers and government is lagging behind practices and ambitions in other utilities (Accenture, 2001, p.20). The publication seems to signal that more ambition is needed to grasp the potential. The publication boils down to an almost desperate exclamation: "Water supply industry, take the lead!" (Accenture, 2001a, p.43). These two scenario-studies together confirm the lack of a sense of urgency. The momentum seems to have disappeared while there is still enough to improve upon.

Also after the second benchmark different companies initiate diverse initiatives to reduce the costs. For example, in the region Amsterdam and The Hague, collaboration between four water companies is intensified. Furthermore, three water companies in the west and the center of the country combine forces in the mutually owned co-operative Hydron. It emphasizes the competition for procurement initially it should be active in engineering, ICT, marketing and the laboratory (Vass, 2002). The best known consolidation is a series of consolidations of the multi-utility NUON: besides buying smaller utilities abroad and a number of specialized service companies, it acquired several local and regional energy and water monopolies, and recently merged its water division with two regional water supply companies in the East of the Netherlands. At more or less the same time the Department of Housing, Public Works and the Environment (DHPW) has sent a revised Water Bill to Parliament to ascertain that the ownership of water companies will remain in public hands and within national boundaries. It further contains obligatory benchmarking, and central authority to control tariffs, and oversee large investments.

7 CONCLUSION

The water industry in the Netherlands is indicative of the rise and fall of liberalization in the public arena in at least the Netherlands. Around 1996/97, the water industry was already in the process of consolidation, consumers were satisfied, markets were saturated, and price elasticity was low. The discussions on the revision of the Drinking Water Act, initiated in 1996, opened up Pandora's box on how to liberalize the sector and engineer competition, as illustrated by the various scenarios developed from then onwards. While the drinking water industry favored the status quo and gradual change, the Ministry of Economic Affairs initiated and propagated the liberalization debate; also some renegade water companies like NUON and Delta, actively preparing for multi-utility liberalization and privatization, clearly advocated change from inside the water industry.

The almost perfect performance regarding water quality and environmental performance, and the excessive costs of inset competition and third party access lacking feasibility, prevented radical and disruptive change.

Although the government and the Ministry of Economic Affairs in particular effectively put change as a policy option on the agenda it was unable to take on leadership in the transformation of the industry (and accomplishing yardstick competition and pricing regulation), as it was constrained by a coalition of parliament and the water industry, supporting the status quo. The pro-active water industry, however, initiated voluntary, open benchmark-studies to neutralize criticism, and advocated gradual concentration between the water supply companies. The rather positive image of the sector, backed up with positive data from the industry (with the exception of prices) may have helped to counter the deregulation. A more negative element in this self-assessment trajectory is that the ongoing consolidation of the industry lacks any sound economic basis, while the consolidation itself may reduce the value of the benchmark (Dijkgraaf et al., 2002). Moreover, already the second benchmark-study shows a downturn in eagerness to improve the results.

The prime attention in the impressive series of scenario studies shifted from being relatively more policy-driven, via industry-driven, to relatively more company-driven. The interplay between the speculations in the scenario studies and the representation of data by the various empirical studies resulted in a variety of experiments, collaborations and integration between 1996 and 2001. However, the impetus seems to loose strength: as a result the most recent scenario-studies, especially the one by Accenture in 2001, call for a resolution: Who takes the lead? The absence of a European Water directive as part of the European agenda may have been crucial in neutralizing the national liberalization tendencies. Also the lack of (financial) scandals, and public discontent (e.g. as in the UK) strengthened the position of the incumbents. As the scenario studies show, the water industry prepared themselves for all eventualities, and initiated the benchmark-studies to neutralize criticism.

It took until 2001 before the revised Water Act, already announced in 1996, was finally sent to Parliament. The deregulation trajectory of the coalition governments of social democrats, liberal-conservatives and liberal democrats (i.e the two Kok Cabinets) and in particular of the Ministry of Economic Affair basically ran aground: the idea for economic liberalization and hence creating a dynamic water industry was marginalized in the discussion. Ironically, governmental planning and control, by the other Ministry DHPW, seems to have won. Given the lack of major strides in liberalization on the one hand, and major cost-cuttings over the last years on the other, something like the advised obligatory participation in the benchmark, the marginal efficacy-test for investments, and a modest national tariff regulator seems indeed needed to reinforce the ongoing efficiency drive. However, it is difficult to assess what are the most effective means of change, as British research into these matters indicates (Dean, et al. (1999). More detailed research on these matters is needed.

The result will be that water companies come to operate at arms' length from governmental control, with regional service contracts for both water collection and distribution. To conclude this study we can stipulate that the great expectations to deregulate the industry by the Kok Cabinets were dashed by a combination of a pro-active water industry and a majority in parliament supporting the present public monopoly structure and quality of service levels. Some minor changes, intended or by accident, took place over the last year, yet transforming the industry, such as ongoing consolidation, mandatory benchmarking, and the establishment of a national pricing and investments regulator, also illustrate the victory of regulation (which had not yet been seriously considered in the discussions) and the resilience of (now larger) public monopolies.

NOTES

1. The division into 'free navigation, convoy and pilot' as possible medium term development paths for a policy area such as the provision of Dutch drinking water is derived from the Arnbak et al (1990) study group, that has carried out a research project for the Interdepartmental Information Policy Committee.

REFERENCES

ABN AMRO (1996), De Watersector: Visssen in troebel water, of hoop op een kristalheldere toekomst, Amsterdam.

Accenture (1999), Reflections on performance. Benchmarking in the Dutch Drinking Water Industry 1997. Amsterdam.

Accenture (2001a), Reflections on performance 2000. Benchmarking in the Dutch water industry. Amsterdam.

Accenture (2001b), *Wie neemt de leiding? Het resultaat telt.* Amsterdam

Achttienribbe, G.E. (1997), 'Onwijs over water', *H_2O*, 18 (30): 546-550.

Arnbak, J.C., Van Cuilenburg, J.J. and Dommering, E.J. (1990), *Verbinding en Ontvlechting in de Communicatie. Een studie naar Toekomstig Overheidsbeleid voor de Openbare Informatievoorziening.* Amsterdam: Cramwinckel.

Dijkgraaf, E., R. Aalbers and M. Varkevisser (2002), 'Fusies saboteren eerlijke prijzen op drinkwatermarkt', *Het Financieele Dagblad,* 2 July, 2002: p.9.

Dean, A,Y. Carlisle, and C. Baden-Fuller (1999) 'Punctuated and continuous change: The UK water industry', *British Journal of Management*, 10, S1, 3-18.

EUREAU (1997), *Management Systems of Drinking Water Production and Distribution Services in the EUR Member States in 1996.* Brussels. EUREAU.

Godet, M. (1987), *Scenarios and strategic management.* London: Butterworths.

International Water Supply Association (ISW) (1997), *International Statistics for Water Supply*. London.

Hancher, L., W. Hulsink, and K. Sevinga (1997) 'Netherlands', in: Lewington, I. (1997), *Utility Regulation 1997*, London: Privatization International, pp.125-131.

Kooreman, P. (1993), 'De prijsgevoeligheid van huishoudelijk watergebruik', *Economisch Statistische Berichten*, 78, pp.181-183.

Lindblom, C.E. (1959), 'The science of muddling through', *Public Administration Review,* 19, 79-88.

Little, A.D. (1999) 'Toekomstige bedrijfsmodellen waterleidingbedrijven: verkenning van opties'. Rotterdam. A.D. Little.

Lower House (1997-98), Motie van het lid Feenstra c.s. Herziening Waterleidingwet [Revision Water Law. Motion by Feenstra, a.o.], 25869, nr.2. SDU Uitgevers: The Hague.

Ministerie van Economische Zaken (1998), *Markt en overheid: Analysegroep watersector. Markt activiteiten van waterleidingbedrijven.* The Hague. Ministry of Economic Affairs.

National Utility Service (NUS) (1995), *1994 International Water Price Survey*, Croydon.

OCFEB (1997), 'Mogelijkheden tot marktwerking in de nederlandse watersector', The Hague. Ministry of Economic Affairs.

OFWAT (1993), *Comparing the cost of water delivered, Initial research into the impact of operating conditions on company costs*, Birmingham.

Pont, H. (1999), Waterspiegel, nr.1, maart 1999, p.14.

Pressman, J.L. and A. Wildavsky (1984), *Implementation: How great expectations in Washington are dashed in Oakland* ... (1973). Berkeley: University of California Press.

Quinn, J.B. (1978) 'Strategic Change: Logical Incrementalism', *Sloan Management Review*, 19, 613-627.

Romanelli, E. and M.L. Tushman (1994) 'Organizational transformation as punctuated equilibrium: An empirical test', *Academy of Management Journal*, 37 (5), 1141-1166.

Schoemaker, P. (1995), 'Scenario planning: a tool for strategic planning', *Sloan Management Review*, Winter, 25-40.

Twynstra Gudde (2001), 'Water Voorzien', Amersfoort.

Twynstra Gudde (1997), 'Scenarios voor de herziening van de waterleidingwet', The Hague: VROM.

Vass, P. (2002), 'Competition and restructuring in the UK Water Sector', *Journal for Network Industries*, 3 (1).

VEWIN (1997), Wensen en keuzes. Jaarverslag 1996, Rijswijk.

VEWIN (1997) Water statistics 1996, The Hague

VEWIN (1998), Waterspiegel, 4e jr., nr.2, The Hague.

VEWIN (1999), Water in zicht: Benchmarking in de Drinkwatersector 1997, The Hague.

VEWIN (1999), Waterspiegel, 4e jr., nr.1, The Hague.

VEWIN (1999) Benchmark Special Waterspiegel., 4e jr., nr.4, The Hague.

VEWIN (2001) Water in zicht 2000: Bedrijfsvergelijking in de drinkwatersector, The Hague.

VEWIN (2001b), Waterspiegel, jr.4, nr.4. november, The Hague.

VEWIN, (2002) Water Supply Statistics 2000, The Hague.

VEWIN (2002b) Addendum to Water in zicht 2000, The Hague.

Wack, P. (1985), 'Scenarios: Uncharted waters ahead', *Harvard Business Review*, Sept-Oct. pp.72-89.

Water Services Association (WSA) (1996), *Waterfacts 1993*, London, p. 45.

Wubben, E.F.M., Hancher, L. and Hulsink, W. (1998a), 'Stille Wateren Hebben Diepe Gronden' Deel I: Over vormen van ordening en toezicht in de Nederlandse Waterleidingsector. Erasmus University Rotterdam *Management Report Series*, no.58-1998.

Wubben, E.F.M., Hancher, L. and Hulsink, W. (1998b), 'Stille Wateren Hebben Diepe Gronden' Deel II: Organisatie en regulering van de drinkwatervoorziening in Engeland and Wales, Frankrijk en Schotland. Erasmus University Rotterdam *Management Report Series*, no.59-1998.

Wubben, E.F.M. (ed.)(2000) *The dynamics of the eco-efficient economy. Environmental regulation and competitive advantage.* Cheltenham: Edward Elgar.

PART FOUR

Conclusion

8. Engineering Competition – or Engineering Regulation?

Leigh Hancher

1 INTRODUCTION

The various contributions to this volume touch on a number of sectors which were traditionally organized along monopolistic and often state-owned lines and which have been subjected over the past decade to a process of liberalization. Liberalization is synonymous with the withdrawal of the state's role as entrepreneur – in other words privatization. It is not necessarily the same as de-monopolization as there are many examples of industries being transferred to the private sector without any significant degree of re-structuring. Liberalization is certainly not the same as de-regulation; indeed the past decade has witnessed the steady growth of detailed, complex regulation. Engineering competition is therefore a process – a complex process which involves the transition to liberalized markets where competition can flourish. It is of course a well-known truism that competition is not an end to itself but a means to an end: the reliance on competition to produce goods and services is based on the assumption that market forces can deliver more efficiently and effectively than top-down planned processes and that market forces, if suitably engineered can adequately protect consumers from abuses of market power. This is the function of regulation.

The current debates surrounding the regulation of what are generally characterized as network industries – sectors such as post, telecommunications, energy, railways and water – all of which are dependent on the provision of capital-intensive infrastructures – focus essentially on three issues. Has liberalization worked – has the withdrawal of the state from infrastructure provision been justified? Has de-monopolization been secured to an adequate level so that incumbents are indeed less powerful than before? Is detailed sectoral regulation a necessary as well as a sufficient condition for markets to develop and work properly – could this latter function not be guaranteed by generic competition law principles? At what point in time can generic competition replace sectoral rules? Different disciplines examine these three questions from different starting points and on the basis of different sets of analytical tools. The analysis provided by an economist or a political scientist will differ in many respects from that provided by a legal perspective and yet a full understanding of the process of engineering for competition demands a combination of insights from all three, especially when it comes to the crucial question of assessing whether or not the transition to competition is sufficiently guaranteed so that sectoral regulation can wither away. Added to the debate over these three essential elements is the growing debate on governance – irrespective of whether we assume sectoral regulation is a passing or transitional phase on the way to a fully-functioning market – urgent attention should be paid to the mechanics of regulation and whether the process of regulation meets established standards of legitimacy, fairness and transparency. Competition should not be engineered at any price. The tools employed should be critically assessed. Again multi-disciplinary approaches are inherent in the governance debate. In this short concluding chapter I will examine these issues further, drawing upon the multi-disciplinary contributions to this volume.

2 LIBERALIZATION AND PRIVATIZATION

In his introductory contribution Professor Van Miert suggests that the state should back off from being an entrepreneur but that it still has an important role to play, as a regulator, an enforcer of rules, as promoter of modern infrastructure and as a guarantor of a free and socially balanced society. From this perspective the state should not play a direct role in the provision of network services or network infrastructures but should ensure only that a modern and efficient infrastructure is fully available. Professor Van Miert hints that this could be achieved by the provision of state aid under certain conditions and for certain purposes – for example to promote environmentally friendly forms of power generation. This would be a limited role for the state indeed and in practice it seems that few governments in Europe are prepared to wait on the side-lines of the famous level-playing field, occasionally providing financial incentives to struggling players. The contribution from Professor Vass documents clearly the failure of liberalization in the UK water sector and the transition from share-holder ownership to customer ownership. The recent reversal of privatization of the railways infrastructure in the UK and more recently the Netherlands also indicates that in certain sectors at least, market forces cannot deliver the goods: the state must continue to act as entrepreneur in the market, and not just as guardian of the market. Certainly this process is by no means uniform across all sectors. Privatization in the telecommunications sector is not likely to be reversed even if the economic climate for telecommunications companies in 2001 was not as rosy as in preceding years.

Parker in his contribution to this volume doubts whether the debate about the merits of privatization can be couched in a discussion over the choice between the merits of monopoly state ownership and competitive private markets. The real choice is often between state monopolies and private monopolies or at least firms that remain dominant in their markets for some time. Regulation is about proxy competition – it is about setting the 'rules of the game'. It is also a complex balancing act between advancing the interests of consumers, the interests of investors in the incumbent utility and the needs of potential competitors. The gradual replacement of sector-specific regulatory rules of the game with generic competition based rules may well enhance rather than reduce regulatory risk for the utility firm as the scope for discretionary intervention is arguably enlarged under the latter regime as opposed to the former.

3 RE-REGULATION OR RE-NATIONALIZATION?

The energy sector presents a more complex picture however. The adoption of the European internal market directives for electricity[1] and for gas[2] required as a starting point towards de-monopolization, a certain degree of unbundling. The Electricity Directive required the managerial separation of the transmission function as well as accounting unbundling for all functionally separate activities. The Gas Directive requires only accountancy unbundling. In March 2001 the European Commission issued proposals for revisions of both directives. A central theme in its proposals is the strengthening of unbundling requirements as well as an enhanced role for sector-specific regulation and sector-specific regulators. The European Council or the European Parliament has not yet accepted these proposals. There is substantial debate as to whether for example, the transmission function should not only be fully separated out as a commercial and managerial function but also that transmission assets should be separately owned from generation or distribution assets. It is doubtful whether the Commission has the legal as well as the political power to require such radical re-structuring. Controversial too are the Commission's demands for the creation of sector-specific regulators as opposed to leaving it up to Ministries or competition authorities to regulate the industry. Less controversial it would seem is the Commission's conception of the role and function of transmission system operators (TSOs) and the relationship between the state and this entity. The Commission like any other public authority cannot afford to overlook the continuing concern throughout the electricity and to a lesser extent, the gas industry that new, private investment in production capacity and transmission capacity has not been developing as hoped. In the former, monopolistic world, energy companies could afford to build excess capacity to be used as a buffer to meet sudden fluctuations in demand. The costs of maintaining idle capacity were simply passed through to the customer in final tariffs. In the liberalized, quasi-competitive market this option is no longer so attractive and regulators might be unwilling to allow these costs to be passed on.

Extending transmission capacity is capital-intensive, fraught with environmental and health-related issues and perhaps not always economically attractive for the incumbent TSOs. At the same time there are important bottlenecks between key markets in Europe so that trade in electricity between countries has remained rather static – at approximately 8% of total consumption.[3] Partly at the behest of the Commission and partly as a result of national regulatory action, TSOs have been encouraged to introduce auction procedures as a way of allocating scarce capacity on international interconnectors. This has had the paradoxical result of ensuring that the price difference between national markets is de facto eliminated making cross-border trade less attractive and isolating national markets and their local monopolistic incumbent producers, while at the same time generating substantial windfall profits for the TSOs. This is perhaps a classic example of the type of regulatory failures discussed by Bauer in his contribution to this volume and yet in abstract economic terms, auctioning scarce resources should have provided an optimal solution.

What would have been the better alternative? If we take a closer look at the Commission's plans the solution is two-fold: enhanced national state intervention in the activities of the TSO's and the provision of Community resources to stimulate investment in trans-European infrastructural projects. The Commission expects Member States to take measures to direct their TSOs to invest and at the same time to give the TSOs total control over all assets necessary to carry out their functions. This looks very much like a return to the old days – the state acting as entrepreneur through the TSO which may or may not be in its ownership. Indeed privatization of the TSO function remains an issue in several Member States, while in the Netherlands, the national network company TenneT has been nationalized. This is perhaps not the type of dynamic regulation that Professor Bauer would hope to see emerging in the era of partial competition. It is certainly not regulation of the market or in the market, but it would seem the partial removal of certain functions from the market.

Seen from this perspective Professor Parker's chapter provides a timely reminder of the fact that privatized, de-monopolized companies are not only subject to commercial risk but also to regulatory risk. Regulation is a learning process for both the regulator and the regulated but this process is certainly not 'cost-free'.

4 DE-MONOPOLIZATION AND RE-CONCENTRATION

A major issue surrounding the regulation of the network sector in Europe in particular is the question of whether de-monopolization and privatization processes will not in fact lead to the substitution of a state-owned monopolistic or oligopolistic sector in each Member State with a highly concentrated industries comprising of three or four major players which will effectively dominate the market, eventually even for multi-utility services, in Europe and beyond. Most of the mergers and strategic alliances, first in the telecommunications and more recently in the energy sector have met with approval from the European Commission. As Professor Van Miert notes, in certain cases, approval has been subject to stringent conditions requiring divestiture of certain assets and in some cases has even been made dependent on Member State commitment to the liberalization and re-regulation process. The possibility for large state-owned companies to enter newly liberalized foreign markets, while continuing to enjoy the protection of state ownership in their own markets has given a new twist to the reciprocity debate. Can a Member State which has liberalized its market forbid the purchase of shareholdings in these companies by foreign monopolists? Politically the European Commission appears to have equivocated on this issue, although from a strictly legal point of view any attempts by Member States to impose such restrictions would appear to infringe the European Treaty rules of the freedom of movement of capital. In fact the Commission has taken legal action against Member States which retain strategic golden shares in certain telecommunications companies.

An interesting point which should be made here is that the instruments available to both Member States and the European Commission to deal with market structures and patterns of ownership in the network sectors do not belong to the battery of sector-specific regulations. Take-overs and strategic alliances are regulated according to merger control rules – rules based on generic competition principles. Sector-specific regulation rarely touches on such matters – this set of rules being largely confined to access terms and conditions and tariff matters. This is perhaps ironic, given as Professor Bauer points out in his paper, that a basic issue in arriving at the right mix of sector-specific versus generic competition type instruments is getting the market structure right. In fact the two sets of instruments have to be seen at least to an extent, as complementary – and hence it is perhaps hardly surprising that the Commission uses the opportunity of applying its merger control powers to exact certain undertakings from both governments and from the industry itself. What is perhaps more surprising is the fact that sector-specific regulators have virtually no input into the process of merger control: this is purely the function of competition authorities. Indeed national regulators have limited spheres of influence both functionally and territorially. The foreign activities of a national provider of telecommunications or energy services do not fall within their remit. This of course makes overseas adventures all the more attractive. Co-ordination between national regulators is something which is only just beginning to develop so that engineering cross-border regulation is very much a matter for the future and one which the Commission appears to be anxious to stimulate in its proposals for reforming European telecommunications regulation.

5 MANAGING TRANSITIONS

Without doubt the assumption that sector-specific regulation is a transitional if necessary 'evil' continues to inform both public and academic debate. Eventually sector-specific regulation should be replaced by generic competition rules which apply to all sectors. These latter rules, as is well-known, apply ex post facto and to individual instances whereas sector-specific rules apply ex ante and are generalized in their application. Two particular issues continue to dominate this debate: do we need sector-specific regulators to implement sector-specific rules or can this task be left to a national competition authority? And on the assumption that sector-specific rules can be disregarded, at what point in time should this be possible? The first issue raises questions of governance as well as economic and legal issues. What type of regulatory institution is most suited to perform certain tasks? Some countries, for example the Netherlands, have preferred to set up a single body and confer specialized sectoral powers on different chambers or boards within it while others have preferred to create strong regulators with detailed and complex powers, alongside national competition boards, a notable example being the United Kingdom. The first variant may be a better guarantee against the threat of 'regulatory capture' whereas the second may provide a better expertise over the sector. Looking across Europe and indeed the OECD countries, the institutional picture varies substantially. At first sight this seems surprising given that national regulatory bodies have all been created at around the same time and for the same purposes. Institutional variation reflects different political and constitutional cultures but it also reflects the degree of commitment to liberalization. A weak commitment may mean a weak regulator but as the example of Finland shows, state ownership of a sector may still be combined with strong regulation.

The second issue is perhaps the most complex – at what point are markets sufficiently robust to allow for the withdrawal of sector-specific rules? Benchmarking has become the new concept in this respect but a review of some of the recent attempts to 'measure' competition in certain sectors, such as the European electricity sector, illustrates that this process is very much in its infancy. One highly valid result of studies performed so far is the confirmation that the adoption of formal requirements to liberalise a market is only the very initial stage of a long process. Customer –switching in telecommunications and for energy services remains low in numerous countries and paradoxically it is often in markets where governments have actively intervened to promote switching that the process often takes off.

Again, as Parker stressed in his contribution, it is important nonetheless to recognize that regulation influences the nature of the markets that evolve. This in turn influences management strategy within utility firms. He suggests that instead of resources being attracted to areas of greatest need, with potentially the highest welfare gains, they may be attracted to areas where access is permitted or short-term profit is highest given the regulatory constraints.

6 CONCLUSION

Engineering competition is a complex process of which detailed regulation is a necessary part. The various outcomes of the process are often contradictory and in any event unpredictable for governments, regulators and regulated alike. Regulation itself has to be engineered and like any high precision instrument, it must be carefully maintained, re-adjusted and fine tuned. Inevitably, the performance of regulation – and regulators – will remain subject to critical scrutiny as well as, invariably, criticism. Substitution of sector-specific regulation with generic competition rules is likely to remain an elusive goal in many jurisdictions for the foreseeable future. Indeed we may even witness an early return to some form of state entrepreneurship and more intensified state intervention in key infrastructural sectors. It is sometimes easy to lose sight of the fact that the goals of regulation do not appear to remain uniform over time: in certain markets where capital intensive infrastructure pre-dominates and where such infrastructure cannot be easily duplicated recent developments suggest that regulation is also a tool to correct the perceived short-comings of liberalization. Regulatory instruments are being used not to steer a market towards more competition but to compensate for major market failure – including the perceived failure of the market to produce new investments.

This process in itself will generate interesting issues of governance, and perhaps conflicts between independent regulators who were appointed to balance the interests of shareholders, the general public and consumers, and their increasingly active political masters.

NOTES

1. EC Directive 96/92, O.J. 1996 L 27/1.
2. EC Directive 98/30 O.J. 1998 L.204/1.
3. For a further discussion see the Commission's recent plans on European Energy Infrastructures as announced in IP of 20 December 2001.

Index